SO-AXZ-202

THE AMBIVALENT LEGACY OF ELIA KAZAN

FILM AND HISTORY
Series Editor: Cynthia J. Miller

THE AMBIVALENT LEGACY OF ELIA KAZAN

The Politics of the Post-HUAC Films

Ron Briley

ROWMAN & LITTLEFIELD
Lanham • Boulder • New York • London

Published by Rowman & Littlefield
A wholly owned subsidary of The Rowman & Littlefield Publishing Group, Inc.
4501 Forbes Boulevard, Suite 200, Lanham, Maryland 20706
www.rowman.com

Unit A, Whitacre Mews, 26-34 Stannary Street, London SE11 4AB

British Library Cataloguing in Publication Information Available

Library of Congress Cataloging-in-Publication Data

Names: Briley, Ron, 1949- author.
Title: The ambivalent legacy of Elia Kazan : the politics of the post-HUAC films / Ron Briley.
Description: Lanham : Rowman & Littlefield, 2016. | Series: Film and history | Includes bibliographi-
    cal references and index.
Identifiers: LCCN 2016010652 (print) | LCCN 2016019696 (ebook) | ISBN 9781442271678 (cloth :
    alk. paper) | ISBN 9781442271685 (electronic)
Subjects: LCSH: Kazan, Elia—Criticism and interpretation. | Motion picture producers and direc-
    tors—Political activity—United States. | Motion pictures—Political aspects—United States—
    History—20th century. | Communism and motion pictures—United States.
Classification: LCC PN1998.3.K39 B75 2016 (print) | LCC PN1998.3.K39 (ebook)| DDC 791.4302/
    33092—dc23 LC record available at https://lccn.loc.gov/2016010652

Printed in the United States of America

For my children:
To Pam for a free and independent spirit
To Shane for his work ethic and love of the law
To Meghan for her compassion and beautiful voice
To Ross for the courage to be himself

CONTENTS

ACKNOWLEDGMENTS

I grew up in a poor Texas Panhandle home almost devoid of books. My mother attended high school, but my father left grade school to work during the Great Depression. Later in life, I would discover the joy of books and reading, but what allowed me to survive my youth picking cotton in the fields with my family was an introduction to the movies provided by my semiliterate father. Failing to perceive much purpose in a traditional education, on school nights he allowed me to sit up with him and watch the late show on television. Thus, I often went to bed well after midnight, and we had to be careful not to wake my mother. Despite my rather bleary-eyed days at school, I appreciate that my father introduced me to the works of Henry Fonda, John Wayne, Gary Cooper, Humphrey Bogart, Cary Grant, James Cagney, Clark Gable, Marlon Brando, Joan Crawford, Bette Davis, Elizabeth Taylor, Marilyn Monroe, Vivian Leigh, Greer Garson, and Barbara Stanwyck—the Turner Classic Movie canon; albeit a white community upon which Hollywood did not really expand until the 1950s and 1960s.

It was during these late-night film screenings that my father also introduced me to the films of Elia Kazan. As a young boy, I was especially drawn to the courage of Kazan's heroes in such films as *Gentleman's Agreement*, *Viva Zapata!*, and *On the Waterfront*. Although I was fascinated by *A Streetcar Named Desire*, I did not understand the film until later in life. Also, I cannot imagine that my father watched Kazan's *Baby Doll*, as the sexual themes would have offended him. Nor would the idea that *On the Waterfront* was a metaphor for Kazan's testimony before the

House Un-American Activities Committee (HUAC) have registered with my largely apolitical father. Nevertheless, there was something about the humanity embraced by Kazan and his actors, such as Marlon Brando, that attracted my father and me to these films. This filmmaker with the strange name of Elia Kazan was every bit as good as John Ford.

Even after discovering books, I continued my love affair with the movies but broadened my horizons to include contemporary, art house, and international cinema. As I embraced more liberal politics in the 1960s, I was disappointed with Kazan's decision to betray his friends and associates by naming names before HUAC, destroying the lives of others while he continued to work within the Hollywood system. Despite my political misgivings, I still found much to admire in the cinema of Kazan, but there appeared to be a disconnection between his public, and often extreme, anti-Communist rhetoric and the themes of social justice and individual conscience contained in his films. In fact, in many of his post-HUAC testimony films, Kazan seemed to espouse such leftist views as questioning hierarchy and patriarchy within the family and society, the validity of the American dream, and even the capitalist system itself. It is this discrepancy between Kazan's public politics and his post-HUAC film texts that led me to this book. Kazan was not always an easy person to like. His autobiography and correspondence reveal a tremendous ego and rather sexist attitudes, but there are always those wonderful films that reveal a more complex Kazan. One may certainly criticize the filmmaker for his decision to cooperate with HUAC's unconstitutional investigations into the private political beliefs of American citizens, but the greater issue is that no one should ever have been placed in the untenable position of Kazan, and others in the Hollywood community, of betraying their friends and associates in order to find employment and practice their art.

My interest in film studies was not encouraged during my history graduate school days, but I was delighted when I secured a teaching position at Sandia Preparatory School in Albuquerque, New Mexico, where I was supported in the pursuit of my passion for developing an elective course in film history. Over the next thirty-eight years, the school allowed me to expand my cinema offerings to include a class on world cinema. Although the film classes included considerable reading and writing, not to mention the screening of black-and-white films with more conversation than action and explosions, I appreciate the many students at Sandia Prep who elected to take the courses. The young film scholars at

Sandia Prep, whom I was fortunate to teach, have enriched my understanding of cinema with their astute observations and insights. One of the film texts that we consistently employ in the U.S. History through Film class was Kazan's *On the Waterfront*, and the students were captivated by Brando's performance but divided on the decisions made by Terry Malloy and Kazan to name names. These classroom discussions regarding *On the Waterfront* have certainly contributed to this book, and I would like to express my appreciation to my film students for their inspiration. I would also like to thank Sandia Prep's former head of school Dick Heath for generously providing funds to attend conferences and present my film scholarship. My colleagues at Sandia Prep, with whom I have discussed history, film, and Kazan over the years, have contributed much to my understanding of film and teaching. I would like to thank Paul Ryder, Tom Gentry-Funk, Stacy Moses, Tony Schoepke, and especially Claudio Perez. Cindy Miller's editorial assistance was invaluable in getting this manuscript completed, and I am also indebted to Stephen Ryan and the folks at Rowman and Littlefield for sticking with me.

And last, but never least, is my family, who have listened to countless discussions of Kazan and the blacklist while indulging my passion for cinema. I am so proud of my children, Pam, Shane, Meghan, and Ross. But none of this could happen without the love of my life and the cornerstone of our family, my beautiful and gifted wife, Kathleen Chaffee Briley, who makes every day worth living.

INTRODUCTION

The Post-HUAC Testimony Films

On the evening of March 21, 1999, feeble, eighty-nine-year-old film director Elia Kazan, accompanied by his wife, actor Robert De Niro, and filmmaker Martin Scorsese, ambled onto the stage at the Dorothy Chandler Pavilion to receive an honorary Oscar bestowed by the Board of Governors of the Academy of Motion Picture Arts and Sciences. The audience reaction was mixed. Perhaps about half of the film community present stood and applauded a celebrated filmmaker who was previously honored by the Academy with Oscars for Best Director for *Gentleman's Agreement* (1947) and *On the Waterfront* (1954). Others applauded politely while remaining in their seats, and some, such as actors Nick Nolte and Ed Harris, refused to publicly acknowledge Kazan. The selection of Kazan to receive the honorary Academy Award was a controversial one due to his April 1952 testimony before the House Un-American Activities Committee (HUAC) in which the director named former associates as members of the Communist Party. Kazan's cooperation assured that he would be able to continue with his Hollywood career, while members of the Hollywood community who refused to acknowledge the right of the committee to ask questions regarding their political activities were placed on the blacklist by the film industry and denied employment. The Kazan honorary award reignited the debate over the Hollywood blacklist and the issues of free speech and association raised by Kazan's testimony.

Anti-communists quickly rose to Kazan's defense. Alan Wolfe, a professor of political science at Boston University and a contributing editor to the *New Republic*, wrote a piece for the *Los Angeles Times* in which he was quick to denounce progressive critics of Kazan as Stalinists who refused to acknowledge the crimes of the Soviet Union. Wolfe argued that the blacklist was not comparable to the millions who died due to the tyranny of the Soviet Union. Concluding with resurrected Cold War rhetoric that had worked so well for Ronald Reagan, Wolfe declared, "Funded by the Soviet Union, the U.S. Communist Party put Soviet interests ahead of everything else, shifting positions a bewildering number of times to accommodate its subservient status."[1] Historian Arthur A. Schlesinger, Jr., who was a founder of the anti-communist liberal Americans for Democratic Action and an adviser to President John Kennedy, found common cause with Wolfe. While critical of HUAC and its tactics, Schlesinger, nevertheless, insisted that Kazan deserved credit for "recognizing the horrors of Stalin."[2]

Kazan's critics on the political left, however, perceived the efforts of HUAC to stifle dissent as a far greater threat to American democracy than the Communist Party of the United States (CPUSA). Victor S. Navasky, editor of the *Nation* magazine, argues that Kazan's cooperation with HUAC helped to legitimize the committee's interrogation of American citizens regarding their personal political views. According to Navasky, Kazan's testimony was especially disappointing to those on the political left as the director in both his films and theater projects demonstrated empathy for social justice and the working class. Many believed that with his critical and commercial success, Kazan was in a position to challenge the blacklist. Navasky concluded, "Probably no single individual could have broken the blacklist in April 1952 and yet no person was in a better position to try than Kazan, by virtue of his prestige and economic invulnerability, to mount a symbolic campaign against it, and by this example inspire hundreds of fence sitters to come over to the opposition."[3] Kazan, of course, disappointed Navasky as well as many of his associates, including playwrights Arthur Miller and Clifford Odets, the latter of whom was named by Kazan in his testimony. Filmmaker Abraham Polonsky, who was a victim of the blacklist, recognized Kazan's talent but made it clear to reporter Patrick Goldstein that he had little sympathy for the informant, asserting: "I don't like Kazan, but I try not to confuse my moral hatreds with my aesthetic hatreds. He made a lot of good pictures, so you could say he deserves an award for his work—I just wouldn't want to give it to him. He was a creep. I wouldn't want to be wrecked on a desert island with him because if he was hungry, he would eat me alive."[4]

In disagreement with those on the left and right who wanted to continue the cultural conflicts of the Cold War, Martin Scorsese asserted that the historical and cultural context of the emerging Cold War in the early 1950s placed individuals such as Kazan in an impossible situation, and one was damned no matter what decision was made regarding cooperation with the committee. Scorsese, therefore, argued that Kazan's qualifications for an honorary Oscar should be based exclusively on his considerable filmmaking abilities. In support of Scorsese's position, Bernard Weinraub of the *New York Times* wrote that Kazan "lent his prestige and moral authority to what was essentially an immoral process, a brief but nevertheless damaging period of officially sponsored hysteria that exacted a huge toll on individual lives, on free speech and on democracy." The journalist concluded that to deny Kazan recognition was, ironically, to perpetuate a contemporary form of the blacklist to which Kazan's critics were so adamantly opposed.[5]

But what of Kazan's views on the legacy of his HUAC testimony? The filmmaker certainly earned little sympathy from his critics when he followed his testimony with a paid advertisement in the *New York Times* explaining why it was so important to cooperate with the committee. According to Kazan, the piece in the *Times* was actually the work of his wife Molly Day Thacher Kazan, whose moral certainty provides a differing perspective from the theme of ambiguity often expressed in Kazan's rather massive autobiography, *A Life* (1988). In the statement to which only his name is attached, Kazan maintained that it was his patriotic duty to appear before HUAC as the Communist Party was a conspiratorial organization that posed a direct threat to American democracy. Kazan was a party member from 1934 to 1936, but he abandoned the Communists when they attempted to use him in a proposed takeover of the Group Theatre in New York City. Arguing that secrecy served the Communists, Kazan insisted that it was the duty of liberals to expose Communist colleagues. Kazan concluded, "Firsthand experience of dictatorship and thought control left me with an abiding hatred of Communist philosophy and methods and the conviction that these must be resisted always."[6]

Kazan would never apologize for his naming of names before the committee or for his assertive *New York Times* piece. In fact, when his cinematographer for *America America* (1963), Haskell "Pete" Wexler, suggested that Kazan might employ his 1999 Oscar appearance to make some type of apology to those harmed by his testimony, the reply was reportedly a short and simple, "Fuck you, Pete."[7] Nevertheless, there is a far greater degree of ambivalence in the Kazan autobiography. On the one hand, there is a consistent denunciation of the Communist Party as a criminal conspiracy. Yet there is also doubt expressed that the associates he named were really threats to the fabric of American life. Perhaps this duality is a product of Kazan's ambivalent political principles. He writes: "Politically, I consider myself left of center. I believe there won't be peace in the world until everyone has a dry, clean home and enough to eat. Socialism! Yes. Still I have a decent bundle in the bank and live off the interest."[8] While sympathetic to socialism, Kazan had little positive to say about Stalin and the Soviet Union. He believed American Communists were simply slaves following the dictates of Stalin, and he was embarrassed by the ease with which many of his leftist colleagues shifted from supporting collective security to denouncing capitalist imperialism following the 1939 Nazi-Soviet pact. Thus, Kazan insisted that the government had an obligation to investigate American Communists as subversive threats to the nation's democracy. Kazan proclaimed: "There was no way that I could go along with the crap that the CP was nothing but another political party like the Republicans and the Democrats. I know very well what it was, a thoroughly organized, worldwide conspiracy. This conviction separated me from many of my old friends."[9]

Accordingly, Kazan reiterated that any readers expecting an apology for his actions would be disappointed. Instead, he suggested, "The people who owe you an explanation (no apology expected) are those who, year after year, held the Soviet Union blameless for all their crimes."[10] Yet only a few pages later, the filmmaker returns to the theme of ambivalence. Seeming far less certain of his actions, Kazan writes: "I did what I did because it was the more tolerable of two alternatives that were, either way, painful, even disastrous, and either way wrong for me. That's what a difficult decision means. Either way you go, you lose."[11] These second thoughts seem triggered by his concern for his friend Clifford Odets. Before naming Odets in his testimony, Kazan approached the playwright and essentially asked for his permission. Odets evidently provided Kazan with his blessing, and the playwright later appeared as a friendly witness before the committee as well. Kazan believed that it was a mistake for

Odets to cooperate with HUAC, as the identity of the writer was connected to his championing of the political left in notable plays such as *Waiting for Lefty* (1935), *Awake and Sing* (1935), and *Golden Boy* (1937). Following his naming of names before the committee, Odets was shunned by his former colleagues on the left who previously lionized the man and his work. Kazan suggests that the writer lacked the mental toughness of the director and could not handle the disdain of former associates, leading to the premature death of Odets in 1963.[12]

After treating the death of his first wife, Molly, in the autobiography, Kazan comes close to making the apology he insisted that he would never make. Thinking about Odets, as well as Tony Kraber of the Group Theatre, whom he had implicated in his testimony, Kazan proclaimed:

> I felt that no political cause was worth hurting any other human being
> for. What good deeds were stimulated by what I'd done? What villains
> exposed? How is the world better for what I did? It had just been a
> game of power and influence, and I'd been taken in and twisted from
> my true self. I'd fallen for something I shouldn't have, no matter how
> hard the pressure and no matter how sound my reasons.[13]

The juxtaposition in the autobiography of this "confession" with the examination of Molly's death is interesting. For Kazan seems to give some credence here to the claims of some supporters that Molly was primarily responsible for his decision to give testimony and name names. Molly Thacher was from a prominent New England family that did not approve of her decision to marry a Greek immigrant from Turkey. Nevertheless, Molly was a loyal wife who loved her husband and four children, and Kazan insisted that he reciprocated this love and adoration despite his many extramarital affairs. Although he had great admiration for Molly as a wife and mother, he found her moral certainties to somewhat cramp and limit his freedom. Kazan found himself struggling to fit into Molly's expectations of bourgeois conformity. Thus, he describes the most important relationship of his life with a degree of ambivalence that also characterized many of his films—especially those made following his HUAC testimony. In his relationship with Molly, Kazan always seemed to perceive himself as the immigrant outsider who was never quite accepted into American life despite earning acclaim and financial reward as theatrical director, filmmaker, and writer.

Kazan was born on September 7, 1909, in Istanbul, Turkey, to Athena and George Kazanjioglou (the family name was shortened following immigration to the United States). As Anatolian Greeks, the family suffered considerable discrimination from the Turkish authorities, and Elia Kazan asserted that he often concealed his true feelings behind the mask of an enigmatic Anatolian smile. His uncle Avraam, whose story is told in Kazan's favorite film, *America America*, migrated to the United States and helped the rest of the family to complete their American journey in 1913. Kazan's father, George, continued his career as a rug merchant, but his eldest son did not share his father's passion for commerce. Elia became closer to his mother, who encouraged his education and interest in the arts. Against the wishes of his father, Elia attended and graduated from Williams College in 1930. Although he was often ostracized by his more affluent New England classmates at Williams, Kazan continued his studies at the Yale School of Drama. Believing that he was learning little that would further a professional career in the theater, Kazan dropped out of Yale and was eventually accepted into the Group Theatre, where he studied the Stanislavsky, or method, school of acting taught by Harold Clurman and Lee Strasberg. Meanwhile, Kazan married Yale classmate Molly Day Thacher in December 1932.[14]

It was within the Group Theatre that Kazan developed passion and commitment to a group of performers dedicated to their art. Making himself indispensable to the group as a performer, stage technician, and later director, Kazan went by the name of "Gadget" or "Gadj," a term of appreciation for his willingness to assume so many roles in promoting the Group Theatre. During these years, Kazan was active politically, embracing the proletarian focus of his friend Clifford Odets's plays and joining the Communist Party for two years. And even after leaving the party, Kazan was still accepted by his former comrades. The spirit of the Group Theatre during the 1930s is well captured in the memoir/history *The Fervent Years* by Kazan's friend and mentor Harold Clurman. Placing the work of the Group Theatre within the historical context of the Great Depression and the possibilities for political change fostered by Roosevelt's New Deal, Clurman writes: "The worker in the thirties demanded life free from fear of unemployment and insecurity. The artist in the thirties like the artist in all times was driven by the hope and desire for a fullness of life. He made common cause with the worker. He found new matter for his art, he brought a new understanding to old themes, he related himself more completely to the world as a whole."[15]

Although he would become more critical of political sectarianism on the left, the worldview and milieu of the Group Theatre certainly shaped Kazan as he achieved success as a Broadway director during the early 1940s with plays such as Thornton Wilder's *The Skin of Our Teeth* (1942); *Jacobowsky and the Colonel*, by Franz Werfel and S. N. Behrman (1944);, and Kurt Weill's musical comedy *One Touch of Venus* (1945), featuring Mary Martin. The Broadway acclaim garnered by Kazan convinced Darryl F. Zanuck of Twentieth Century Fox to sign the director to a contract despite Kazan's lack of experience with the medium of film. Kazan's first film with Zanuck was an adaptation of Betty Smith's novel *A Tree Grows in Brooklyn* (1945) that was well received by both film critics and audiences despite the fact that Kazan was receiving on-the-job training as a filmmaker. Kazan was credited with examining a young girl's relationship with an alcoholic father and a life of poverty in the tenements of New York City without resorting to undue sentimentality. His next film at MGM, however, proved to be a more negative experience for the novice filmmaker, as in the production of *Sea of Grass* (1947) he was overwhelmed by the film's stars Spencer Tracy and Katharine Hepburn. Kazan was able to regain his equilibrium after returning to Zanuck and Fox, inserting a degree of documentary realism into his crime film *Boomerang!* (1947), starring Dana Andrews. And he earned a Best Director Oscar for his work on *Gentleman's Agreement* (1947), focusing on the topic of anti-Semitism in America and featuring Gregory Peck. The film was also honored with an Oscar for Best Picture and considered by many critics to be an insightful social-problem film, but Kazan argues that the film was intentionally "thin," for it was aimed at a middle-class audience that Kazan was accusing of anti-Semitism. The goal was to get the film-going public to accept the picture as well as the responsibility for making things better. Kazan told interviewer Jeff Young, "There is nothing in it that will mess up an audience psychologically."[16]

Kazan's next film, *Pinky* (1949), was also perceived as a social-problem film. The legendary John Ford was originally tapped to do the film for Fox, but Ford dropped out of the project and Kazan agreed to pick up the production as a favor to Zanuck. *Pinky* tells the story of a young black woman in the South passing for white until she is confronted by her racial past when she becomes engaged to a white man. The picture further established Kazan's reputation as a progressive filmmaker, but *Pinky* is not a work in which Kazan took particular pride. He viewed completing the film as a favor to Zanuck and had little to say about the film's commentary on race relations in the American South. Kazan did, however, assert that the film's black star, Ethel Waters, had little tolerance for white people, including John Ford, but she made somewhat of an exception for an Anatolian Greek.[17] After his disappointment with *Pinky*, Kazan was determined to do a film on his terms. The result was *Panic in the Streets* (1950), in which Kazan eschewed big-name stars in favor of Richard Widmark, Jack Palance, and Zero Mostel. Kazan especially enjoyed working with Mostel, who would later express his disapproval of the director's HUAC testimony. With *Panic in the Streets*, however, Kazan seemed less concerned with his actors and more focused on location shooting and making New Orleans the star of the film. In describing *Panic in the Streets*, Kazan asserted that he wanted to make "a film that could be understood using only the eyes of a deaf person. And to shoot it in the style I had found to be my own—on location, without a set, everything real, true, ordinary, totally convincing."[18] The film has a documentary feel to it, and in terms of politics it is interesting to note that the hero of the film, played by Widmark, is a public official attempting to stave off an outbreak of plague in New Orleans. A decade later in *Wild River* (1960), Kazan was much more ambivalent regarding the activities of a government representative from the Tennessee Valley Authority.

Meanwhile, Kazan was continuing to draw accolades for his work on Broadway. In 1947, he helped to establish the Actors Studio, a nonprofit acting workshop emphasizing the method style of acting in which actors were trained to achieve greater realism by relating events in the play or film to personal experiences. And on the stage and screen, Kazan was praised as a director who could elicit outstanding performances. Kazan also began his relationship with Arthur Miller in 1947, directing *All My Sons* and earning his first Tony Award for direction. The Kazan and Miller collaboration went on to achieve even greater success with *Death of a Salesman*, which opened on Broadway in February 1949 and ran for 742 performances. Kazan identified personally with *Death of a Salesman* as the character Willy Loman reminded the director of his own father, and the play's ambivalent depiction of American capitalism certainly resonated with Kazan. Thomas H. Pauly, in his study of Kazan and American culture, concludes that with their sympathetic but insightful treatment of

Loman, Miller and Kazan achieved "a fully developed character whose troubled mind and compulsive behavior reflected the defects of his society."[19]

Kazan also began another collaboration in 1947 that would extend into the 1960s. On December 3, 1947, Kazan directed Tennessee Williams's *A Streetcar Named Desire*, which ran for 855 performances at the Ethel Barrymore Theatre. In the role of Stanley Kowalski, actor Marlon Brando emerged as a major figure on the American stage and, later, in Hollywood. Brando also established a strong working relationship with Kazan, which was strained by the director's HUAC appearance. Directing *A Streetcar Named Desire* with a degree of sympathy for the character of Blanche, Kazan described the theme of the play as "a message from the dark interior. This little twisted, pathetic, confused bit of light and culture puts out a cry. It is sniffed out by the crude forces of violence, insensitivity and vulgarity which exist in our South—and this cry is the play."[20]

Kazan was initially opposed to directing the film version of the play, but he was eventually prevailed upon by Tennessee Williams to do the picture for Warner Bros. Although assured by Jack Warner that there would be no changes to the Kazan edit of the film, alterations were made by the studio to satisfy complaints from the Catholic Church and Legion of Decency objecting to the film's implication that Stanley and his wife Stella might reconcile following the rape of Blanche. While the changes proposed by the church censors failed to impact the film's box office and critical acclaim, Kazan was furious. Unable to secure the release of his version of *Streetcar*, Kazan penned a letter to the *New York Times* complaining of censorship. In a letter to Martin Quigley, the publisher of several trade publications including the *Hollywood Reporter* and a Catholic who helped to draft the Production Code in 1929, Kazan asserted that he was proud of *Streetcar* and the entire film crew "tried, to the best of our ability, to tell the truth as we saw it." The director also challenged Quigley as to what right the Catholic Church had to exercise moral authority over cinema in a democratic society. An unimpressed Quigley replied, "The American constitutional guarantees of freedom of expression are not a one-way street. I have the same right to say moral considerations have a precedence over artistic considerations as you have to deny it."[21]

The confrontation helped convince Kazan that the Catholic Church and Communist Party were similar in regard to their secrecy and moral certainty, but it was Kazan's former association with the Communist Party that caused the filmmaker problems with his next project.[22] Kazan and his friend, novelist John Steinbeck, were seeking approval from Zanuck and the Fox studio to begin production on their Emiliano Zapata script. The studio chief was concerned about the marketability of a film on the Mexican revolutionary leader during the anti-Communist crusade of the Cold War. Rumors of Kazan's past association with the Communist Party and assumptions that the director would be called to give testimony before HUAC troubled Zanuck. But the director was finally given the green light for *Viva Zapata!* However, Kazan believed that the opportunity to film in Mexico was denied by Mexican Communists who wanted to dictate how Zapata was presented to film audiences.[23] The film was completed and released before Kazan's HUAC appearance, but in considering the ambiguity of Kazan's political perspective in his post-HUAC film work, *Viva Zapata!* deserves considerable attention.

After Kazan's HUAC testimony, the director was often perceived as a right-wing figure whose voice and art were dedicated to serving the anti-Communist crusade and denouncing progressive causes. A close analysis of Kazan's cinema following his testimony provides evidence for more ambivalence and ambiguity than political consistency. These film texts suggest that despite his opposition to the Communist Party, Kazan remained a man of the political left who was often critical of capitalism. For example, in *Viva Zapata!* Kazan and Steinbeck are Cold War liberals in their depiction of the fictional character Fernando Aguirre (Joseph Wiseman) as an opportunist Communist whose Leninist vanguard of the proletariat elitism demonstrates little concern for the common Mexican people. On the other hand, Kazan and Steinbeck were sympathetic to the cause of land reform championed by the revolutionary Zapata, who eschewed personal fame and fortune. Thus, Kazan and Steinbeck may be interpreted as Cold War liberals focusing their attention upon the threat that Communist professional revolutionaries will hijack legitimate reforms for their own devious ends.

The political ambiguity of *Viva Zapata!* was apparent to many on the political right who continued to question the sincerity of Kazan's HUAC testimony. Zanuck urged Kazan to make a clearly anti-Communist film, and the result was *Man on a Tightrope* (1953), featuring Fredric March, whose political loyalties were also the subject of anti-Communist inquiry. Somewhat reluctantly, Kazan agreed to do the film, which lacks the political complexity of his other post-HUAC films and was also a major box office flop. The film is based on the true story of a traveling circus that risked arrest, imprisonment, and death for fleeing Communist Czechoslovakia to reach the freedom of Austria and the West. *Man on a Tightrope* certainly fits into the simplistic anti-Communist film genre produced by the studios to demonstrate their opposition to domestic Communism and support of the Cold War to halt the expansion of the Soviet monolith.[24] In the hands of Kazan, however, this propaganda genre becomes somewhat more sophisticated. According to film scholar Lloyd Michaels, a key element of the director's cinema was the theme of power, which became more pronounced following the HUAC hearings. Michaels asserts that Kazan's embracing of human dignity, while becoming increasingly suspicious of institutionalized power, whether it resided in the family, government, or economic system, "seemed to coalesce with Kazan's own fall from grace and confrontation with authority during the HUAC hearings."[25] For Karel Cernik (Fredric March) in *Man on a Tightrope*, this source of power to be resisted was the Soviet system, while in *On the Waterfront* (1954), Terry Malloy (Marlon Brando) confronts a corrupt waterfront union.

The acclaimed *On the Waterfront*, which earned Kazan another Best Director Oscar in addition to an Academy Award for Best Picture, is often perceived as containing key autobiographical elements in which Terry Malloy represents Kazan. Just as Kazan testified against Communist Party influence in the entertainment industry, Terry must take a stand against the corrupt union controlling the waterfront. The film is usually interpreted as justifying Kazan's cooperation with HUAC. *On the Waterfront*'s conclusion, however, also provides an alternative and more ambivalent political reading. While the workers now follow Terry rather than the corrupt Johnny Friendly (Lee J. Cobb), Mr. Upstairs remains in command of the waterfront, and the workers still exercise little independence within a closed system. Thus, the final shots of *On the Waterfront* may be read as a condemnation of capitalist exploitation.[26] A detailed analysis of Kazan's other post-HUAC films reveal similar ambivalent themes and suggest that perhaps we should not unequivocally embrace Kazan's declaration of "no regrets." The leftist sympathies of his youth for the impoverished immigrants residing in the tenements of New York City and his early experiences with the Group Theatre were not so quickly erased from his political consciousness. Hidden behind what Kazan often described as the Anatolian smile was a questioning of capitalism and materialism, which he shared with former colleagues whom he betrayed in his HUAC testimony. Kazan also displayed a fear of authority, which was present in his reactions to Turkish officials, his father, his first wife, studio heads, the Communist Party, and HUAC.

Kazan followed the success of *On the Waterfront* with another picture that appealed to both audiences and critics. Adapting part of Steinbeck's massive novel *East of Eden* to the screen in 1955, Kazan completed his first film in color and introduced movie audiences to James Dean—although Kazan was not overly impressed with Dean and preferred Brando for the lead role. In the conflict between Cal Trask (James Dean) and his father, Adam (Raymond Massey), we see elements of the troubled relationship between Kazan and his own father in addition to influences from *Death of a Salesman*. Again the American dream is brought into question as, despite the best efforts of Cal, his father is unable to achieve his goal of exporting produce through refrigerated boxcars. Kazan embraced the theme of ambivalence in his film of the Steinbeck novel, asserting: "That's my specialty because that's what my life experience has been. I very rarely have a pure emotion. Even my feelings about America are ambivalent. In all my films I knock it, and tear it down. I'm highly critical. I love Southerners, whom I criticize more than anyone else."[27] And it would be toward the South that Kazan would turn in a trilogy of films whose ambivalence proved too much for most film audiences.

After *East of Eden*, with which Kazan was not totally satisfied, the director pursued another collaboration with Tennessee Williams. Kazan was a great admirer of the playwright, and following *A Streetcar Named Desire* he worked with Williams to bring *Cat on a Hot Tin Roof* to the Broadway stage in 1955. With *Baby Doll* (1956), Kazan was drawing on two of Williams's one-act plays, *27 Wagons Full of Cotton* and *The Unsatisfactory Supper*.[28] During filming in Mississippi, Williams tended to maintain some distance from Kazan, as he was peeved with the changes the director had asked him to make in the third act of *Cat on a Hot Tin Roof*. *Baby Doll* is a rather strange film with an unconventional and somewhat Southern gothic plot dealing with the conflict between Silva Vacarro (Eli Wallach) and Archie Lee Meighan (Karl Malden) over their cotton crops, a burned down cotton gin, and Archie Lee's young bride, Baby Doll (Carroll Baker). While Kazan insisted that the film was about the changing South, critics tended to focus on the film's sexuality, and Kazan was again embroiled in a controversy with the Catholic Church. Pushing back against New York's Francis Cardinal Spellman, who urged Catholics to stay away from the film or risk damnation, Kazan urged Jack Warner to resist censorship from the church, asserting that *Baby Doll* "has grotesque and even tragic elements, but essentially the viewpoint is comic and affectionate. It will certainly not be sordid. They'll have to take my word for that. But where I think we must fight hard is the admissibility of the grown-up subject at the core of this script. If we can and do, why then we may well have a picture that will really interest everyone and which people will leave their homes to see."[29] In the final analysis, *Baby Doll* was approved by the Production Code, but the film received a condemned rating from the Legion of Decency. Whether concerned about their immortal souls or confused over the story line, audiences stayed away from *Baby Doll*. Nevertheless, it was a film of which Kazan was proud, and while it lacked some of the political themes explored in other post-HUAC testimony films, *Baby Doll* certainly presents Kazan as a rebel artist who was willing to push the envelope on issues of sexuality and censorship.

Kazan's *A Face in the Crowd* (1957) also failed at the box office, but today it enjoys a solid reputation as a film well ahead of its time. *A Face in the Crowd* tells the story of Larry "Lonesome" Rhodes, played by Andy Griffith with a bravado performance that defies his laconic role as Sheriff Andy Taylor in the revered *Andy Griffith Show*. Rhodes is a folksy Southern entertainer who employs music, humor, and demaguery to rise from an Arkansas jail cell to the pinnacle of political power as a presidential kingmaker. Rhodes has an appetite for power, sex, and money as he recognizes the possibilities that the new medium of television, in conjunction with Madison Avenue advertising, offers for selling products such as the vitamin supplement Vitajex—which Lonesome links to increasing male sexual potency well before the arrival of Viagra—as well as presidential candidates. Before Joe McGinniss and *The Selling of the President, 1968* and *Madmen* there was *A Face in the Crowd*.[30] But the Kazan film is a complex text in which Rhodes falls even more rapidly than he rose once the people understand his contempt for them. While *A Face in the Crowd* seems to endorse a populist solution, a closer reading of the film indicates that the downfall of Rhodes is due to the loss of support from his corrupt manager and sponsor, the elite Marcia Jeffries

(Patricia Neal), who discovered and loves Lonesome but must now destroy the Frankenstein monster she created.

It is also interesting to note that the presidential candidate whom Lonesome is grooming is not a liberal; rather Senator Fuller (Marshall Neilan) is a right-wing figure concerned about the rise of the Soviet Union and how government programs such as Social Security are a threat to traditional American values of individualism and are paving the way for Soviet collectivism. *A Face in the Crowd* was based on a short story written by Budd Schulberg, with whom Kazan had collaborated for *On the Waterfront*. But Kazan made clear the contemporary political origins of the film in an interview with Michel Ciment, commenting:

> The impulse came partly from the story itself but even more from a series of conversations we had about—well, about everything. About TV—its power—hypnotic, potentially dangerous and still, at times, brilliantly effective for good. We talked of how much more powerful Huey Long would have been if he had TV at his disposal. We talked about the famous Nixon broadcast, when the question of his financial backers turned somehow into a defense of his children's dog. . . . We talked about the way public figures are now coached for their broadcasts and how the medium can make a performer as a politician overnight—or break a man that fast, too.[31]

And Kazan was on target, for the United States elected a former actor President in 1980, and one of the leading candidates for the presidency in 2016 is a billionaire businessman turned reality television star. *A Face in the Crowd* certainly indicates that Kazan's political ideology was complex, and he could not be reduced to simply a soldier in the anti-communist cause.

The final film in Kazan's Southern trilogy had been a long time in gestation and reflects changes in the filmmaker's political perspective. Initially, *Wild River* (1960) was to focus on a heroic representative of the New Deal and Tennessee Valley Authority who travels to Tennessee to convince people living in the region that they must abandon and sell their land to make way for the progress that the government-constructed dam project would bring—the control of devastating floods and provision of electrification for people lacking modern conveniences. Over the course of time, Kazan became more cognizant that progress often comes with considerable cost, and he grew more sympathetic to those who resisted the government's relocation plans. Thus, in *Wild River* Montgomery Clift is cast as Tennessee Valley Authority representative Chuck Glover, who often projects a sense of uncertainty in regard to his duties. His nemesis is a family matriarch, Ella Garth (Jo Van Fleet), who refused to vacate her property. The plot is complicated by Glover's love affair with Ella's widowed granddaughter, Carol Garth (Lee Remick), and the jealousy of Carol's local boyfriend. In the end, Ella Garth is forcibly evicted from her family home, and she dies shortly thereafter as Glover surveys the "progress" of the dam from a plane flying over the area. The conclusion of the film demonstrates considerable ambiguity as Kazan displays empathy for Ella Garth, telling interviewers Stuart Bryson and Martin L. Rubin: "I love Mrs. Garth, the old lady. She was wrong in terms of progress, the way the world had to move. Absolutely wrong, intolerably ornery, unbending. But a kind of person I like. I like obdurate people—what's called inner directed. The kind who will stand up and say, 'I'm not going to change.'"[32]

Wild River was another film of which Kazan was quite proud, but like the other pictures of the Southern trilogy, it was unsuccessful at the box office. The film did, however, earn considerable praise from European critics, and Kazan blamed much of *Wild River*'s failure to resonate with American audiences on the reluctance of Twentieth Century Fox to promote the picture. Nevertheless, many critics and film historians perceive the Southern trilogy as essential films for understanding the cinema of Kazan and the director's worldview. In his book on Kazan's cinema as reflecting the perspective of an American outsider, Brian Neve observes that going back to his days in the Communist Party, Kazan was fascinated by the American South. In 1937, he served as an assistant director for the progressive Frontier Films documentary *People of the Cumberland*, and he often traveled to the South. Neve believes that Kazan was drawn to the Southern people, who were forced to accommodate change, whether it was the economic progress of the New Deal or the civil rights movement of the 1950s and 1960s.[33] In this reading, the people of the South are defined as white, as are all the protagonists in Kazan's Southern films. Kazan was not a racial bigot and does not stoop to the broad racial stereotyping that characterized so much of American cinema in the 1940s and 1950s. The black characters in the background are treated with respect, but they remain in the background. The theme of ambiguity is, therefore, quite prevalent in Kazan's Southern trilogy and in the filmmaker's reaction toward the gathering civil rights movement.

Yet with *Splendor in the Grass* (1961), Kazan expressed a degree of identification with the youth culture that would consume the 1960s. Based on a story by playwright William Inge, whose *The Dark at the Top of the Stairs* (1957) was successfully staged on Broadway by Kazan, *Splendor in the Grass* presents the tragic love story of Deanie Loomis (Natalie Wood) and Bud Stamper (Warren Beatty). Bud's nouveau riche father, Ace Stamper (Pat Hingle), does not want his son to marry a poor girl. Instead, he expects Bud to enter Yale and find a more suitable mate for climbing the American social ladder. Due to parental interference, Bud and Deanie break up, and the pressures of the dissolved relationship lead to Deanie being institutionalized after a failed suicide attempt. Meanwhile, Bud is miserable at Yale and flunks out, while his father commits suicide as his financial empire collapses with the onset of the Great Depression. Bud marries a young Italian woman and becomes a farmer. Deanie leaves the mental hospital and plans on marrying a young doctor to whom she was introduced at the institution. She and Bud meet for one last time, and they part as friends, remembering what might have been. The script resonated with Kazan, reminding him of the troubled relationship with his own father as well as the doubts about the American dream, which he found so compelling in *Death of a Salesman*. While he dealt compassionately with the difficulties poor Southern whites experienced in confronting progress and change, Kazan has little patience for the Midwestern middle-class parents of *Splendor in the Grass*, who crush the dreams of their children. In fact, Kazan unfavorably compares the parents of *Splendor in the Grass* with the conformist consumer culture of the American middle class in the 1950s. Speaking of the parents from *Splendor in the Grass*, Kazan asserted:

> They murder a rare and a fine thing, namely romantic love, a most precious thing. And they do it throughout, repeatedly and consistently in the name of the Eisenhower virtues. They do it for their children's good. They do it with a sense of not being appreciated and understood. They do it also with a sense of self-righteousness, that only they are holding the fort for what is right. They do it to SAVE their children. They do it firmly, without self-doubt, completely within their tradition. They are the great American middle class. They are absolutely perfect in the middle of this tradition. They are the killer. All their rules are

business rules, what is practical, what will make the most money. They are the dominators and the castrators. [34]

The venom unleashed here hardly seems to coincide with the friendly witness who defended American values against the assaults of the conspiratorial Communist Party. Kazan, ever the outsider, certainly remained a fervent critic of American bourgeois values, and the commercial success of *Splendor in the Grass* helped provide a foundation for confronting his immigrant experience in Kazan's most personal film, *America America*. Based on family history and his uncle Avraam's journey to America, the film reveals Kazan's complex views on the immigrant experience and the American dream. [35] The production was a troubling one, as Kazan scrambled to gain financing for the film and struggled with Turkish censors, which induced the director to move filming to Greece. Introducing elements of Italian neorealism into the film, Kazan sought a degree of authenticity by casting Stathis Giallelis, a young Greek nonprofessional actor whom the director reportedly discovered sweeping an office floor, in the lead. In addition, Kazan was going through a difficult time in his personal life. While he remained married to Molly, his mistress Barbara Loden, who appeared in *Wild River* and *Splendor in the Grass*, gave birth to the couple's child. Despite these problems and challenges, *America America* was Kazan's favorite film.

Stavros Topouzoglou (Stathis Giallelis) is an Anatolian Greek who dreams of migrating to America. The Turks harass his family and Armenian friends, so his father sends Stavros to Constantinople with the family fortune to prepare the way for other family members to follow his path to the capital. Stavros, however, is swindled out of his money, and he has to survive by serving as a *hamal* or human beast of burden on the loading docks. But Stavros does survive, even though he kills a man and is almost murdered for joining a revolutionary group. He ends up rising in society through a proposed marriage to a woman he does not love but whose father is a wealthy merchant. Stavros deserts his betrothed and finds passage to America as the paid lover of Sophia Kebabian (Katharine Balfour), a young Turkish woman married to an older American businessman. When her husband discovers the affair, Sophia denounces Stavros, who is almost deported. He is able, nonetheless, to enter the country by assuming the identity of his dead friend, Hohanness (Gregory Rozakis). At Ellis Island, the authorities change his name to Joe Arness. And despite everything that has happened to him, Stavros kisses the ground when he sets foot on American soil. In a brief epilogue, Joe is shown shining shoes and sending money back to Turkey so that his family may join him in the promised land. The film is an ambiguous text that raises serious questions about the American dream.

While *America America* earned Oscar nominations for Best Picture and Kazan as Best Director, reviews were mixed, and the film failed to do well at the box office. Kazan resented that many of the negative reviews focused on the film's length at over three hours or the difficulty of understanding Giallelis's English dialogue, delivered with a thick accent. The timing was also poor, as shortly before the film's release, President John F. Kennedy was assassinated. Audiences were not in the mood for the often-depressing tale of Stavros's American odyssey. Instead, the Oscars that year went to the bawdy and comic *Tom Jones* and its director, Tony Richardson. While many Americans attempted to honor the legacy of Kennedy by supporting President Lyndon Johnson in enacting the legislative agenda of the slain leader, Kazan's film presented a much more conflicted portrait of the nation. Asserting that he had a love/hate relationship with the United States, Kazan concluded:

> I think of the United States as a country which is an arena and in that arena there is a drama being played out and the protagonists are not always sympathetic figures and the light where they perform their actions is murky and we often see that they are not the best of possible acts. But even in the worst of times, I have seen that the struggle is the struggle of free men. Mistakes are made. There are tragedies. Shameful episodes. Betrayals. But the struggle continues. [36]

These observations reflect political ambivalence rather than the moral certainty of the HUAC testimony.

The disappointment over the reaction to *America America* was exacerbated by a personal crisis. On December 14, 1963, Molly Thacher Kazan died of a cerebral hemorrhage, and Kazan went into a period of depression. He continued in his leadership at the Repertory Theatre of Lincoln Center—a project and position strongly supported by Molly. He renewed his relationship with Arthur Miller and staged the playwright's *After the Fall* in 1964, with Barbara Loden in what many considered to be the Marilyn Monroe lead. Kazan maintained his relationship with the actress, whom he married in 1967. The marriage was tumultuous, but the couple stayed together until Loden died from cancer in 1980. Meanwhile, Kazan grew disenchanted with Lincoln Center and resigned from his position in 1965. Disappointed with his recent experiences in Hollywood and on the stage, Kazan pursued a new career as a novelist. Although his books sold well, his writing was not well received by critics.

Nevertheless, *The Arrangement* (1967) was a best seller, and Kazan agreed to direct the film for Warner Bros. In hindsight, Kazan regretted committing to direct the film and blamed the studio for failing to support the film. In his autobiography, Kazan details how he lobbied for Marlon Brando to play the lead. Despite the actor's weight gain, which distressed Kazan, the director believed that Brando might have saved the film. Instead, he selected Kirk Douglas, who Kazan concluded was simply not right for the role. Also, perhaps Kazan was too close to the material. He considered the novel to be autobiographical in theme, if not in fact, as the protagonist seeks to establish his freedom against a society and family that attempt to control the individual.[37]

The Arrangement focuses on advertising executive Eddie Anderson (Kirk Douglas), who has a beautiful mistress, Gwen (Faye Dunaway), and a loving wife, Florence (Deborah Kerr). While many of his associates perceive Eddie as having achieved the American dream, in reality he is miserable, engaging in conflict with his mistress, wife, father, and attorney, who all attempt to control his life and limit his individuality. Eddie is thwarted in his efforts to attain happiness on his terms, and he ends up being committed to a mental institution. The film received poor reviews, and Kazan did not believe that audiences wanted to understand the film. The filmmaker asserted that the characters of *The Arrangement* were not individuals but prototypes of American society in the late 1960s. While many films, such as Westerns or gangster genres, used metaphors to discuss contemporary problems, Kazan insisted that *The Arrangement* was an honest film that made audiences uncomfortable when they realized that "the people on the screen are the epitomization of the people watching the screen." Kazan concluded, "And the climax of my film simply says that our society condemns a man who breaks the mold as erratic and finally dangerous, and so therefore one way or another restrains him."[38] Thus, Eddie Anderson becomes Kazan—a man whose individuality and artistry were limited by marriage, the Communist Party, HUAC, and studio heads.

The poor reception given to *The Arrangement* once again convinced Kazan to withdraw from filmmaking and pursue the more lucrative arena of popular novels. The experience of his son Christopher's generation with the Vietnam War, however, encouraged the filmmaker to experiment with *The Visitors* (1971). Christopher Kazan's script was loosely based on Daniel Lang's *New Yorker* story "Casualties of War," which was later made into a 1989 feature film starring Sean Penn and Michael J. Fox. Experimenting with low-budget filmmaking, Kazan shot *The Visitors* in seven weeks on a budget of $170,000, using the Kazan country home in Connecticut for location shooting. Kazan also saved money by shooting in 16 mm film, which reduced processing costs, while working with a nonunion crew of four and actors who were willing to work without formal contracts.

The Visitors tells the story of a young couple in rural Connecticut, Bill Schmidt (James Woods) and Martha Wayne (Patricia Joyce), who are unexpectedly visited by Bill's former Vietnam buddies, Mike Nickerson (Steve Railsback) and Tony Rodriguez (Chico Martinez). Bill is uneasy about the visitors as during the war he had testified against his fellow soldiers for raping and murdering a Vietnamese girl. After a tension-filled day, the visitors beat Bill and rape Martha. *The Visitors* is a brutal film, but it brought the Vietnam War home to Americans—something that most filmmakers were reluctant to do during the course of the conflict. While Kazan was a critic of the Vietnam War, the political message of the film is ambivalent as the visitors are not presented as murdering monsters but rather as victims of the war. The certainty with which Kazan approached informing in *On the Waterfront* is missing from *The Visitors*. Although the film was well received at the Cannes Film Festival, Kazan believed that continuing fallout from his HUAC testimony prevented the film from attaining the coveted Palme d'Or. Few in the United States saw the film, as its American distributor, United Artists, did little to promote it.[39]

A disenchanted Kazan again pulled away from filmmaking, but he was lured back into the Hollywood arena for a final time by producer Sam Spiegel, with whom Kazan created *On the Waterfront*. This time the project was *The Last Tycoon* (1976), based on the final and unfinished novel of F. Scott Fitzgerald. The model for Fitzgerald's character of filmmaker Monroe Stahr was MGM Studio's boy wonder Irving Thalberg, who died at age thirty-seven—a victim of poor health and overwork. While the erratic Spiegel sometimes drove Kazan crazy, the director was eager to work with Harold Pinter as a screenwriter and newcomer Robert De Niro, who was cast in the title role. Although Kazan ended up being somewhat disappointed by the love story that was crafted by Pinter, there were a number of plot elements that drew the director to the film project. Seeking to make a quality film, Monroe Stahr is beset by many problems, including overwork, a failed love affair, and difficulties with screenwriters, union representatives, actors, and producers who make it impossible for him to make his film the way he desires. At the conclusion of *The Last Tycoon*, Stahr is relieved of his responsibilities by the studio, and he walks across an empty studio lot into a dark and deserted soundstage. In many ways, *The Last Tycoon* becomes a metaphor for Kazan's own life and career. The film failed to resonate with audiences at the time of its release, but like many of Kazan's films, *The Last Tycoon* earns a better reputation today.[40]

The Last Tycoon proved to be Kazan's last film, although he continued his writing career as a novelist. He married for a third time, wedding Frances Rudge in 1982, and the marriage endured until the director's death in 2003. Kazan was increasingly out of the public eye during the 1980s and 1990s, but the publication of his autobiography in 1988 and an honorary Oscar in 1999 brought the filmmaker back into the spotlight and reinvigorated debate over his HUAC testimony. Kazan's decision to legitimize HUAC and name former friends and associates made the director a pariah to the Hollywood left and to many liberals. His *New York Times* advertisement following the testimony cemented his reputation as an unapologetic collaborator. In his denunciation of the Communist Party, Kazan seemed to exacerbate the worst excesses of the Cold War and Second Red Scare.

A closer examination of Kazan's post-HUAC cinema, however, reveals a more complicated picture. From *Viva Zapata!* to *The Last Tycoon*, Kazan's films suggest that the director maintained an allegiance to many of his progressive principles going back to the Group Theatre days of the 1930s. In addition, the film texts demonstrate a degree of ambiguity regarding issues of informing and moral authority. While Kazan's autobiography failed to provide a direct apology for his collaboration with HUAC, his discussion of naming names indicates a far greater degree of ambivalence than he exhibited publicly in 1952. *A Life* also embraces a fierce individualism that Kazan lamented was always being checked by various forces and people in his life: Turkish authorities, his father, the Communist Party, his first and second wives, HUAC, critics, and studio heads. This discontent was often masked by his Anatolian smile, which was permanently wiped away by his death on September 28, 2003, from natural causes in New York City. Nevertheless, Kazan's cinema lives on, and in his post-HUAC films we are able to see the complexity of an artist, individualist, and progressive who was more than a right-wing collaborator.

I

VIVA ZAPATA! (1952) AND COLD WAR LIBERALISM

Novelist John Steinbeck and Elia Kazan's film project on the Mexican revolutionary leader Emiliano Zapata was released several months before Kazan's HUAC testimony in the spring of 1952. The film's topic and timing led many political observers of both the Right and the Left to carefully peruse the film in order to better ascertain the filmmaker's true political sensibilities. After all, the decision to make a film sympathetic to a revolutionary leader did not exactly coincide with the Hollywood blacklist and anti-Communist film genre of the 1950s and early Cold War. Some doubted that Kazan was sincere in his HUAC confession, but the director and Steinbeck insisted that the character of Fernando Aguirre as the Communist who betrays the populist Zapata, demonstrates the fundamental anti-Communist theme of the picture. Steinbeck and Kazan were Cold War liberals dedicated to the global struggle of the United States against Soviet Communist expansion, yet they were also progressives who worried about the impact of unfettered capitalism on the poor. Thus, *Viva Zapata!* may be perceived as a Cold War film text seeking to find an indigenous reform "third way" between the exploitation of the people by professional Communist revolutionaries and an unregulated global capitalist free market. The film celebrates Zapata as a hero who was willing to walk away from power—something Kazan insisted that a Communist would never do.

There was little ambivalence in the anti-Communist statement made by Kazan in April 1952 after a January private testimony in which the filmmaker admitted his former membership in the Communist Party but refused to name former associates. After considerable soul-searching, described in his autobiography, Kazan made the decision to name names. He wrote the committee that he wanted to amend his January 14 testimony, proclaiming: "I have come to the conclusion that I did wrong to withhold these names before, because secrecy serves the communists, and is exactly what they want. The American people need the facts and all the facts about all aspects of the communists in order to deal with it wisely and effectively. It is my obligation as a citizen to tell everything that I know."[1] Nevertheless, *Viva Zapata!* appears to offer a more ambiguous treatment of the ideological commitments Kazan made in his letter and testimony. Kazan was also suspect in some quarters due to his association with Steinbeck, whose politics were often misunderstood.

Steinbeck was a New Dealer and champion of the downtrodden Okies and migrant farm workers, but he increasingly moved to the political right in the 1950s and 1960s and supported Lyndon Johnson's anti-Communist crusade in Vietnam. While Steinbeck's writings were often denounced by conservatives in the 1930s, the California writer was hardly the favorite author of Communists. For example, Steinbeck's 1936 novel, *In Dubious Battle*, introduces Communist protagonists who will exploit people and engage in any tactics necessary to bring about their vision of a better world. Thus, Steinbeck perceives Communists as opportunists for whom the ends justify the means. Although it was denounced and banned upon publication in 1939, *The Grapes of Wrath* was hardly a revolutionary text. Despite Tom Joad's assertion to his mother that he would be there every time a cop is beating up a guy or a hungry newborn baby cries, Steinbeck's solution for the Great Depression is the "one big soul" advocated by Preacher Jim Casy. Rose of Sharon's charitable breast-feeding of the starving old man at the novel's conclusion represents the sharing and sense of caring that would allow the common people to persevere and is a far cry from a proletarian revolution.[2]

In his frequent travels to Mexico, Steinbeck found that the peasants of that nation exemplified many of the same admirable qualities he found in the Joads, and he began his research on the heroic Zapata. Steinbeck claimed to have interviewed almost anyone who knew Zapata, and he was also influenced by Edgcumb Pinchon's *Zapata the Unconquerable* (1941). The novelist worked on the script from 1948 to 1950, and although Kazan would later take credit for rewriting much of the screenplay, Steinbeck scholar Robert E. Morsberger insists that "Steinbeck not only collected oral history but got a first-hand sense of people and places. His personal involvement contributed to *Viva Zapata!*'s authenticity and helped make it more compelling than the melodramatic, sentimental, or textbookish 1930s film biographies of assorted statesmen, inventors, composers, and artists." Morsberger concludes that Steinbeck's script was the culmination of the novelist's thoughts on power and revolution, with which he was wrestling for over twenty years. Thus, Morsberger writes, "Zapata's role is that of an agrarian reformer, not a revolutionary remolder of society."[3]

Kazan was enthusiastic about Steinbeck's work and sought the backing of Darryl Zanuck and the Fox Studio for the picture. Early in the spring of 1950, Kazan and Steinbeck were summoned to the Palm Springs estate of the producer, who wanted numerous changes to the script—many of which the director later ignored. But Zanuck insisted that the film conclude with somewhat of a Western cliché. Zapata was to ride a white horse, and after the leader was assassinated, the last shot of the movie would be the horse running free in the mountains. Steinbeck was appalled, and Kazan thought the concept to be rather corny but concluded that "the idea worked out well in the end."[4]

Following Zanuck's approval of the project, Kazan and Steinbeck began to look into filming *Viva Zapata!* in Mexico. His experience with the Mexican authorities, however, drew Kazan into another political controversy. Kazan recounts that Steinbeck believed they could gain support for the film from the Mexican government through the intervention of Gabriel Figueroa, who served as president of the Syndicate of Film Technicians and was perceived as Mexico's leading cinematographer. Figueroa was initially pleased that the Americans wanted to film in Mexico, but according to Kazan, the Mexican cinematographer's attitude changed when Zapata's name was mentioned. Figueroa observed that Zapata was a great hero to the Mexican people and that a film on the national icon by an American filmmaker and featuring an American actor in the title role would require official approval. He asked for a copy of the script to examine over the weekend. Kazan and Steinbeck surrendered the script, but the director was quite suspicious of Figueroa. He told Steinbeck that he believed Figueroa was delaying because he needed to run the film past his Communist colleagues, who would formulate the official party position on *Viva Zapata!* Kazan considered that his reservations were confirmed when Figueroa returned and asked for major changes in the screenplay.[5]

According to Kazan, the party was especially upset over the film's emphasis on Zapata's failure to take power. In a letter to the *Saturday Review*, Kazan wrote: "No Communist, no totalitarian, ever refused power. By showing that Zapata did this, we spoiled a poster figure that the Communists have been at some pains to create." Kazan concluded: "In his moment of decision, this taciturn, untaught leader must have felt, freshly and deeply, the impact of the ancient law: power corrupts. And so he refused power. The man who refused power was not only no Communist, he was that opposite phenomenon: a man of individual conscience."[6] To Kazan, the party line to which the director was apparently exposed in Mexico confirmed his decision to name names before HUAC. He informed Steinbeck of Communist efforts in the 1930s to take over the Group Theatre that led Kazan to resign from the party. An angry Kazan also complained to the novelist of Communist efforts to make Budd Schulberg rewrite his novel *What Makes Sammy Run?* and to discipline writer Albert Maltz because he had dared to challenge the party line on literature and socialist realism.[7]

When Steinbeck and Kazan returned to the United States, Zanuck agreed that Mexican interference would make it impossible to go forward with filming *Viva Zapata!* on location in Mexico. Zanuck, however, surprised the director by his continuing support for the picture, which would now be filmed on the American side of the border near the small town of Roma, Texas. Kazan decided to be honest with Zanuck and told the producer that he had once been a member of the Communist Party and that he would likely be called before HUAC. This confession did not cause Zanuck to waver in his decision to put *Viva Zapata!* into production. An appreciative Kazan praised Zanuck for "telling the Mexicans, their official state censor and their department of Defense, their generals and their politicians to make their own film, he'd make his." Although Kazan would later be disappointed with Zanuck's failure to make *On the Waterfront*, the director concluded that he would rather engage in open conflict with tycoons like Zanuck than "deal with the men, consulting in secret, who'd made my old friend Albert Maltz crawl in public and tried to make a man I didn't yet know Budd Schulberg rewrite his novel."[8] Certainly his experience in Mexico seemed a contributing factor to Kazan's decision to cooperate with HUAC, but he still had trouble convincing some anti-Communist critics that *Viva Zapata!* was not pro-Communist in its political orientation.

He reassured Zanuck on numerous occasions that the picture was anti-Communist, pointing to the character of Fernando Aguirre and Zapata's decision to walk away from the presidency of Mexico. Kazan told Zanuck that the character of Fernando was introduced to thwart political criticism of the film by the Right. According to Kazan, "This personage was put in there as an embodiment of our feelings about the communists." In his desire to attain power, Fernando betrays both President Francisco Madero and Zapata. Kazan concludes: "If this character is not completely destructive of the Communist as he operates in politics and society, I don't know what is. Please remember, dear Darryl, that we put this man in with an eye towards possible attacks in the future. This picture is not only pro-democratic, but it is specifically, strongly, and uncontrovertibly anti-communist."[9] The significance of the Fernando character, however, was lost upon Twentieth Century Fox president Spyros Skouras. A Greek immigrant, Skouras believed that it was the duty of those new to the country to avoid controversy and to demonstrate their allegiance to America. Thus, he wanted Kazan to sign a letter that would absolve the studio from any responsibility for the politics of *Viva Zapata!* Kazan refused to sign the letter, and the director reiterated that *Viva Zapata!* was an anti-Communist film, proclaiming: "The point of Communist activity is to gain power, then use it. No Communist in history has ever given it up once he'd gained it. Zapata does precisely that."[10] Skouras remained unconvinced, urging the director to cooperate with HUAC and the Federal Bureau of Investigation. He even gave Kazan a copy of the anti-Communist memoir *I Led Three Lives*, by Herbert Philbrick, and insisted that the director make an overtly anti-Communist film. With Zanuck's support for *Viva Zapata!*, Kazan was, at least for the moment, to resist making an anti-Communist genre film.

In terms of casting, Steinbeck preferred Mexican actor Pedro Armendariz, who bore a physical resemblance to Zapata. For commercial appeal, Kazan and Zanuck believed that it would be necessary to have an American actor portray the Mexican hero. Zanuck's candidate was Tyrone Power, who had convincingly portrayed Spanish and Mexican characters in such films as *The Mark of Zorro* (1940), *Blood and Sand* (1941), and *Captain from Castile* (1947). Kazan's choice was Brando, whom Zanuck thought was too inexperienced, but following the actor's Academy Award nomination for *A Streetcar Named Desire*, Zanuck withdrew his objections.[11] Thus, the casting of *Viva Zapata!* followed the Hollywood tradition of white American actors portraying ethnic roles. The exception to this rule for *Viva Zapata!* was Anthony Quinn, whose mother was Mexican and father Irish, in the role of Zapata's brother Eufemio—a role for which Quinn would win an Academy Award as Best Supporting Actor. To portray Zapata's upper-class wife, Josefa, Jean Peters, the girlfriend of producer Howard Hughes, was selected to project an aristocratic image. As for the important political role of Fernando, Canadian actor and Broadway veteran Joseph Wiseman was tapped by Kazan, while the heavily Mexican American population of Roma provided some authenticity for the extras portraying participants in the Mexican Revolution.

The film was dependent upon Brando in the title role, and Kazan was delighted with his performance. The director pointed out to Brando that as a peasant, Zapata was not a man of words. Instead, the peasant keeps his thoughts to himself and conveys his emotions through more subtle facial expressions and mannerisms. In assessing Brando's performance as Zapata, Kazan proclaimed: "But no one altogether directs Brando. You release his instinct and give it a shove in the right direction. I told him the goal we had to reach, and before I'd done talking, he'd nod and walk away. He had the idea, knew what he had to do, and was, as usual, ahead of me. His talent in those days used to fly."[12] Brando was also complimentary of Kazan's directing of *Viva Zapata!*, but he was disappointed with Kazan's decision to name names before HUAC. In describing his work on *A Streetcar Named Desire* and *Viva Zapata!*, Brando asserted that Kazan was "the only one who ever really got into a part with me and virtually acted it with me." Brando appreciated the fact that Kazan respected his actors enough to provide them with time and space to interpret their characters. But Brando did have some reservations regarding the production of *Viva Zapata!* For example, he believed that Kazan "made a mistake in not requiring everyone in the cast to speak with a Mexican accent. I affected a slight one, but it wasn't well done, and most of the others spoke standard English, which made it seem artificial."[13] Questions of authenticity regarding his portrayal of Zapata were evident in the actor's belief that in the final analysis, his rendering of the Mexican revolutionary leader was "too romanticized for the real Zapata, too soft, too sweet."[14]

Viva Zapata! begins with a visit by Mexican peasants in 1907 to the presidential palace of Porfirio Diaz, who ruled the country from 1876 until overthrown by Francisco Madero in 1911. Diaz (Fay Roope) addresses the peasants as "my children" and treats them in a condescending manner. The farmers are concerned that their traditional lands are being intruded upon by the growing haciendas and large plantations. The advice of their president is for the peasants to work within the system and verify the boundary markers of their landholdings. The farmers express gratitude toward their president and begin to shuffle out of the room. One of them, however, pauses to remind Diaz that to verify the boundaries it will be necessary for the farmers to cross the fences constructed by the large land owners. Perturbed by the question, Diaz quickly asserts that there will be no problems as long as the peasants follow the law. He then asks the outspoken farmer for his name and circles the name of Emiliano Zapata. The next scene shows families crossing the fences to find the rocks and boulders that mark the traditional holdings of the people. Betraying the promise made by Diaz, the people are massacred by armed guards and soldiers employing modern means of destruction, such as machine guns. This treachery leads Zapata to become a rebel against the Diaz regime.

In the film's opening segment and portrayal of Diaz as one who cared little for the common people, Kazan and Steinbeck demonstrate their support for progressive political principles. To bring about the economic modernization of Mexico, Diaz invited the investment of European and American capitalists in the development and exploitation of his country. The result was an increase in foreign trade, mining production, industrialization, and railroad construction. While this expansion benefited the Mexican upper class, the majority of Mexicans remained in poverty. Only a quarter of the population was literate, while in 1900 29 percent of all male children died within a year of their birth.[15] This economic inequality helped to foster the Mexican Revolution and the rise of Zapata, in addition to underscoring the reservations of Steinbeck and Kazan for unfettered capitalism.

The film next depicts Zapata as a rebel hiding in the mountains of his native Morelos along with several comrades, including his brother Eufemio. His hiding place is breached by Fernando Aguirre, and Zapata is immediately suspicious of this unarmed man who approaches the rebels with a typewriter rather than a gun. Fernando's goal is to convince Zapata that he should join the liberal Francisco Madero in his struggle to over-throw the Diaz regime. Eufemio views the rather frenetic Fernando as crazy and proposes that he be executed—a decision that would make some sense in hindsight. His brother, however, is unwilling to either kill Fernando or commit to his cause, but he sends his trusted comrade Pablo (Lou Gilbert) with Fernando to find out more about this Madero. While a fictional character, Fernando is essential to the Steinbeck and Kazan characterization of *Viva Zapata!* as an anti-Communist film. Fernando is intended to represent the professional Communist revolutionary who, as the elitist vanguard of the proletariat, is willing to use anyone in the process of fostering violent revolution. Thus, in the early moderate stage of the revolution, Fernando is supporting Madero, but when change is not rapid and radical enough to satisfy him, Fernando will desert the liberal Madero. Kazan told interviewer Jeff Young that *Viva Zapata!* allowed the filmmakers "to show metaphorically what had happened to the commu-nists in the Soviet Union—how their leaders became reactionary and repressive rather than forward thinking and progressive." Thus, Fernando was an opportunist Stalinist. The director, however, did defend himself from allegations that he was an anti-intellectual for depicting Fernando in such a negative light. Kazan insisted: "To me someone with a lively reflective, disturbing, and investigative mind is the greatest fun in the world to be with. But I do feel that a lot of intellectual society people are just cheerleaders. They say things that they know their friends already agree with. Banalities are couched in high-falutin [*sic*] language, and nothing is the result of their own experience."[16] A man without emotion, Fernando would eventually betray both Zapata and the promise of the Mexican Revolution.

Although he was given a positive report by Pablo on the trustworthi-ness of the reformer Madero, Zapata decided to pursue more personal than revolutionary goals. He was in love with the aristocratic Josefa, whose father did not approve of the courtship. To make himself more presentable to the affluent family, Zapata applied his skills as a horse handler for one of the large haciendas. This effort at bourgeois confor-mity reminds one of Kazan's own efforts at attaining respectability with his marriage to Molly Thacher and her prominent New England family. Zapata, however, could not prevent himself from expressing sympathy with the common people, who were abused by his patron, Don Nacio, and the authorities, who always sided with the elite. He administers a beating to a horse trader who strikes a starving boy, and then Zapata offers a less than heartfelt apology. He is finally arrested for attacking soldiers who arrested an elderly peasant for stealing corn from what used to be his land. But Zapata's championing of the common people does not allow his arrest to go undetected.

As a group of soldiers on horseback place a noose around Zapata's neck and force him to walk rapidly to keep up with the mounted soldiers, men, women, and children begin to follow the soldiers and their prisoner. Through the pounding of stones together, the peasants are able to communicate Zapata's arrest—a strategy Anthony Quinn asserted that he witnessed when he was growing up in Mexico. Soon a small army of peasants, many of them armed with machetes, have joined the procession, informing the soldiers that they are there to guard the prisoner from the troopers. Increasingly intimidated and beginning to fear for their lives, the soldiers surrender their prisoner to the people and beat a speedy retreat. It is a powerful and inspiring scene of spontaneous revolution far from the scheming Fernando. The power of the people again underlines the progressive principles of Kazan and Steinbeck's script and politics.

Zapata is now committed to the revolution and is appointed by Madero as a general in command of the Army of the South. While Zapata is depicted as a victorious commander, the film does not include the battle scenes originally envisioned by Kazan due to budget reductions by Zanuck, who was becoming increasingly concerned about the commercial possibilities of a film deemed insufficiently anti-Communist. The lack of action is compensated with a greater emphasis on the courtship of Josefa, as her family recognizes that the political winds in Mexico now seem to be blowing away from Diaz and toward Madero and Zapata. Zapata is reciting proverbs to Josefa when the news arrives that Diaz has fled the country and the revolution is over. As everyone celebrates and drink flows freely at the wedding of Josefa and Zapata, an intoxicated Eufemio confronts Fernando, wondering why he does not share in the joy and instead avoids drink and sexuality. Fernando does not participate in the celebration as for him the revolution and violence are only beginning, establishing the Communist figure as "the cold, tight-lipped revolutionary, immune to pleasure and totally dedicated to the massive killing he considers inevitable and imperative."[17]

The wedding night includes a fictitious scene in which Zapata confesses to his bride that he is illiterate, and he asks Josefa to teach him to read and write. According to historians and biographers, Zapata, as a product of rural Mexico, was not well educated but certainly literate. This curious scene has the peasant acknowledging the advantages of the upper class, which he would like to extend to all of the Mexican people. In many ways, it seems reminiscent of Kazan's own marriage to Molly Thacher. Speaking of Zapata, Kazan told interviewer Michel Ciment: "He wanted both a peasant woman, and a woman of a higher social class, with more education and greater refinement. What he did was to go outside his class. He moved up into the middle-class, and he had to court her in the old fashioned ways; he got dressed up as a middle-class landowner. And in a way it was his first betrayal of himself, to court a woman that way and to marry that type of person."[18] In a similar fashion, the immigrant Kazan sought the respectability of Molly Thacher and her family. And while in the film Zapata seems to be interested in only one woman, the historical Zapata was involved with many women, just as Kazan pursued numerous extramarital affairs while professing his love for Molly.

The aftermath of the Diaz regime failed to usher in the period of peace and prosperity desired by the Mexican people. Zapata was disappointed with the slow pace of agrarian reform as Madero (Harold Gordon) surrounds himself with advisors and military figures from the previous government. In response to Zapata's complaints, Madero says that land redistribution is a complicated matter that will require considerable study. The new president asks for time and trust, but Zapata asserts, "You cannot plant and harvest time." Among his advisors, Fernando encourages Zapata to distance himself from Madero, who is betraying the promise of the revolution, while Pablo insists that the well-intentioned president needs the support of Zapata. Zapata decides to follow Pablo's counsel and agrees to Madero's demand that his men surrender their arms. Unknown to Madero, General Victoriano Huerta decides to take advantage of this situation and launches a military operation against Zapata and his followers. An angry Zapata now heeds the advice of an excited Fernando and takes up arms against the Madero government, while Pablo's pleas that he negotiate with the president are ignored. Meanwhile, Madero becomes a virtual prisoner of General Huerta, who eventually orders the execution of the president and assumes power.[19]

The Mexican Revolution entered a bloodier phase as Zapata fought to topple the Huerta government. During this fighting, a war-weary Zapata recognizes that his troops require discipline, and he issues an order that soldiers fraternizing with the enemy, many of whom were relatives in this civil war, would face execution. This directive leads to the arrest of Pablo, who was communicating with family members and still seeking to find some type of negotiated peace. To maintain a sense of order among his men, Zapata understands that his directive must be followed, so with great sorrow he personally accepts the responsibility of killing his friend. Fernando reassures Zapata that he had no choice, but the professional revolutionary also seems to embrace the growing violence.

Huerta resigned on July 8, 1914, blaming the collapse of his regime on the military intervention ordered by American president Woodrow Wilson—an intervention whose impact is ignored by *Viva Zapata!* The ensuing period was complicated, as the revolutionary victors failed to agree on a reform agenda and a division of power among Zapata, Pancho Villa, Venustiano Carranza, and Alvaro Obregon. *Viva Zapata!* condenses this political maneuvering into the December 1914 meeting between Villa and Zapata at Xochimilco on the outskirts of Mexico City. In this scene, Villa (Alan Reed) asserts that with his background as a bandit, he is in no position to assume the presidency and that it is Zapata's responsibility to fulfill the promise of the revolution. A reluctant Zapata accepts the mantle of reform and the presidency. But in the next scene, it is quite clear that Zapata is uncomfortable in the presidential palace with Fernando now serving as his secretary and advisor. Reminiscent of the film's opening, a delegation of peasants from his native village come to complain about his brother Eufemio, who is taking their land. Zapata becomes defensive, pointing out Eufemio's many contributions to the revolution but promising the villagers that he will look into the matter and concluding that they will have to "trust" him. When he circles the name of the peasant who was most outspoken in his criticism, Zapata realizes that he is allowing power to corrupt him. He gathers his saddlebags and rifle, preparing a return to his roots in Morelos. Fernando pleads with him to come to his senses as they are now in a position to enact the promise of the revolution. Zapata is not assuaged by Fernando and walks away from power, while the professional revolutionary decides to stay in Mexico City and will seek to destroy Zapata while serving the Carranza government. This scene is crucial to the arguments of Kazan and Steinbeck that *Viva Zapata!* is an anti-Communist film, for no Communist would willingly surrender power.

The film, however, does not end with this renunciation of power. Instead, Zapata returns to the people and the struggle for land reform—the type of leftist ambivalence that concerned Darryl Zanuck. Zapata confronts his brother, who has seemingly succumbed to the corrupting influence of power and wealth. Living on the estate given to him by the state for his service to the revolution, Eufemio has expropriated the land of the peasants and insists that he is entitled. It is the argument offered by the Communist Party as a new privileged class, as well as by the pigs in George Orwell's *Animal Farm*. A disappointed Zapata urges the peasants to fight for their land, not to depend upon leaders who may change and betray them. Zapata is spared a potential violent confrontation with Eufemio when his brother is killed by one of the peasants whose wife was claimed by Eufemio. With a personal example of the dangers presented by power and corruption, Zapata takes up the struggle against the Carranza government, although the complexities of the Mexican Revolution are again passed over—perhaps in a desire to not offend the Mexican authorities, whose support was deemed essential to the Cold War containment of the Soviet Union.

The last section of the film features a revolutionary Zapata hiding in the mountains with Josefa, who has now taken on a more peasant persona making tortillas, as her father feared. But Josefa appears happy, although she is terrified that her husband will be killed. The Carranza government organized a plot to assassinate Zapata, and the film's conclusion is loosely based on fact. An officer in Carranza's army offers to defect and turn a large arsenal over to the revolutionaries if Zapata will personally accept the weapons. Josefa suspects a plot to murder her husband and begs Zapata not to make the transaction. But Zapata says that the arsenal is essential for the revolutionary cause and that even if he is killed, the struggle for freedom and reform will continue. The revolution is not dependent upon one man. Josefa retorts that her marriage is dependent upon one man, but Zapata believes that his responsibilities extend beyond his domestic obligations. Zapata is betrayed and assassinated in a barrage of gunfire. Prominent in organizing the ambush is Fernando, who now works for the Carranza government and considers Zapata a threat to the centralization of power in the hands of the state. Ever the opportunist, Fernando is the professional revolutionary who is willing to betray friends and principles in the support of power. It is the culminating anti-Communist statement of the film.

Steinbeck and Kazan, however, provide a degree of ambivalence in the film's conclusion and suggest that the visions of Zapata regarding land reform and equality are alive and well despite the best efforts of men such as Huerta, Carranza, and Fernando. A distraught Fernando is upset that Zapata's white horse escapes the ambush and roams free in the mountains—a touch that Zanuck had insisted on including in the film. Meanwhile, the common people assert that the bullet-riddled body that the authorities identify as Zapata could be anyone; the real Zapata, like his white horse, is in the mountains, free and waiting for the people to call on him again if needed. In other words, the progressive principles of the revolution remain alive. It is a political message that undercuts the anti-Communist theme associated with the character of Fernando.[20]

The film opened to mixed reviews from the film critics, and it is interesting to note that many of these commentaries made no mention of Fernando. Instead, the critics were focused on the film's themes regarding social revolution. A generally sympathetic Bosley Crowther of the *New York Times* described *Viva Zapata!* as "lively a swirl of agitation as had been stirred in quite a time; the Mexican rebel leader, whom Marlon Brando plays, is recalled as a man of savage passion devoted to the poor and oppressed. He is also recalled as a champion of matchless integrity, unswerving in his belief in the people—a romantic ideal in every way." The review also praises the work of Kazan, Quinn, and Steinbeck, and Crowther concludes that "the best features of this drama are the visual aspects it presents of social injustice and unbalance in a primitive and misgoverned land."[21] Other critics, however, were unimpressed by the politics of *Viva Zapata!*, asserting that the Steinbeck script was essentially revisiting the populist rebellion of Tom Joad and *The Grapes of Wrath* in an environment very different from that of the Great Depression and New Deal. Thus, *Holiday* described the film as suffering from "a tedious and oratorical screenplay by John Steinbeck," while *Life* complained of Steinbeck's "mouthfuls of political platitudes."[22] The *New Yorker* found the screenplay's views on revolution to be "murky" at best, and the *New Republic* lamented that the film was dominated by "squelchy aphorisms of a kind we have heard before from the Okies."[23]

These reviews described the revolutionary ardor of Steinbeck and Kazan as being out of place during the Cold War. On the other hand, the Communist Party *Daily Worker* took a different approach, branding *Viva Zapata!* as Trotskyist and insisting that Kazan had taken a brave revolutionary leader in Zapata and made him into an ineffective and wavering intellectual. In replying to these criticisms, Steinbeck and Kazan indicated that progressive principles were still important to both of them. Steinbeck told Laura Hobson of the *Saturday Review* that he had attempted to interview every living person he could find in Mexico who was associated with Zapata and all described him as a common man of the people who uttered such phrases as "a strong people do not need a strong man."[24] In an interview with Michel Ciment in the early 1970s, Kazan went even further in embracing the revolutionary potential of *Viva Zapata!* Proudly acknowledging that the Communists had denounced *Viva Zapata!* when it premiered in the early 1950s, he pointed out that in the late 1960s the New Left, abandoning the intellectual straitjacket of Stalinism, embraced the film. Kazan proclaimed that young radical groups such as the Puerto Rican Young Lords loved and studied *Viva Zapata!* just as they did Gillo Pontecorvo's *The Battle of Algiers* (1966), for both of the films allowed them "to understand what their problem was going to be. The scenes of the revolution and of the unity of the people around Zapata, how the people gathered around a cause, was something they felt was going on with them. It became a film they showed like an educational picture, on the technique and the nature of a revolution. The change in what the Left is reversed the attitude toward the picture."[25] Endorsing *The Battle of Algiers* is certainly a long way from HUAC and the anti-Communist characterization of Fernando, providing further evidence as to the complexity of Kazan's political ideology.

Viva Zapata! was also criticized for its lack of historical accuracy. Journalist Carlton Beals complained that the notion of Zapata denouncing power was "absurd." The revolutionary's retreat from Mexico City was simply a matter of expediency. In addition, Beals found the character of Fernando to be an awkward insertion that was "utterly devoid of Mexican savor."[26] In response, Kazan claimed considerable anecdotal evidence for his depiction of Zapata based on Steinbeck's extensive interviews with revolutionary veterans. The director also believed that many on the political right were too quick to dismiss Zapata simply because the Communists claimed the Mexican leader. In a letter to the *Saturday Review*, Kazan wrote: "Whenever the Communists stake a claim to any concept or person that people value, the ever-anxious Right plays into their hands with cooperating regularity. If they would treat the Communist claim to peace, to free speech—and to men like Zapata—with the same good sense and laughter that greets the Communist claim to the invention of the bicycle, it would make life easier for those of us who really value those things."[27]

Rather than focusing on whether Kazan captured the historical reality of Zapata and the Mexican Revolution, Kazan's biographer Richard Schickel argues that *Viva Zapata!* may be read as a critical allegory of the Russian Revolution, in which Madero becomes a tragic figure much like Alexander Kerensky and the Provisional Government in Russia, betrayed by the Bolsheviks, even going so far as to suggest that Zapata was a Trotsky figure who was assassinated by the Stalin-like Fernando.[28] In the sweep of his film, however, Kazan's perceptions of the Russian Revolution do not fit quite so neatly into Schickel's allegory. Kazan was an admirer of the Soviet revolutionary filmmakers, such as Sergei Eisenstein and Alexander Dovzhenko, whose sweeping portrayals of the Russian people embraced the revolutionary hope of progressive change. In addition, the director revered the neorealism of Italian filmmaker Robert Rossellini. Thus, Kazan employed historical photographs of the Mexican Revolution to provide his film with a sense of realism. In the *Archiva Casa Sola*, Kazan discovered the *Historia Grafica de la Revolucion* collection, and he based the look of his film on these historical photographs as archetypal, for they displayed "a great quality of underplaying horror, that is, there'd be horrors and drama and death there, but it was taken as a matter of course. It was the nature of a revolution to show that and deal with it."[29] Along with this historical portrayal, Kazan did not want to dismiss the possibility of revolutionary change. While disappointed with the outcome of both the Russian and Mexican Revolutions, Kazan asserted that he did not mean to suggest that revolution was necessarily futile. He told Michel Ciment that at the conclusion of the film, the people still believe in Zapata, "and he was trying to create the revolution again, that he did educate himself to a point—in other words, we tried to say that there is a next step, that he was beginning to find it, and that he didn't. We had that in mind, anyway. And in the end the ritualistic Leftist becomes a murderer and kills Zapata."[30] In this commentary, Kazan reflects the Cold War liberalism to which he and Steinbeck adhered. The film director still believed in the progressive principles of his youth regarding the government's duty to provide decent health care, housing, and economic opportunity for all citizens. Yet the anti-Communist Kazan still perceived Communist Party members such as Fernando to be selfishly limiting the possibility for fundamental change. Accordingly, *Viva Zapata!* was the first of many film texts providing evidence of Kazan's complex political ideology. In his study of Kazan's cinema, Brian Neve argues that Fernando is more of a dated 1950s Cold War character, while the progressive principles espoused by Zapata have a more lasting impact. Neve insists: "In a longer perspective, the Fernando character, a product in part of contemporary political pressures, seems a reasonable if unfocused comment on the exploitation of popular revolution by opportunistic leaders. In an era when Joseph McCarthy and others were using the Communist scare to promote their own agenda of conservative populism, the film provides visual imagery that strikingly reflects a more progressive, grass roots populist vision."[31]

It is also worth noting that despite taking considerable liberty with the details of Zapata's life, Kazan seemed to accurately portray the larger historical truth of Zapata's struggle for justice. For example, Harvard historian John Womack, Jr., in his definitive study *Zapata and the Mexican Revolution*, praised the Kazan film. Noting the compression of events and creation of composite characters to fit the film within a two-hour Hollywood framework, Womack nevertheless believed that *Viva Zapata!* was a distinguished achievement that "quickly and vividly develops a portrayal of Zapata, the villagers, and the nature of their relations and movement that I find still subtle, powerful, and true."[32] In a similar vein, Zapata biographer Samuel Brunk describes the Mexican leader as quite similar to the figure portrayed by Brando in *Viva Zapata!* While not directly addressing the film text, Brunk concludes that Zapata was sincerely dedicated to fundamental land reform for the peasants of Mexico, but in the final analysis he was betrayed by Carranza and other former supporters. While representing those who have lost in Mexican history, Brunk argues that Zapata nonetheless "stands for the lasting ability and willingness of the dispossessed to maintain their dignity and to resist." Brunk acknowledged that Zapata was a tragic hero "destroyed by very human feelings as he tried to change his world. But those who have kept his memory alive most conscientiously, in the fields and villages and even the cities of Mexico and beyond, understand the value of his effort."[33] Thus, Brunk's academic biography strikes a similar note to Kazan's *Viva Zapata!* with the revolutionary leader still embodying the hopes and dreams of the common people.

Viva Zapata! earned five Academy Award nominations, including nominations for Steinbeck, Brando, and Quinn, although the film's only Oscar win was Quinn for Best Supporting Actor. Receiving mixed reviews, the film opened well, but attendance rapidly fell off, and *Viva Zapata!* failed to earn a profit in its initial release. Zanuck insisted that the timing was wrong for a historical picture such as *Viva Zapata!* Reflecting on successful Fox movies such as Tyrone Power in *The Mark of Zorro*, Zanuck concluded they should have dropped the historical references to Zapata and just constructed the protagonist as a Mexican "Robin Hood" figure. He told Kazan, "It came out at a time when audiences were reaching for pure escapist entertainment and not willing to listen to any messages or historical lessons even about an exciting and colorful Mexican bandit."[34] In response, Kazan believed that Zanuck never understood *Viva Zapata!* He informed Michel Ciment: "I still don't know why he did *Zapata*. I guess because I'd made money for the company and he was looking for something exciting and unusual; maybe he liked some things about it. I don't know. It seemed very foreign to him, at that time. I don't think *Grapes of Wrath* was about people he knew. But *Zapata* just bewildered him."[35]

And perhaps the politics of *Viva Zapata!* were just too ambivalent for Zanuck and film audiences. After all, shortly following the film's release, Kazan made his public testimony before HUAC, denouncing the international Communist conspiracy. On the other hand, he had just released a film featuring a Mexican revolutionary, admired by Communists, as its tragic hero. It is certainly not clear that the insertion of Fernando as a critique of professional Communist revolutionaries, attempting to hijack the aspirations of the common people for democracy and land redistribution, was understood by mainstream audiences. Therefore, during the height of the Second Red Scare and McCarthyism, a film such as *Viva Zapata!* was viewed suspiciously by those on the political right. Zanuck believed he had a plan to thwart these critics. It was time for Kazan to make an overtly anti-Communist film. Finally succumbing to studio pressure, Kazan agreed to direct *Man on a Tightrope*—a poorly received movie that led to a rupture in the relationship between Kazan and his producer and a picture that lacked the ambivalence that continues to make *Viva Zapata!* such an interesting film.

2

KAZAN AND THE ANTI-COMMUNIST FILM GENRE

Man on a Tightrope (1953)

The early 1950s were a terrible time in Hollywood as the studios blacklisted writers, directors, and performers whose politics were questioned by HUAC, which was invited to the film capital by the Motion Picture Alliance for the Preservation of American Ideals in order to rid the film industry of supposed Communist influence. The Red Scare in Hollywood was also part of a labor dispute in which Screen Actors Guild president Ronald Reagan worked with the studios and Roy Brewer, president of the International Alliance of Theatrical Stage Employees Union, to crush the Conference of Studio Unions, which was accused of being a Communist front union. In addition, the film industry was facing economic challenges from the spread of television and suburbia, keeping the baby boom generation in their homes and automobiles, while the *Paramount* Supreme Court decision (1948) curtailed the monopolistic practice of the studios owning their own theater chains. It was within this turbulent atmosphere that Kazan was called before HUAC and eventually decided that he would cooperate and name former associates.

In his recent study of Hollywood politics, historian Steven J. Ross has tried to somewhat downplay the political partisanship associated with informing by emphasizing the post–World War II insecurities plaguing industry executives. Ross writes:

Concerned about potential audience backlash at the box office, studio heads moved to limit the unprecedented activism of their former employees. The financial success of the studio system made it possible for actors and actresses to make unprecedented amounts of money, but at the cost of restricting their freedom by tying them to lengthy contracts that gave studio heads the ability to shape a star's image and control his or her offscreen activities. Studios were willing to tolerate some partisan activism, but stars who strayed too far from the political mainstream had their careers cut short, blacklisted or graylisted by fearful industry executives.[1]

Many who suffered through the blacklist were far more critical of the Hollywood establishment. For example, screenwriter Lillian Hellman titled her memoir of the blacklist *Scoundrel Time*, denouncing the efforts of HUAC to interrogate American citizens regarding their political views and highlighting her refusal to inform when called before the congressional committee in 1952.[2] Screenwriter Dalton Trumbo, who was a member of the Hollywood Ten, went to prison for contempt of Congress when he challenged the right of HUAC to inquire about his political beliefs. In his political memoir, *The Time of the Toad*, Trumbo asserted that individual liberties were under siege in the United States. The writer believed that if intellectuals really wanted to preserve freedom of speech, it would be necessary to defend the rights of everyone, including Communists. Trumbo had little patience for the friendly witness, such as Kazan, writing: "He must determine for himself whether, by casting aside the immunity with which he is clothed, he wishes to assist the committee in its pursuit of an illegal end. He must consider the precedent which his act establishes. He must decide whether he wants absolution and approbation at such hands."[3]

Kazan, of course, insisted that while he had little use for the committee, his testimony was an important step in defeating the Communist criminal conspiracy, which did not deserve the protection of the Constitution. Critics of Kazan, however, insisted that the filmmaker was more concerned with preserving his lucrative Hollywood career than saving the country from conspiracy. For example, Hellman maintains that Kazan told her executives at Twentieth Century Fox threatened that he would never make another film if he did not cooperate with the committee.[4] The expression of such fears led scholars Larry Ceplair and Steven Englund, in their study of the blacklist, to conclude: "In short, it finally came down,

not mainly to disillusionment, not to prison even—neither of which ne-
cessitated informing—but to the blacklist. This was the material, obvious,
and basic 'American' truth that no one cared to mention at the time, and
very, very few have admitted years later. The reality which informed
informing was this: four dozen witnesses so feared losing their careers
and their income that they cooperated."[5] In his examination of informing,
Victor S. Navasky related these fears to moral lapses in which "the citizen
delegated his conscience to the state."[6] Kazan, the Greek immigrant with
the Anatolian smile, always considered himself the outsider who was
intimidated by authority, whether it be Turkish officials, the Communist
Party, HUAC, or studio heads, any of whom might endanger his liveli-
hood. Thus, on a psychological level his informing and striking out
against the Communist Party might be interpreted as the perpetual outsider attempting to fit in as a patriotic American. Ironically, this act made
him a pariah whose informing would remain an issue when he received
his 1999 honorary Oscar.

But in April 1952, when he named names, Kazan could not admit to
such conflicting thoughts. Instead, he embraced the anti-Communist
cause and produced a film, *Man on a Tightrope*, that lacked the sense of
ambivalence that would characterize the rest of his film career. The Hollywood anti-Communist film genre included such pictures as *The Iron
Curtain* (1947), *The Red Menace* (1949), *I Married a Communist* (1949),
The Whip Hand (1951), *Invasion, U.S.A.* (1952), *Big Jim McClain*
(1952), *My Son John* (1952), and *I Was a Communist for the FBI* (1952).
These films were characterized by stereotypes such as the Communist
villain who has no emotions or respect for religion and human life. In
these films, American society is fundamentally sound, but many young
Americans and minorities are naive and subject to Communist propaganda. For example, in *My Son John*, Robert Walker portrays a young man
who is seduced by an Ivy League education and a State Department job to
abandon the simple patriotic values of his family. After realizing their
son's betrayal and conversion to Communism, the parents chastise him,
his father literally thumping John over the head with a Bible, while his
mother observes that unlike his brothers, who served in the military, John
never played football. In denouncing the conformity of Communism,
however, these film texts embrace another type of conformity—the ideology of anti-Communism, which was used to criticize New Dealers as well

as advocates for women's liberation, civil rights, and union democracy. Thus, film historians Peter Roffman and Jim Purdy conclude:

> Like HUAC, these films rely on their own internal logic which betrays a tendency toward the very totalitarianism that they are supposedly combating. Any of the beliefs and freedoms that fail to conform precisely to the values of the American people are held up as suspect, as the means by which the Communists infiltrate and poison the country. So, although America is glorified as the land of freedom where everyone can speak and think for himself, the threat of communism is simultaneously located in that very exercise of free thought.[7]

In addition to the anti-Communist ideology enforcing its own brand of conformity and totalitarianism, the anti-Communist film genre contributed to Hollywood's failure to explore social problems—a trend that had been promising in the immediate postwar period and to which Kazan contributed with such films as *Gentleman's Agreement* (1947) and *Pinky* (1949). Ceplair and Englund write, "Never daring in the first place, the studios withdrew before the lengthening shadow of HUAC and McCarthy into the dictated confines of patriotic conformity and circumscribed creativity. Controversial or 'social' subjects, at best only a minor portion of previous production schedules, were no longer even countenanced as story material at the majors."[8] Yet after his HUAC testimony and the modest box office receipts for *Viva Zapata!*, Kazan found himself making his own anti-Communist film to silence critics who insisted that *Viva Zapata!* was insufficient in its denunciation of Communism.

According to Kazan, Zanuck argued that the director would need to do an anti-Communist film in order to demonstrate his loyalty, and he had just the right property for a new film. Zanuck proposed that Kazan film Robert Sherwood's script *Man on a Tightrope*, based on the story "International Incident" by Neil Paterson, about a circus that escaped Communist Czechoslovakia for freedom in Austria. Kazan did not want to do the film, complaining about the quality of the script. He understood that Sherwood was a gifted writer who wrote the screenplay for *The Best Years of Our Lives* (1947) and the intimate history *Roosevelt and Hopkins* (1945), a book Kazan much admired. Nevertheless, he initially declined the project, asserting, "Because it's badly written, all-black or all-white characters, typical propaganda stuff, and I'd only be doing it to satisfy a pack of red-baiters who want my ass."[9] Zanuck persisted in his demands, observing that many in Hollywood, including the producer, continued to harbor doubts about Kazan's politics. This argument seemed to have some impact on Kazan, and he agreed to accompany Sherwood on a journey to Bavaria to meet the Brumbach Circus and ascertain whether their story was truthful or simply propaganda.

Kazan was impressed when he met the circus performers in Bavaria and decided to do the film; however, his reservations regarding the Sherwood script, in which the love stories eclipsed the drama of the escape, were on target. The film was based on the actual escape of the Brumbach Circus from East Germany, but the script changed the plot slightly to the Cirkus Cernik fleeing Communist Czechoslovakia. Kazan was delighted to be filming on location and working with a German crew, whom he grew to admire as they helped him to move beyond being a "stage-bound director."[10] Kazan was also inspired that the crew stuck with the film despite threats from the East German government against relatives still living under that regime. He admired the toughness of his German crew, who survived the devastation of World War II and were uncomplaining about the rigors of shooting on location in a cold and damp environment. Impressed with these people who were rebuilding their lives after military defeat, Kazan concluded: "I became unburdened of self-pity. It was such a relief to be out from under the heavy issues, to be up against the simplest one, survival, and to enjoy the rough comradeship of my crew. I determined to accept what they had accepted, that one part of my life was over, and not to look for support or friendship where I'd once had it. I determined to look everyone in the eye when I got back home and tough it out, as my crew was toughing it out."[11]

During filming, Kazan also became enamored with the circus troupe. He was especially friendly with a dwarf who was employed in the comedy routines, and the two became inseparable drinking partners. The dwarf introduced Kazan to the other performers, and the filmmaker was amazed by their pride as artists despite the rather humbling circumstances of their small and impoverished circus. Always describing himself as an outsider with his Anatolian smile, Kazan found that he had much in common with the circus folk, observing: "I came to see that circus people were outsiders to any society—freaks, in fact—and since we were so compatible, I must be the same. That identity suited me that year, and I made the circus my home, hung out there all day long, day after day, and was accepted as a member."[12]

While hardly outsiders, the cast assembled by Kazan lacked big name stars, although Fredric March as circus manager Karel Cernik is a notable exception. March was a major Hollywood and Broadway star, appearing in the acclaimed *Best Years of Our Lives*, written by Sherwood. He and his wife, Florence, had worked with Kazan on the stage in Thornton Wilder's *Skin of Our Teeth*. Both of the Marches' politics were under scrutiny, and it was becoming difficult for Frederic March to obtain roles. Kazan scoffed at the notion of March as a Communist and considered him to be an honest liberal. The director also enjoyed drinking and carousing with March when the actor's rather proper, but more political, wife was not around. While March would portray a courageous anti-Communist, in a casting of apparent opposites Adolphe Menjou was selected to play his nemesis, a Communist official investigating the circus. Menjou, an associate of Ayn Rand, was active in the Motion Picture Alliance for the Preservation of American Ideals and welcomed HUAC to Hollywood, testifying before the committee and denouncing the Red Menace in the film industry. On the film set, however, Menjou was apparently professional and kept his political opinions to himself.[13] Terry Moore, another protégé of producer Howard Hughes, played Cernik's daughter and served as the love interest for newcomer Cameron Mitchell. Gloria Grahame, whom Kazan described as "a slightly over the hill siren," was cast as Cernik's wife, who has a passion for the circus lion tamer.[14] Richard Boone, who later in the decade gained fame as Paladin in the television series *Have Gun Will Travel*, portrayed the devout Communist informer who sought to block the circus's escape.

As Kazan began working on the film, he dismissed any thoughts that *Man on a Tightrope* would be just another anti-Communist genre propaganda picture. Writing to Zanuck, Kazan asserted that it was essential to downplay the love stories and focus on the important political implications of the escape plan. Kazan wrote: "This is a story above all others, that should not be conventionalized. We're dealing with something red hot, something that will be seen and judged by very serious standards because it deals, in miniature, with the central issue of our day. It must have about it the stamp of complete truth."[15]

The significance to which Kazan was elevating *Man on a Tightrope* seems related to the ostracism, and perhaps guilt, he was experiencing regarding his HUAC testimony. In letters and interviews, Kazan began to denounce as Stalinists those who did not share his break with Communism. And *Man on a Tightrope* emerged as a cinematic statement in support of what Kazan considered his courageous decision to name names. Lacking the ambivalence of later films such as *On the Waterfront*, *Man on a Tightrope* could not carry this weight. Writing to Sherwood, Kazan proclaimed how fortunate he was to testify before HUAC and clear the air. The director asserted: "The Communists had done violence to everything I believed in, and still somehow I stayed silent and shrugged it off and minimized and looked the other way."[16] But it was not quite so easy for the filmmaker to dismiss the criticism of former friends and associates. During the filming of *Man on a Tightrope*, he wrote his wife Molly that he was reading *Witness* by Whittaker Chambers, who named Alger Hiss as a Soviet spy. Identifying with Chambers, Kazan acknowledged that he also paid a great price for his testimony and insisted: "But I'm really proud of what I've done. You know you always told me that I should be, but I would never answer that I was. Because I wasn't until I read Chambers. God knows he's fruity, but he saw his duty and he done it."[17]

Thus, Cernik in *Man on a Tightrope* was a Kazan or Chambers figure, but this confession analogy would work better with Terry Malloy in *On the Waterfront*. In discussing *Man on a Tightrope* later with interviewers, Kazan returned to the theme of guilt. However, he insisted that he did not suffer guilt for naming names but rather was ashamed of how long he had waited to denounce the Communist threat. Kazan told Michel Ciment that he hoped a film such as *Man on a Tightrope* would lift his guilt. Kazan observed: "I mean, I was really ashamed at being so terrorized, so immersed in Stalinism. Many of my friends are still unable to face the truth of that situation. The Stalinists here are so terrorized and so automated that they can no longer take stands."[18] In a similar vein, Kazan told Jeff Young that making *Man on a Tightrope* played an important role in helping him break with Stalinism. Describing his attachment to and break with Communism, Kazan said: "It's akin to a kind of religious faith. After all, Stalin was as bad as Hitler, maybe worse. Hitler killed six million Jews. Stalin killed the same number of people, maybe more. He was a monster, but your mind, once you've been a committed Communist, doesn't want to face that fact. So in a way the film was an important purgative thing for me to do. In another sense, it was a simple play of sweet affectionate people against ritualized violence."[19]

This level of affection for the circus people provides a degree of respect for individualism and artistic integrity, which raises *Man on a Tightrope* beyond the anti-Stalinist tract with which Kazan was becoming increasingly comfortable. In his production notes for the film, Kazan described *Man on a Tightrope* as "an ode to individualism," featuring circus folk as the "least uniform, the most individualistic, the oddest, the most eccentric" of people in society. Thus, the filmmaker concluded that the circus was an excellent symbol for a healthy democracy as "it has room for all kinds, it has need for all people."[20] And like any good democracy, politics were of secondary concern to the circus performers, who are prodded into action by the efforts of the Communist government in Czechoslovakia to threaten and control their way of life. Thus, in their rebellion the circus members are struggling for the right of the individual conscience to be expressed and heard.[21] But in the immediate wake of his HUAC testimony, Kazan did not seem to realize that to many individuals, the interrogations of Joseph McCarthy, HUAC, and Loyalty Review Boards could be just as threatening to freedom of conscience as a grand Soviet inquisitor. This more complex approach to the political environment of the Cold War was too much absent from *Man on a Tightrope* to make the film one of Kazan's best.

Accordingly, Kazan wrote associate producer Gerd Oswald that the deterioration of the Cernik circus should mirror the decline of Eastern Europe under Communist rule. Kazan explained that the Cernik circus was once an excellent circus that performed before the crowned heads of Europe. After World War II and the triumph of Communism, the circus is in disarray. There is no money for new costumes, tents, rigging, and machinery. Everything has a tattered and patched look as the government, which now technically owns the circus, has little time and money for the enterprise. Kazan asserts, nevertheless, that the film should demonstrate to viewers that the circus is "held together by sheer will power. And this is the fact. It is maintained by the spirit, the bravery and the fortitude of its owner, Cernik, who would not give up." Joined by his loyal performers, Cernik projects a valiant assertion that the show, indeed, must go on. Kazan suggests to Oswald: "And as we watch their act, we must feel despite shabbiness and the poverty that the circus is succeeding in giving a good show. In fact we forget the patches and the shabbiness and the worn out equipment. We feel only the brave spirit of the circus."[22] Indeed, in the black-and-white cinematography of Georg Krause, Kazan did get the downtrodden but resilient look that he desired for the film. *Man on a Tightrope*, however, is limited by its rather one-dimensional political perspective, which was fairly typical of the anti-Communist film genre.

The film begins with a performance in which clown and circus manager Karel Cernik (Fredric March) pretends to fall from a tightrope, but he catches himself just in time to the delight of the small crowd. The shabby, but entertaining, little circus is obviously only hanging on by a thread as Cernik is beset by personal, economic, and political problems. Cernik's daughter, Tereza (Terry Moore), is engaging in a relationship with Joe Vosdek (Cameron Mitchell), whom the father does not trust, as Joe is new to the circus and no one seems to know anything about his background. Tereza's mother is deceased, and Cernik is married to a younger woman, Zama (Gloria Grahame), who is carrying on an affair with the circus lion tamer. She finds her husband weak and indecisive. In addition, sinister figures in trench coats, representing the state security apparatus, are monitoring the performance. The ominous presence of the Communist state is also evident in an early scene when a police/military vehicle forces the circus off the road to make way for a truck convoy of political prisoners.[23]

Cernik is then summoned to police headquarters in Pilsen for an interrogation. He is reminded by the Communist officials that while once his family owned the Cirkus Cernik, he is now only the manager, as the circus is controlled by the government on behalf of the people. And to continue its performances, the Cirkus Cernik will need to maintain its state permit. In a scene that is rather heavy-handed in its anti-Communist propaganda, Cernik is criticized for failing to implement propaganda skits dictated by the government to poke fun at Jim Crow and the imperialistic foreign policy of the United States. The circus manager assures the authorities that he has tried the dictated skits, but audiences did not find them amusing, so they were dropped from the show. Having no patience for such excuses, the authorities inform Cernik that if he wants to continue managing the Cirkus Cernik, the propaganda pieces will be reinstated. In addition, the interrogators are concerned about one of the show's longtime performers, "The Duchess." It seems that she waved a French flag during a recent performance, but Cernik interjects that she was just attempting to honor her deceased French husband. Cernik is ordered to fire "The Duchess," but the manager retorts that she is an elderly woman who might not be able to survive without the support of the circus. This plea is met with strong silence from the authorities, who, in the standard Holly-wood anti-Communist film formula, lack any sense of compassion or emotion. After Cernik is dismissed, one police interrogator writes him off as "a dull, uncomplicated clown." On the other hand, propaganda chief Fesker (Adolphe Menjou) disagrees, believing Cernik to be a devious and dedicated man who "deserves to be watched."[24] This conversation will eventually lead to the arrest of Fesker and introduces the idea that Com-munists do not trust one another as they maneuver to demonstrate their loyalty not to people but to an abstract ideology and the state.

The audience learns that Fesker's suspicions are well founded, as upon returning to the circus, Cernik is planning a daring escape that will take the circus across the border into Austria. Cernik believes that Joe is a spy who is revealing his plans to the police. When he confronts Joe, Cernik learns from his daughter the rather convoluted story that Joe is a native of Czechoslovakia who moved to America with his mother. He joined the American army during World War II, but Joe deserted in order to search for his businessman father, who was apparently killed by either the Nazis or Soviets. The story adds little but confusion to the film, and Kazan was on target in his criticism of the screenplay, to which he could not get Zanuck to make necessary changes.

As Cernik continues to plot his escape, he is visited by his major circus rival, Barovik (Robert Beatty), who seems to have prospered under the Communist regime with a nice car and fancy Russian attire. Barovik has learned of Cernik's plans to flee the country and wants to purchase surplus equipment that will be left behind. Cernik is rather surprised that his rival has not informed the state police, but Barovik retorts, "We're both circus men, first, last, and always." In the conversation, Kazan again reveals his respect for the circus people, suggesting that their adherence to their art and individuality are a democratic shield against blind obedi-ence to ideology and authority. To cover their conspiracy, the two circus men engage in a tumultuous fight, after which Barovik secretly wishes Cernik good luck.

Cernik now makes his move to cross the Austrian border. The border crossing includes considerable drama, which is enhanced by cross-cutting editing. But some of the drama is negated by plot elements not essential to the suspense. For example, Zama is again drawn to her husband when he seemingly proves himself to be a "real man" by engineering the daring escape and slapping her for being unfaithful. Meanwhile, Fesker arranges for Cernik to obtain a permit to perform near the border so that the circus man will be apprehended attempting to flee the benefits of state socialism. Before he is able to detain Cernik, Fesker is arrested for issuing the illegal permit by a rival security officer seeking to improve his status with the state.

The escape plan calls for the circus to approach the border crossing as if getting ready for a performance, with all circus members in their costumes. Disguised as a Czech soldier, Joe engages the border guards in gunfire as the circus performers attempt to cross a bridge into freedom. The escape is almost thwarted by Cernik's friend and lieutenant for twenty years, Krofta (Richard Boone), who is a spy for the Communist authorities—highlighting Kazan's perception of betrayal on the part of Communists who are committed to their ideology. Krofta vows to stop this "criminal escape" and claims to be the "leader of the tent men, the real workers of the circus." This champion of the proletariat pulls a gun on Cernik and promises to turn him over to the secret police so that all involved in the plot would be exposed. Cernik and Krofta grapple over possession of the gun, and in the struggle Krofta is killed and Cernik seriously wounded. Despite the death of several other circus members, including the lion tamer, Jaromir, (Paul Hartman) who finally shows courage beyond the lion cage, the escape is successful. After crossing the border and achieving his dream, the heroic Cernik dies, but Zama, whose love for her husband has been rekindled, assumes the role of circus manager and tells the saddened circus members that the Cirkus Cernik owes the children of free Austria a performance. And the film concludes as it began, with the clowns dancing, but this time on free soil.

The film's ending reflects Kazan's belief, expressed to Zanuck, that *Man on a Tightrope* must dramatize "the arrival of the circus into the Free World—and what this means. I'm repeating it is important. The ending should concern only our main story which is not a love story and not a personal story, but the story of an escape of a group of individuals."[25] The film's final scene does not quite carry the punch envisioned by Kazan, as the motive for Zama's newfound dedication to the circus appears to spring from love for her husband and honoring his personal sacrifice rather than the desire to make a political statement. Nevertheless, Kazan's film did establish an anti-Communist martyr in Cernik—perhaps reflecting Kazan's own sense of martyrdom at the time. He was to continue the exploration of this theme with *On the Waterfront*, but the character of

Terry Malloy presents a more complex individual and ambivalent motivation than the one-dimensional Cernik, who sacrificed his life to strike a blow against the Communist state.

Kazan had enjoyed the location shooting of the film in Germany and believed that with careful editing, *Man on a Tightrope* showed promise. Zanuck, however, assumed the editing duties without consulting the director, privileging the love story over the political statement that Kazan desired to make. Also, similar to most films of the anti-Communist genre, *Man on a Tightrope* was a failure at the box office. Nevertheless, film critics were somewhat supportive of Kazan's picture, as it was a cut above the usual mindless propaganda of the genre.

The *New York Times* credited Kazan with having "the artistic acumen to concentrate more on movement and characterization than on politics." Most of the review in the *Times*, however, then proceeded to discuss the politics of the film. For example, the reviewer wondered whether Communist authorities would really invest so much time and energy into the investigation of a circus but concludes that the theme of common people "chafing against bondage of any sort appears to be real and touching." After crediting Fredric March with portraying a courageous man of conviction, the review concludes that *Man on a Tightrope* was "not only an arresting melodrama but a vivid commentary on a restricted way of life in our perilous times."[26] Arthur Knight of the *Saturday Review* also gave *Man on a Tightrope* a strong endorsement, arguing that the film was "an unusually absorbing picture, given added stature by its implications in our world today." Perhaps indicative of the clumsy propaganda that characterized most anti-Communist pictures, Knight credits Kazan with staging *Man on a Tightrope* as an "adventure" film in which "there are no wild anticommunist speeches, the characters are never allowed to become grotesque political symbols."[27]

Despite these positive reviews, *Man on a Tightrope* was a flop. Nevertheless, Kazan was basically pleased with his work, blaming the film's failure on Sherwood's script, Zanuck's editing of the picture, and the studio's lack of support in promoting the movie. After his sojourn in Germany, Kazan returned to New York City with increased resolve that he, just as Cernik, had done the right thing in confronting the Communists. Writing in his autobiography, Kazan proclaimed: "Just as my circus had, I'd survived all threats, spoken and implied, and was going on. The thing was to be hardy, no matter what the 'weather,' not to expect the comforts of position, the constant flattery of praise or the false assurances of comradeship. I would be what I had to be—tougher than my enemies—and work harder." Kazan concludes that his best and most original films were made after his HUAC testimony. The filmmaker was convinced that freed from the shackles of Communism, he, like the Cirkus Cernik, was now able to honestly and fully present his vision. The director proclaimed: "The films after April 1, 1952 were personal, to come out of me, fired by what I've been describing. They're films I still respect."[28] Many critics would agree with Kazan's statement with the exception of *Man on a Tightrope*, which in the final analysis could not avoid the moralistic certitude of the propagandistic anti-Communist film genre. In his next film project, *On the Waterfront*, Kazan returned to the complexity and ambivalence that made *Viva Zapata!* a notable work of cinema and would characterize the filmmaker's post-HUAC testimony films.

3

THE AMBIVALENCE OF INFORMING

On the Waterfront (1954)

On the Waterfront is the most acclaimed of Kazan's films. It received eleven Academy Award nominations and won eight Oscars, including Best Picture, Best Director for Kazan, Best Actor for Marlon Brando, Best Supporting Actress for Eva Maria Saint in her debut role, Best Cinematography for Boris Kaufman, and Best Screenplay for Budd Schulberg. The film is often interpreted as a justification for Kazan's HUAC testimony, as Terry Malloy (Brando) gives evidence against many of his former associates in a corrupt waterfront union. Although Kazan insisted that the film was primarily about the abuses suffered by long-shoremen at the hands of union leaders in cahoots with organized crime, he did eventually acknowledge the parallels between Terry and himself present in the film. Nevertheless, the film's conclusion raises serious questions about this allegory and the validity of informing. While Terry's actions do succeed in the removal of the corrupt Johnny Friendly (Lee J. Cobb) as leader of the union, Mr. Upstairs, the capitalist who really runs the docks and from whom Friendly took his orders, is still firmly en-trenched in power. This ambivalent conclusion raises serious questions as to whether informing really brought any fundamental change to the lives of the longshoremen. In addition, the implied condemnation of capitalist exploitation on the waterfront suggests that Kazan's progressive politics were still important to the filmmaker. The more simplistic anti-Communist principles of *Man on a Tightrope* gave way to the complexity that characterized Kazan's later films.

On the Waterfront was in gestation well before Kazan's HUAC appearance. Initially, the waterfront picture was to be a collaboration between Kazan and his good friend Arthur Miller, who was working on a screenplay titled *The Hook*. However, the politics of anti-Communism led to a rupture between Miller and Kazan, although the two would work together again on Miller's play *After the Fall* (1964). In addition to their progressive politics and collaboration in the theater, Kazan and Miller shared an interest in the actress Marilyn Monroe. And it was Kazan who introduced Miller to his future wife. These relationships were pursued while Miller and Kazan were in Hollywood attempting to obtain studio approval for their script. After Zanuck passed on doing the film for Twentieth Century Fox, Miller and Kazan sought to interest Harry Cohn of Columbia Pictures in the project. To make sure that Cohn would meet with them, they brought their secretary along—Marilyn Monroe disguised as a Miss Bauer. Cohn's interest was drawn to Miss Bauer, but according to Kazan the studio chief never seemed to recognize that she was one of his contract players.[1]

In his autobiography, Kazan asserts that he and Miller were making progress with Cohn until the studio executive called for a meeting with Roy Brewer, a staunch anti-Communist and head of the International Alliance of Theatrical and Stage Employees. As a union leader who discredited his opponents by labeling them as Communists, Brewer was primarily concerned that the projected film include a strong anti-Communist subtext.[2] He suggested that the protagonist should reject a reporter from the Communist *Daily Worker*, asserting that the union had no use for Communists. Brewer insisted: "The greatest problem in the union is the communist. The racketeers are much less a menace to labor than the communists."[3] When Miller seemed to show little enthusiasm for making the proposed change, Brewer countered that a failure to include the scene might be perceived as an effort to curry favor with Harry Bridges, the Australian-born president of the International Longshoremen whom the United States was attempting to deport for his alleged Communist connections and a man both Miller and Kazan admired.[4] Even if Miller agreed to make the proposed changes, Brewer considered the film to be controversial, and he was not sure that he could obtain support for the film from the American Federation of Labor. The meeting concluded with what Kazan interpreted as a somewhat challenging comment from Brewer directed at Miller, asserting, "If you plan to make the picture, make it." Kazan and Miller were devastated by the meeting and were no longer convinced that Cohn would go forward with production. Kazan concluded: "It had been a dreadful scene. A man we'd never met, who had nothing to do with the artistic values of our script, seemed to believe he had the power to decide whether or not we could go ahead with the film. We felt humiliated, so much so that we couldn't discuss the problem. We told our secretary, Miss Bauer, only the basic facts."[5]

A discouraged Miller left for the East Coast, but Kazan was delighted when Cohn continued to greenlight *The Hook*. Meanwhile, Miller was supposedly working on changes to the script while also trying to deal with his deteriorating marriage and a growing attachment to Monroe. Kazan assumed the film was on schedule until he was called away from a budget meeting to take a call from Miller, who informed his collaborator that he was withdrawing *The Hook*. The author failed to provide a detailed explanation as to the reasons for his action. Kazan, however, seemed to suspect that Miller was under some type of political pressure. Without directly accusing Miller of being a Communist or influenced by the party line, Kazan later argued: "I think Art saw the Un-American Activities Committee coming and there was something that developed in his personal life that made him not want to have that film done. Things were much touchier then, people were threatened and on trial and being forced to take stands."[6] Kazan's biographer Richard Schickel seeks to confirm Kazan's suspicions of Miller by engaging in a little McCarthyism of his own, suggesting that the writer's script was influenced by Vincent James Longhi and Mick Berenson, who were associated with the Communist-influenced American Labor Party. Schickel concludes with a conspiratorial observation that before beginning *Death of a Salesman*, Miller traveled to Europe with Longhi, where he was introduced to leftist intellectuals.[7]

In his memoir, *Timebends*, Miller presents a very different account of what happened to his collaboration with Kazan on *The Hook*. According to Miller, he was not present at the meeting with Brewer, Kazan, and Cohn, but Kazan conveyed to the playwright that Brewer insisted that Communists be inserted for the organized crime figures exploiting the longshoremen. If such changes were not made, Kazan told Miller that Brewer threatened the projectionists in his union would refuse to exhibit the picture. Moreover, the Federal Bureau of Investigation was concerned that making the film might cause problems on the nation's waterfronts during the Korean War, when an uninterrupted flow of supplies and troops were required for the war effort. In other words, if the Communist theme was not included, the picture would be un-American and almost an act of treason. Miller writes: "Nearly speechless, I said that I knew for a fact that there were next to no Communists on the Brooklyn waterfront, so to depict the rank and file in revolt against Communists rather than racketeers was simply idiotic, and I would be ashamed to go near the waterfront again."[8] Miller concludes that he would not make such a compromise, and thus he withdrew his screenplay.

Despite Miller's departure, Kazan was still interested in the waterfront story, and at the urging of his wife Molly, the director approached Budd Schulberg, who was also working on a script dealing with the waterfront.[9] Schulberg had deep Hollywood connections as his father was a Paramount producer during the 1930s and 1940s. After a brief writing stint with Paramount, Schulberg published the critically acclaimed Hollywood novel *What Makes Sammy Run?* (1944). The writer was also a member of the Communist Party, but after his novel was heavily criticized by Hollywood Communists such as John Howard Lawson, Schulberg left the party. Following service in the navy during World War II, Schulberg published *The Harder They Fall* (1947) and *The Disenchanted* (1950), in addition to writing Hollywood screenplays. In 1951, he was called before HUAC and named names of former associates in the Communist Party. When approached by Kazan, Schulberg was working on a screenplay based on a series of newspaper articles by journalist Malcolm Johnson exposing the exploitation of longshoremen by racketeers and organized crime. Although Schulberg claims that he never saw a draft of Miller's screenplay and only knew what Kazan told him about *The Hook*, Miller's biographer Martin Gottfried argues that much of Schulberg's script was lifted from Miller's work. Richard Schickel, in a somewhat detailed examination of both scripts, finds little merit to Gottfried's allegations, pointing out that Miller's *The Hook* did not include the characters of Charlie Malloy and Father Barry, who are essential for the Kazan film.[10]

Issues of alleged plagiarism aside, it is clear from Kazan's early correspondence with Schulberg that issues of waterfront corruption were of considerable interest to the director, who initially perceived the film as more than a commentary on informing and his HUAC experience. Kazan wrote to Schulberg, expressing his delight that International Longshoreman Association officer Mike Clemente, the reputed overlord of the East River docks, was indicted for income tax evasion and perjury. The figure of Johnny Friendly was reportedly based upon Clemente. Schulberg, who attended all forty sessions of the Waterfront Crime Commission, was also a confidante of many longshoremen who were still supporters of union activist Pete Panto, who was lured from his home and murdered in 1939. This unsolved crime may be related to the murder of Joey Doyle, with which *On the Waterfront* begins. Thus, Kazan told Schulberg that he hoped that their film would bring some reform to the waterfront and change such corrupt practices as the "shape up," in which union bosses controlled the longshoremen by issuing a brass token to favored workers who would be assured employment. But even in this early stage of forging a script, Kazan seemed to be making connections between his informing and Terry's testimony. For example, Terry's courageous act of informing must bring about some reform for the workers. Kazan was distraught about Stalinists, and in this letter he seems to place Miller in that camp, who despaired of any hopes regarding the reform of a corrupt capitalist democracy, and the director asserts that their waterfront film must provide hope that Terry's action will bring about positive change. Kazan concludes: "I've been thinking about our picture being good for a long time. It can be, if its final thinking is not about the waterfront but about the operation of a democracy. About how a democracy moves, and how a democracy grows, and what a democracy must learn and do etc. The worth of our picture will depend finally on the size of its moral view point."[11]

Despite such lofty ambitions, Hollywood producers were less than enthusiastic about the proposed film. Zanuck was hesitant about what he considered to be another picture like *Viva Zapata!* that would sell few tickets. The director countered that the film would not be controversial, with support coming from the Catholic Church as well as Roy Brewer. Kazan informed Zanuck that Father John M. Corridan, the waterfront priest upon whom Father Barry was modeled, was working closely with Schulberg and the archdiocese was supportive. While Schulberg did not directly mention the Communist issue, Brewer was also on board with the new script and the removal of Miller from the project. Despite his less than satisfying experience with *Man on a Tightrope*, Kazan perceived the waterfront story as an anti-Communist film. Kazan wrote: "The moral, in other words, will be somewhat as Father Corridan has stated it in many public interviews—one of the most effective ways of rooting out Communism is to take back from them the genuine grievances they exploit for their own purposes. In other words, see to it that decent, law-abiding Americans can do the clean-up jobs that need to be done."[12]

By also emphasizing the film's love story and promising to secure Marlon Brando for the lead, Kazan believed that he had Zanuck's support. A confident Kazan and Schulberg journeyed to California, where on May 25, 1953, Zanuck informed them that he would not be doing the picture. According to Kazan, Zanuck proclaimed: "It's exactly what audiences do not want to see now. Who gives a shit about longshoremen? I even tried making Terry a member of the FBI, but it didn't work."[13] The producer concluded that in order to compete with the threat posed by television, the studio would be making its future pictures in Cinema-Scope, and there was simply no room for a film with a gritty Italian neorealism look.[14]

While disappointed with Zanuck, Kazan and Schulberg still believed in their film, and the pair remained in Hollywood, hoping to interest another producer in the project. While drinking at their hotel, Kazan and Schulberg encountered independent producer Sam Spiegel, who agreed to package their proposal to United Artists with Frank Sinatra in the lead. Meanwhile, Spiegel continued to pursue Brando for the role of Terry Malloy. Brando, however, was hesitant to work with Kazan again, as the liberal activist actor disapproved of Kazan's HUAC testimony. Kazan asserts that after Spiegel arranged a meeting between the reluctant actor and the director, Brando agreed to accept the role because the film was to be made on location in New York and New Jersey, which would make it possible for Brando to see his psychoanalyst every afternoon.[15] Brando's account of his decision to accept the role was a bit more complicated. Based on his previous experience, Brando clearly admired Kazan as an artist, but his politics were troubling for the actor. In his memoir, *Songs My Mother Taught Me*, Brando maintained that the film was really "a metaphorical statement" by Kazan and Schulberg to justify "finking on their friends." Brando states that he confronted the director about his actions, but Kazan insisted that the Communist Party was a criminal conspiracy to take over the world, expressing no regrets for his testimony. The actor disagreed, believing that people were deeply hurt by Kazan's cooperation with HUAC. Brando proclaimed, "It was especially stupid because most of the people named were no longer communists. Innocent people were also blacklisted, including me, although I never had a political affiliation of any kind. It was simply because I had signed a petition to protest the lynching of a black man in the South." He concluded, "To this day I believe that we missed the establishment of fascism in this country by a hair." Kazan was also a hypocrite according to Brando, for the director turned on his friends but was willing to cooperate with the Mafia in order to obtain permission for filming along the waterfront. [16]

Despite all these objections, Brando agreed to do the film, although it was to be his last collaboration with Kazan. The director was delighted with Brando's performance as Terry, terming it one of the greatest portrayals in the history of American cinema. Kazan was also appreciative of Spiegel's efforts to get the film made, even though he was often exasperated by the producer's efforts to interfere with the production. Nevertheless, after securing Brando as Terry, Spiegel repackaged the film with a higher budget and distribution deal with Harry Cohn and Columbia. Sinatra, who was preparing to play Terry, was upset, but the actor was able to reach a financial settlement with Spiegel. Kazan credited the producer with being essential to the making of the picture, cutting costs and making valuable contributions to the script. [17] The director concluded: "I believe we would have had a failure without Sam, and a fiasco with Zanuck. That is the reason that no matter what Sam did, I never turned against him." [18]

Depicting the waterfront with the gritty look employed by Italian neorealist filmmakers, *On the Waterfront* begins with Terry using his pigeons (a motif for informers as stool pigeons) to lure young Joey Doyle to a roof where he is thrown to his death by associates of union boss Johnny Friendly (Lee J. Cobb, who was another member of the production who cooperated with HUAC). [19] Terry is somewhat distraught, thinking that the union enforcers (played by former professional fighters Two-Ton Tony Galento, Abe Simon, Tomi Mauriello, and Roger Donohue) were simply "going to lean on him a bit." Friendly appears to be sympathetic to Terry, a former boxer whose contract was once owned by the union boss. Friendly, however, could not take any chances with Doyle, who was willing to testify before the Waterfront Crime Commission and expose the corruption of the union in forcing workers to pay kickbacks for their employment and accept "payday loans" at exorbitant rates of interest. He

gives Terry some money to "get his load off," and the former fighter will
be assigned an easy job the next day in the loft. Charlie (Rod Steiger),
who was considered one of the brains in the union because he had two
years of college, informs Terry that he has a real friend in Johnny and
should not forget it. A self-made man who clawed his way up from
poverty to leadership of the union, Friendly asserts: "We've got the fattest
piers and the fattest harbors in the world. Everything moves in and out,
and we take our cut."

The next morning as jobs are handed out for the day in the shape up,
Terry notices Edie Doyle (Eva Marie Saint) and secures her a token so
that her father may work. Meanwhile, the waterfront priest, Father Barry
(Karl Malden), calls for a meeting at the church to discuss what happened
to Joey Doyle. Learning of this gathering, Friendly and Charlie dispatch
Terry to monitor the meeting and make sure there will be no more witnesses before the Crime Commission. The meeting at the church is
sparsely attended, and a frustrated Father Barry is unable to get anyone to
break the code of silence. Nevertheless, union goons attack the church
and administer a beating to longshoreman Kayo Dugan (Pat Henning).
This effort at intimidation, however, backfires, as Dugan tells Father
Barry that he is willing to testify against Johnny Friendly.

During the confusion, Terry helps Edie escape the assault on the
church. Terry is obviously attracted to Edie and reminds her that they
attended parochial school together. He assumes that she does not remember him, but Edie clearly recalls the school rebel whom the priests and
nuns tried to beat into obedience. After leaving Terry, Edie disappoints
her longshoreman father, Pop (John Hamilton), by asserting her independence, informing him that she will not be returning to school until she
discovers who murdered her brother.

Edie also believes that she can reform the bad boy Terry, to whom she
is drawn. She goes to visit Terry at his rooftop pigeon coop, where he
shows his soft side with the birds, and Edie agrees to have a beer with
him. Both charming and introspective, Terry shares his difficult life with
Edie, describing his life as an orphan raised by his brother and career as a
good fighter who was forced to "throw" fights by Friendly. The couple
ends up at a rather boisterous wedding, where they enjoy dancing until
Terry is summoned by Friendly. The union leader is upset that Terry
failed to alert him to the possibility that Dugan was testifying before the
Crime Commission. As punishment, Terry will lose his "cushy" job and

be sent back to hard labor in the hold. Charlie chastises his brother for becoming involved with Edie, who is evidently clouding his judgment. An interesting aspect of this scene is that Friendly has obtained a copy of Dugan's testimony. Clearly the web of corruption extends into official circles well beyond the reach of Friendly, suggesting that corporate and government figures are orchestrating much of the corruption—a theme that becomes even more obvious in the film's conclusion.

The next day Terry is working with Dugan, who has received Joey's jacket from Edie, in the hold unloading cargo. Terry tries to warn Dugan that Friendly is aware of his secret testimony, but before he is able to disclose this information, one of the union's crane operators drops a load of crates on Dugan, and the informer perishes in what is labeled as an industrial accident. Father Barry administers the last rites to Dugan, asserting that Dugan's death is a crucifixion. When some of the union thugs attempt to silence the priest, Terry, the former boxer, springs to his defense. The scene in the hold, where the longshoremen are unloading crates, includes major Christian symbolism, an essential motif in the film. Background shadows in the shape of crosses are apparent throughout Father Barry's oration, and the shot of the priest with Dugan's body being lifted out of the hold suggests the theme of resurrection as they ascend out of the darkness and hell in the hold into the light.

At this point, Terry is wavering in his loyalty to the corrupt union's code of silence. He confesses his involvement with Joey's death to Father Barry, who urges him to share this revelation with Edie. Unable to handle this information from the man with whom she is falling in love, Edie flees from Terry, whose conscience has been primed by the pleas from the priest and the young woman. These developments are noticed by Friendly, who tells Charlie that he must guarantee his brother's silence or it will be necessary for the union to murder Terry, just as Joey and Dugan were eliminated.

In one of the most famous scenes from the movie, Charlie and Terry are in the back of a taxi, where the older brother attempts to convince his sibling to maintain the code of silence. Terry chides Charlie for not looking out for him, explaining that he could "have been a contender" but instead he is a bum because when Terry had an opportunity against Wilson in Madison Square Garden to get a shot at the title, Charlie and Friendly forced him to lose the fight so they could cover their bets. Recognizing the validity of Terry's accusation, Charlie lets his younger brother out of the cab and asserts that he will try to work things out with Friendly. However, this act of reconciliation with his brother leads to Charlie's murder by Friendly and his henchmen.

After departing from Charlie, Terry goes to Edie's apartment and breaks down the door when she refuses to open it. Clad only in a white slip, Edie asks Terry to leave, but instead he embraces her in a violent kiss and her resistance melts. This scene seems to reflect the sexist idea that no means yes, and it reinforces many of the gender stereotypes of the 1950s and Kazan's own ideas toward women as revealed in his autobiography. While they are embracing, a voice calls out from the street that Charlie wants to see Terry. Edie and Terry run out of the apartment into an alley, where a truck attempts to run them down. Evading the deadly vehicle, they discover Charlie's body hanging from a hook like a slab of meat—fulfilling the foreshadowing of Charlie as "a butcher in a camel-haired coat." A distraught and armed Terry then goes to look for Friendly at his bar. The union boss is not present, but Father Barry arrives to prevent Terry from killing someone. After a confrontation in which the priest slugs Terry for telling him to "go to hell," Father Barry convinces Terry that the best way for him to gain revenge is through publicly testifying against Friendly before the Crime Commission.

In a crowded courtroom, Terry testifies that Friendly was responsible for the murder of Joey Doyle. An angry Friendly has to be restrained from attacking the informer and cries out that Terry will never be able to work on the waterfront again. Following his testimony, Terry is ostracized by the community for "ratting" and informing—and here the connection with how many in Hollywood responded to Kazan's HUAC appearance is rather obvious. A young member of Terry's old gang, "The Golden Warriors," turns on his mentor and kills Terry's pigeons. Confronted with this degree of hostility, Edie suggests that they leave the docks and move out west. Instead, Terry grabs the longshoreman's hook and dons Joey's jacket, heading to the docks to demand that Friendly allow him to work. Terry proclaims to Friendly that he is proud of informing, and the two men begin to fight. As the former boxer starts to get the best of Friendly, his henchmen enter the fray and administer a severe beating to Terry. After witnessing Terry's challenge to Friendly, the longshoremen offer to ignore their corrupt former leader and follow Terry. Father Barry and Edie help Terry struggle to his feet, and, carrying the longshoreman's hook over his shoulder as his personal cross to bear,

Terry stumbles toward Mr. Upstairs, who is imploring Friendly to get the workers organized and on the job. The scene is certainly reminiscent of Jesus, bleeding profusely around the temple from the cross of thorns, carrying his cross through the streets of Jerusalem on the way to his crucifixion, which in the final analysis, according to Christian theology, will free the people as Christ died for their sins. In a similar fashion, Terry becomes a Christ figure who sacrificed his life and then arose from the beating administered by Friendly's thugs to lead the workers to freedom and redemption. And if Terry represents Kazan and his former association with the corrupt Communist Party, then the filmmaker himself becomes a Christ figure.

But is the conclusion of the film really this simple? For example, the figure of Mr. Upstairs introduces a degree of ambiguity into the narrative. He seems to be a capitalist character controlling the docks and to whom Friendly must answer. We see a photograph in Friendly's bar of the union leader shaking hands with Mr. Upstairs, and the film includes a shot of him from behind watching a televised account of Terry's testimony. To accent his upper-class standing, Mr. Upstairs tells a butler serving him a drink that if Mr. Friendly should call, he is not available. Thus, Mr. Upstairs requires a new person to control the workers, and perhaps this will be Terry. The final shot of the film shows Terry and the longshoremen entering the warehouse and a door closes behind them, perhaps implying that rather than being freed into a new world of light and hope, they are still trapped within a corrupt system. Friendly may have been dumped in the water by the workers, but Mr. Upstairs, who would seem to have the connections for obtaining Dugan's secret testimony, is still firmly in place, and the exploitation of the longshoremen continues. In his study of the theme of ambivalence in the film, Kenneth R. Hey argues that cinematographer Boris Kaufman's closing shot of the warehouse "symbolizes both protection and entrapment. The workers, having for the moment regained control of their union, must face the problem which originally brought unions into existence: how can the laborer maintain autonomy and dignity in a capitalist society."[20] Thus, Hey suggests that while Kazan and Schulberg are anti-Communists, they remain progressives, concerned about the exploitation of the working class, and the ambiguous figure of Mr. Upstairs demonstrates that considerable reformation of the capitalist system is required. Hey's conclusions underscore the complexity and ambivalence that characterize Kazan's post-HUAC films.

Other critics, however, were far more skeptical in their reading of the film's conclusion. Writing in the film journal *Sight and Sound*, British film critic Lindsay Anderson, who emerged as a major filmmaker during the 1960s, described *On the Waterfront* as "fascist." The longshoremen in the film were blind followers of authority figures, shifting allegiance from obeying Friendly to lining up behind Terry—the new Messiah figure. Anderson believed the filmmakers treated the workers with little respect, although he acknowledged that the film's conclusion certainly alluded to capitalist exploitation. The critic, however, asserted that perhaps the greatest political shortcoming of the film was the failure to systematically investigate the reasons for the corruption and poor working conditions inflicted upon the longshoremen.[21] In his influential book on post–World War II cinema, *Seeing Is Believing*, Peter Biskind agreed that *On the Waterfront* exhibited little respect for the longshoremen. Biskind argues that because of Terry's humanity and compassion, Father Barry and Edie, who have middle-class aspirations, perceive him as the type of person they can mold to fit into the post–World War II conformity of the liberal consensus. Terry will help to reform the docks while he and Edie move out to the suburbs, leaving their working-class origins in the dust. Biskind writes: "By the end of *On the Waterfront*, Terry has been maneuvered into more than betraying his pals, he has betrayed his own class as well. The values that replace his old ones are mainstream, middle-class values disguised as morality, and the lesson the film teaches is that it is smart to climb out of your class. There's nothing at the bottom except long hours and low pay."[22] Thus, Biskind perceived the film as being about the social control of the working class by the corporate liberal consensus.

Kazan tended to dismiss his critics by simply asserting that his film was about the well-documented problems of crime and corruption on the waterfront, but he did eventually come to acknowledge that there were parallels between his HUAC appearance and that of Terry before the Crime Commission. Accordingly, Kazan told interviewer Jeff Young that like Terry he testified because it was the right thing to do, and that he did not cooperate simply to go on working in Hollywood, as he could continue to earn a lucrative living in the Broadway theater, which refused to institute a blacklist. He named names because it was his duty to expose a criminal Stalinist conspiracy. Kazan proclaimed: "In some ways the whole experience made a man out of me because it changed me from being a guy, who was everybody's darling and always living therefore for people's approval, to a fellow who stood on his own. It toughened me up a lot. I'm not afraid of anyone."[23] This comment also would seem to work pretty well for Terry Malloy.

Examining *On the Waterfront* as an intentional or unintentional parallel between Kazan and Terry raises some troubling questions that tend to undermine the more politically progressive interpretations of the film. First, the filmmakers certainly appear to be aligning themselves with conservatives, as the union movement was on the defensive in the postwar period after the gains of the New Deal and war years. The conservative backlash sought to establish connections between unionism and Communism, especially within the Committee for Industrial Organization (CIO), and unions were discouraged through state right to work laws and the congressional passage of the Taft-Hartley Act. In response to the Red Scare and McCarthyism, the CIO was purging union leaders who were accused of Communist connections.[24]

Within this context, the waterfront union and Johnny Friendly may be read as parallel with Joseph Stalin and the Communist Party, claiming to be the workers' friend but in reality exploiting the working class and living well off their labor. Similar to the pigs in George Orwell's *Animal Farm* (1945) and the Communist Party in the Soviet Union, the union leaders dress and live better because, in the words of Charlie, "We're entitled." Johnny Friendly also appeared to be Terry's benefactor, taking him to ball games at the Polo Grounds, but in reality the fighter was exploited to cover bets for the union leader. What Terry does is expose the real face of the waterfront union, whose power and influence are based upon extortion and murder. And Terry is able to accomplish this with the aid of religious figures Father Barry and Edie, who encourage the development of his conscience and the act of confession. This religious theme in *On the Waterfront* fits in well with the film's allegory, as many Americans viewed the Cold War as a struggle between Communist atheists and a Christian America. Feeding into this perspective is the attack by the union thugs on the church, an action reminiscent to many Americans of the way the Soviets were seeking to crush Christianity in Eastern Europe.[25] Armed with this religious righteousness, Terry is able to denounce Friendly and the union as a criminal conspiracy, just as

Kazan perceived the Communist Party to be a clear and present danger to American democracy.

But does this allegory really work? Did the Communist Party within the United States, and especially Hollywood, represent the type of threat posed to the longshoremen by Johnny Friendly and his henchmen? There were certainly Soviet spies in the United States, but there were not too many government secrets to be uncovered at Hollywood cocktail parties. So the major concern in the film capital was that Communist screenwriters would be able to sneak propaganda into American films. The collaborative nature of studio filmmaking, however, made such an enterprise exceedingly difficult, and leftist screenwriters considered it to be a coup if they were able to have a villain or a shady character that was a banker or businessman. An exception to this generalization might be such World War II films as *Mission to Moscow* (1943) and *Song of Russia* (1944), which were made when the Soviets were American allies and taking on the brunt of the fight against Nazi Germany. Nevertheless, Schulberg insisted that informing was a patriotic duty to assure freedom of speech and conscience. Undermining the *On the Waterfront* Communist allegory somewhat, the writer acknowledged that leftist propaganda and censorship in Hollywood was hardly the equivalent of Stalin's gulag, but he asserted that Communism in the film industry must be exposed and denounced.[26] Most film scholars tend to argue that anti-Communists overemphasized the threat posed by Communists in the film industry, and thus Kazan's allegory equating the Communist Party in the New York theater and Hollywood with the murderous Johnny Friendly does not really work. Describing the Communist influence in Hollywood during the 1930s and 1940s, Larry Ceplair and Steven Englund conclude: "Communist screenwriters did not revolutionize, Stalinize, communize, Sovietize, or subvert the output of the film industry. . . . If the majority of the films made from their scripts seem politically indistinguishable from the films made from the scripts of non-radical screenwriters, it is not necessarily because they lacked skill or determination, but because the studio executives were more skilled and determined—and by far more powerful."[27] And in his study of politics in the film capital, historian Steven J. Ross argues that while there is considerable conflict between the Hollywood left and right, conservatives have historically outmaneuvered liberals and radicals as the right "sought, won, and exercised electoral power."[28]

Despite these conclusions questioning the influence of the Communist Party in Hollywood and undermining the Kazan allegory, the director continued to emphasize the persistence of Stalinism on the American left and among those who denounced his HUAC testimony. Like Terry, Kazan was exposing a criminal conspiracy, but the director's allegations of Stalinism were also undercut by Mr. Upstairs and the continuing exploitation of the longshoremen. This interrogation of the capitalist system reflected the progressive principles espoused by Kazan and Steinbeck in *Viva Zapata!* and that would continue to influence Kazan's cinema in the 1960s. The ambivalence of *On the Waterfront*'s conclusion was noted by critic Pauline Kael, who observed parallels between the Kazan classic and *The Godfather* (1972), another film perceived as a critique of American capitalism. Kael wrote:

> In *The Godfather* we see organized crime as an obscene symbolic extension of free enterprise and government policy, an extension of the worst in America—its feudal ruthlessness. Organized crime is not a rejection of Americanism, it's what we fear Americanism to be. It's our nightmare of the American system. When "Americanism" was a form of cheerful, bland official optimism, the gangster used to be destroyed at the end of the movie and our feelings resolved. Now the mood of the whole country has darkened, guiltily; nothing is resolved at the end of *The Godfather*, because the family business goes on. Terry Malloy didn't clean up the docks at the end of *On The Waterfront*; that was a lie. *The Godfather* is popular melodrama, but it exposes a new tragic realism. [29]

This note of cynicism was not shared by most critics and film audiences, who embraced *On the Waterfront* and wanted to believe that a corrupt system could be reformed. For example, A. H. Weiler in the *New York Times* praised Kazan's direction of Brando, observing: "Under the director's expert guidance, Marlon Brando's Terry Malloy is a shattering poignant portrait of an amoral, confused, illiterate citizen of the lower depth who is goaded into decency by love, hate and murder. His groping for words, use of the vernacular, care of his beloved pigeons, pugilist's walk and gestures and his discoveries of love and the immensity of the crimes surrounding him are highlights of a beautiful and moving portrayal." The review, however, failed to notice the film's ambiguous ending, concluding, "Despite its happy ending, its preachments and a somewhat slick approach to some of the facets of dockside strife and tribulations, *On the Waterfront* is moviemaking of a rare and high order."[30] Lee Rogow in the *Saturday Review* found that Brando's acting, Kazan's direction, and Kaufman's cinematography elevated Hollywood cinema to the level of realism achieved by post–World War II European neorealism, but the reviewer also missed the film's theme of ambivalence, describing the conclusion as "pat and slick."[31] In a similar vein, *Commonweal* suggested that "the final scenes have the quality of making a saint," while a more conservative *Time* review believed that the film placed too much sentimental faith in the common man.[32] As for Kazan, he had certainly meant to interject a note of ambiguity in the film's conclusion, but he did not want to convey a sense of hopelessness for the longshoremen even though Anthony de Vicenzo, upon whom the Brando character was partially based, sued the filmmakers for breach of privacy and the case was settled out of court.[33] Kazan, nevertheless, believed that the actions of men such as Terry did move the progressive cause of reform forward and that the film itself promoted change on the waterfront. In a 1971 interview, the director asserted: "I think democracy progresses, as the French say, *reculer pour mieux sauter*; you go back, you go a little more forward. We're in a constant state of tension. I believe in Marxism, you know—I believe that one thing affects the other, I believe in interplay, in the dialectic. But I never meant that when they go back to work at the end of the film, there isn't going to be that same corruption starting up a month later."[34]

While not all critics recognized the theme of ambivalence contained in the film's conclusion, Kazan expressed some satisfaction that he was able to promote reform and progressive principles in *On the Waterfront*. But he took even greater pleasure in the film's commercial success and eight Oscars, which he interpreted as vindication for the personal attacks and ostracism he suffered following his HUAC testimony. Writing in his autobiography of the *Waterfront* Oscar recognition, Kazan proclaimed: "But you can understand that I was tasting vengeance that night and enjoying it. *On the Waterfront* was my own story, every day I worked on that film, I was telling the world where I stood and my critics to go and fuck themselves."[35] In addition, the success of *On the Waterfront* provided the filmmaker with a sense of independence from studio control in selecting his projects, and on his next film, an adaptation of Steinbeck's *East of Eden*, he would also serve as a producer. In his study of Kazan's cinema, Sam Girgus suggests that the filmmaker was abandoning his leftist ideology. Girgus writes:

> He was abandoning one system of belief and body of ritual for another, trading in lingering nostalgia toward the proletarian passion of the Left for a new idealism about another political religion: America. In this light, *On the Waterfront* becomes a transitional film that functions for Kazan as an important bridge to personal fulfillment and identity within a refurbished American ideology. In contrast to communism, the American ideology emphasizes values of individualism and self-reliance that more accurately reflected Kazan's beliefs and felt experience as he matured and succeeded.[36]

This reading of Kazan's cinema, however, tends to ignore *On the Waterfront*'s critique of capitalism as well as the ambiguity toward the American dream expressed in *East of Eden*. In explaining the troubled relationship between Cal Trask and his father, Adam, Kazan is revisiting the conflict with his own father, who was disappointed that his son did not follow a career in business. While Kazan's father and Adam Trask pursued the American dream through hard work and determination, success and happiness seemed to elude the two men, and much was sacrificed in pursuit of the dream. Rather than celebrating America, *East of Eden* continues to document Kazan's questioning of American capitalism even while denouncing the evils of Communism. Except this time Kazan was unable to prevail upon Brando to accept the role of Cal Trask, and the troubled father-son relationship is addressed through the eyes of an emerging stage and screen presence—James Dean.

4

FATHERS AND SONS AND THE COST OF PURSUING THE AMERICAN DREAM

East of Eden (1955)

While Kazan's HUAC testimony led to a rupture with Arthur Miller and many former associates, the director maintained his friendship with John Steinbeck. The novelist defended Kazan for naming names, refusing to embrace playwright Lillian Hellman's defiance of the committee at the expense of Kazan's decision to cooperate. Writing from Paris in May 1952, Steinbeck asserted:

> But I understand there is a great fuss and feathers over his statement as opposed to Hellman's. One can never know what one could do until it happens. I wonder what I would do. I'll never know I guess. And I don't even know what I wish I would do. Isn't that strange. I understand both Hellman and Kazan. Each one is right in different ways but I think Kazan's took more courage. It is very easy to be brave and very hard to be right. Lillian can settle smugly back in a kind of martyrdom but Kazan has to live alone with his decision. I hope I could have had the courage to decide to do what he did.[1]

Thus, Kazan valued Steinbeck's loyalty, and despite some reservations regarding *Viva Zapata!*, the filmmaker had enjoyed his collaboration with the writer, and he approached Steinbeck about a film version of his epic novel *East of Eden* (1952). The novelist's last critically acclaimed book was *The Grapes of Wrath* (1939), and with *East of Eden*

Steinbeck sought to reclaim his status as one of America's predominant authors. *East of Eden* is a massive book that attempts to trace in fictional terms the history of the Steinbeck family in Southern California and the Salinas Valley. While the novel earned mixed critical reaction, readers loved the book, which emerged as a best seller. Kazan admired the book, but the novel's multigenerational story was a problem. Initially, Kazan contemplated a series of films with the novel as source material, but he eventually rejected this idea in favor of concentrating on the book's final section. *East of Eden* concludes with the sibling rivalry between Cal and Aron Trask for the affections of their father, Adam, and Aron's girlfriend, Abra. It is essentially the biblical story of Cain and Abel, culminating in the symbolic death of Aron and a reconciliation of sorts between Cal and Adam.

Despite his great respect for the novelist, Kazan believed that it would be best to assign the screenplay to a professional scriptwriter and suggested Paul Osborn, the director's friend and Connecticut neighbor. Kazan explained that as producer and director, independence he earned following the success of *On the Waterfront*, he had secured a distribution deal with Warner Bros. and was taking his expanded responsibilities quite seriously. The director blamed himself for the collaborators' Zapata project not reaching its full potential. He concluded that *Viva Zapata!* was "too diffuse," and the same was true for *East of Eden*'s initial outline. Believing that the script should concentrate on the figure of Cal, whom James Dean was later cast to play, Kazan diplomatically suggested that Steinbeck abandon the screenplay. In a letter to the novelist, Kazan wrote: "I have no false modesty. I'm a fertile director. But stress director. The ideas I have are basically director's ideas. I'm not a first rate constructionist—I know that. And a first rate novelist and a first rate novel should have a first rate screen technician. I don't want to take any goddamn chances with this one. It's no time for self-favoring. There is too much at stake." Kazan concluded: "*Eden* is the toughest job of dramatization I've ever seen—and for one reason. It's so rich! There's so much of it! Even when you take the last fourth, there's much too much."[2] His gentle approach to removing Steinbeck did not sit well with the author, but Steinbeck was involved with his efforts to write a Broadway musical and agreed to let Osborn draft the screenplay. The Broadway musical proved to be a disaster, but Steinbeck was pleased with Kazan's film, writing to his friend Ritchie Lovejoy: "It's a real good picture. I didn't have anything to do with it. Maybe that's why it might be one of the best films I ever saw."[3]

Kazan next turned to the casting of the film. For the role of Aron, a young film and stage veteran, Richard Davalos, was selected, but his performance is usually dismissed as "wooden"—in fairness, this negative assessment may be due to playing opposite Dean, whose acting electrified many audiences. For the part of the patriarchal Adam, Raymond Massey, perhaps best known for his screen portrayals of Abraham Lincoln, was chosen. Kazan seemed to recognize that the conservative Massey had little patience for the method acting and apparent arrogance of Dean. Massey would carefully memorize his lines and then be frustrated when Dean would alter the dialogue. The traditionalist was also offended by the young actor's use of profanity on the set. All this antagonism was encouraged by Kazan, who told journalist Richard Schickel: "Do you think I would do anything to stop that antagonism? No, I increased it. I let it go. I let it go . . . because it was the central thing I photographed. . . . The absolute hatred that Ray Massey felt for Jimmy Dean and the hatred Jimmy Dean felt for Ray Massey. That's precious man. You can't get that. I mean, you can pretend to have it, but you don't. You hopefully arouse it. You get me? Arouse it. You hopefully stimulate them and in that case I didn't have to. It was there."[4]

The director was also pleased with Julie Harris from the Actors Studio in the role of Abra. In an interview with Jeff Young, Kazan expressed his appreciation for Harris's patience with Dean and credits the actress with helping to elicit an outstanding performance from the petulant young actor. Kazan described Harris as "both a girl and a woman, an extraordinary person. Her soul is beautiful. It comes out of her eyes and her voice, the way she touches things. At the same time she has a plain look. She was just exactly right. She has a wonderful combination of purity and sexual awareness. When you go with that kind of woman it's very intense."[5] Kazan often asserted that *East of Eden* was one of his most personal films, and this perspective is usually attributed to the director's identification with the conflict between father and son. Yet in a conversation with Michel Ciment, the director revealed that Abra's character reminded him of his own wife Molly Thacher, who also tried to help and understand a bad boy and outsider. Kazan observed: "And my first wife saw the good in me, and she was sympathetic to me—when we were young, and first together, and first married, and had children, it was a blessing that she had that for me. It didn't last long—only five or six years—but maybe nothing like that can last long because I developed one way and she developed another. It was autobiographical that picture—more personal than anything I've ever done."[6]

Nevertheless, the most important casting for the film was James Dean as Cal Trask. Kazan had wanted Brando for the role, but he was rebuffed by the actor. As a director, Kazan had elicited one of the greatest performances in American cinema from Brando as Terry Malloy in *On the Waterfront*, but the actor's political objections to Kazan's testimony prevented further collaborations. As a second choice, Dean evoked a mixed response from the director. In his autobiography, Kazan describes his first meeting with the enigmatic actor. Dean was asked to pay the director a visit at his New York City office. Kazan asserted that the young actor was slouched on a couch in the waiting room, "looking resentful for no particular reason." The director countered by keeping Dean waiting, and when he was finally ushered into Kazan's presence, the belligerent attitude was dropped. Kazan found it difficult to engage Dean in conversation, so the actor proposed to the director that they take a ride on Dean's motorcycle through the streets of New York. Kazan concluded: "I didn't enjoy the ride. He was showing off—a country boy not impressed with the big-city traffic." Nevertheless, the director was convinced that Dean was Cal Trask, and he sent the young man to visit Steinbeck in his New York apartment, and the novelist concurred with Kazan's judgment.[7]

Kazan's reaction to Dean on the set for *East of Eden* was inconsistent. In *A Life*, Kazan asserts that the young actor had little technique and was attempting to emulate his hero, Brando. The director also disapproved of Dean as a youth cult figure, complaining about the negative fashion in which his friend Nicholas Ray portrayed the parents in Dean's *Rebel Without a Cause* (1955). Proclaiming his impatience with Dean's cult status, Kazan insisted that Dean's characters, including Cal Trask, were "self-pitying, self-dramatizing, and good for nothing."[8] But these comments were written when Kazan was an older man, and during the production of *East of Eden* there seemed to be greater empathy with youthful rebellion against the patriarchy and the struggles Kazan experienced with his own father. Also, *Splendor in the Grass* would later embrace the challenge of young lovers against the tyranny of their parents. Thus, in numerous interviews Kazan did have more positive things to say about Dean, although the director would always prefer Brando.

East of Eden was Kazan's first film in color and CinemaScope, and he believed that Dean was perfect for these cinematic innovations. The director told Michel Ciment: "Dean had a very vivid body; and I did play a lot with it in long shots. And CinemaScope emphasized Dean's smallness. When he runs in the bean fields, there's a big thing like that, wide, and you see Dean running through it, looking like a little child."[9] And Kazan asserted that the sense of vulnerability Dean conveyed as Cal and in his personal life made the young actor attractive to film audiences. In his notebook on the production, Kazan described Dean as an emotional cripple who was often "writhing in pain" on the screen. The director acknowledged that Dean certainly had natural talent, but his lack of proper training made it difficult for the young actor to stretch himself. After stating that Dean was not particularly intelligent, Kazan concluded:

> Directing him was gratifying because he always caught something of the spirit of the youth which considered itself disenfranchised by the preceding generation. But there was an element of self-pity here and I found this irksome. He had considerable innocence but not as an adjunct of strength or courage, but of hatred and a kind of despair. His imagination was limited; it was like a child's. To direct him was somewhat like directing Lassie the dog; the director dealt in a series of rewards and threats and played a psychological game with him. He had to be coddled and hugged or threatened with abandonment.[10]

Kazan told Jeff Young that Dean was "a sick child" who needed close supervision, so the director moved the actor into the dressing room next to him on the Warner Bros. lot in order to keep an eye on him. The director also credited Julie Harris with nurturing Dean through the film. Kazan denied that he disliked Dean, but he concluded: "He was a very, very neurotic kid. You can't not like a guy with that much pain in him. Later, however, when he got a taste of power, he enjoyed it and became abusive."[11]

Dean biographer David Dalton suggests that perhaps the volatile young actor was not the right choice to provide the sense of reconciliation between father and son that Kazan sought in the final scene of the film as Cal seeks to comfort the dying patriarch. In the confrontation between Adam and Cal Trask, Kazan perceived the conflict with his own father. Describing *East of Eden* as his most personal film, the director proclaims that one hates and rebels against his father, but finally the son stops fearing him and comes to understand and forgive the sins of the father. And Dean shared a similar confrontational relationship with his father, but the actor never reconciled with his parent, leading Dalton to conclude: "The difference between Jimmy and Kazan, however, is that Jimmy never forgave and never accepted. By using Jimmy as the protagonist in the movie, Kazan had unwittingly selected a lethal weapon that would eventually be used to cut away the debilitating compromises of the family." And perhaps Kazan did see this destructive potential as he described Dean as Cal Trask, proclaiming: "I chose Jimmy because he was Cal Trask. There was no point in attempting to cast it better or nicer. Jimmy was it. He had a grudge against all fathers. He was revengeful, he had a sense of aloneness and of being persecuted."[12] Although Kazan often expressed impatience with the post–World War II youth generation, he played an essential role in promoting cultural rebels James Dean and Marlon Brando, who both challenged the conformist assumptions of the postwar liberal consensus. In *The Unfinished Journey*, historian William Chafe describes the 1950s as a period of paradox in which the consumer culture of the era was being undermined by forces of change that would virtually explode in the 1960s. Chafe writes: "Even within the popular culture itself there existed substantial evidence that safety and conformity exercised only limited appeal. While many applauded the moves of Doris Day and Rock Hudson that showered cuteness and conventionality, the major stars of the decade were James Dean and Marlon Brando, individuals through and through. . . . Here was a cry for the individual to reject the self-deception of consumer culture."[13] Thus, whether it was his intention or not, Kazan perpetuated his ambiguous political legacy by promoting rebel images that would undermine the postwar consensus with its twin pillars of anti-Communism and belief that capitalist expansion could solve all the nation's problems.

East of Eden begins with Dean as Cal Trask mysteriously following a well-dressed older woman through the streets of Monterrey, California, as she makes her way to a house on the outskirts of town. Cal loiters outside the house and finally throws a stone against the building, and a man emerges. Cal asks to see Kate (Jo Van Fleet). The boy is told to leave the premises, but before he departs, Cal shouts that he hates Kate.[14] The next shot is one of the most powerful from the film, as Cal is depicted alone and cold on top of a freight train riding back to his home in Salinas. This shot establishes the loneliness and vulnerability of Cal throughout the film.

After Cal returns to Salinas, film viewers are introduced to the Trask family. Adam Trask (Raymond Massey) is a respected farmer and stern father who raised two sons, Cal and Aron (Richard Davalos), alone, but Adam clearly favors Aron. Cal, Aron, and Aron's girlfriend, Abra (Julie Harris), meet Adam at his icehouse, where he shares his dream of shipping fresh lettuce to the East via refrigerated railroad cars. Adam is a Willy Loman figure who believes in the American dream of hard work and entrepreneurship. The film is set in 1917, and the nation is on the eve of entering World War I. Seeking to impress the father with his business acumen, Cal observes that with a war looming there is money to be made in raising beans to feed the soldiers and a war-ravaged Europe. Adam dismisses Cal's idea, insisting that he is interested in big ideas that will bring progress to the region and not simply in making profits off the war. Rebuffed by the patriarch he is trying so hard to please, Cal takes refuge in his father's icehouse. While brooding, he spies upon Aron and Abra, who are making marriage plans. It is obvious that Cal has feelings for Abra, and in his rejection the young man takes out his frustration upon his father's pet project, violently pushing huge blocks of ice down the loading chute.

Later that evening at the dining table, Adam rebukes Cal for his behavior. He forces the son to read from the Bible and seeks to impose upon the son his absolutist and puritanical views of good and evil. In response, Cal tries to learn more regarding his mother, about whom Adam will not speak other than to say that she died when the two boys were infants. After this unsatisfactory conversation, Cal again hops a freight train and journeys to Monterrey, where he again attempts to visit Kate. It is the evening, and it is rather obvious that Kate is running a bordello. Before Cal can speak with her, he is removed from the property by the sheriff (Burl Ives), who tells Cal the true story of Kate. The sheriff relates that rebelling against the isolation and puritanism pushed by Adam, his mother shot Adam and fled from the home that had become a prison. Thus, Cal and Kate are similar in their relationship with Adam, but Cal still believes that he may gain the love of his father.

The brothel scenes are certainly important to the film as Kazan made it clear that in his film he was attempting to denounce puritanism, which still exercised considerable influence over American life and culture during the 1950s. Kazan asserted that *East of Eden* offered an opportunity for one to attack "the absolute Puritanism of 'this is right and this is wrong.' I was trying to show that right and wrong get mixed up, and that there are values that have to be looked at more deeply than in that absolute approval-or-disapproval syndrome of my Left friends."[15] Thus, *East of Eden* returns to the post-HUAC themes of ambiguity. In addition, Kazan continued to combat the censors representing the production code, a problem that would become even more pertinent to his next film, *Baby Doll*. The Breen office objected to Kate running a house of prostitution and not being "punished" for her endeavors. In response, Kazan argued that he would not be presenting a "whore house" as some type of social club as director Fred Zinnemann did in *From Here to Eternity* (1950). Instead, the house of prostitution would be presented as a dull place of business that would not be attractive to the film audience. Kazan maintained: "Of course we would not show customers doing anything except lounging, sleeping, reading. No drinking. A whore house is an incredibly dull place. No slamming of doors in this picture. No towels, no Negro maids, no cuteness, no humor."[16] Kazan prevailed with *East of Eden*, but it is interesting to note that in making his case for presenting prostitution, the director was engaging in a form of puritanism that perhaps reflected his views on sexuality and women. In his autobiography, Kazan proudly extols his many sexual escapades, but he did not have to resort to paying for sex. Of course, one might argue that he was often simply using his power as a director, which represented another form of currency.

Issues of sexuality would be front and center in controversies over *Baby Doll*, but for *East of Eden* the father/son conflict remained dominant. After learning the truth about Kate, Cal seems more eager than ever to please his father, perhaps wanting to earn the love once bestowed upon Kate before she rejected Adam's controlling influence. Cal throws himself into helping Adam achieve his dream of shipping refrigerated lettuce to the eastern market. The train carrying the lettuce is dispatched with considerable fanfare, and Adam for once seems proud of Cal. However, a snowstorm in the Rockies blocks the train, leading to the melting of the ice and destruction of the lettuce crop. Adam is crushed. It takes more than hard work to realize the American dream. The film seems to suggest that capitalist success is more dependent on luck than the work ethic. Again we see the ambivalence of Kazan's post-HUAC cinema regarding American capitalism. Cal refuses to accept this failure and seizes upon an entrepreneurial plan to recover Adam's losses so that he may again attempt to realize his dreams. The son decides to speculate in the beans future market by partnering with a local businessman, Will Hamilton (Albert Dekker), but he needs $5,000 cash to enter the arrangement. A determined Cal then travels once again to Monterrey, where he is finally able to meet his mother and convince her to loan him the money.

As Cal invests his time and money secretly in bean futures and production, the United States enters the World War I, and the community seems to become consumed with an orgy of patriotism—exposing the insecurity and vulnerability often experienced by immigrants such as Kazan. Adam serves on the local draft board, but Aron is a pacifist and does not enlist. This potential source of conflict between father and son, however, is not really explored in the film. Meanwhile, Cal runs into Abra at a carnival, and while they ride the Ferris wheel, he kisses her. Abra is attracted to Cal, but she tells him that she remains in love with Aron. At this point, a mob attacks a local German merchant for his ethnicity and alleged lack of patriotism—an example of intolerance that was all too common during World War I and perhaps reminded Kazan of the conformity demanded by the Communist Party in the 1930s and expected by HUAC and anti-Communists during the early years of the Cold War. Following the dispersal of the mob, Cal and Aron fight over Abra.

Despite her manifestation of love for Aron, Cal shares with Abra his plans to compensate his father for his financial losses. Cal is encouraged by Abra and plans to give Adam $10,000 on his birthday. During the birthday celebration and before Cal is able to bestow his gift, Aron announces his engagement to Abra. Adam is enthusiastic, proclaiming, "I couldn't have wished for anything nicer." Although Aron's announcement has somewhat stolen his thunder, Cal bravely presents his hard-earned cash gift to Adam. But Cal is crushed when Adam asserts that he cannot accept the gift because the money was earned by exploiting wartime markets and conditions. In analyzing Adam's rejection of the money, Kazan observes that the father wanted the money and Cal got it for him, but Adam struggled with the amoral nature of American capitalism, which created millionaires during the war through profiteering. Kazan notes: "Fortunes were made in corrupt ways during the war—like what they did with the beans, by buying something in advance for such-and-such a figure, and then they'd get a much bigger figure. The country was fighting so that democracy would live, and at the same time it was being corrupted by the money philosophy that it lived under."[17] Of course, this war profiteering was hardly limited to World War I, and the Cold War, during which Kazan became an informer, hero, or victim—depending on one's point of view—fostered what President Dwight Eisenhower called the military-industrial complex. And more contemporary conflicts such as the Iraq War have boosted the profits of oil companies and corporations such as Halliburton. War profiteering themes in *East of Eden* provide further evidence of Kazan's ambivalent views regarding capitalism.

There seems to be nothing that Cal can do to please his father, and to strike back against the patriarch, Cal attacks the favored son. Cal confronts Aron and challenges his brother to accompany him to Monterrey to "look at the truth." He takes Aron to Kate and introduces him as "your other son." An angry Cal takes a shocked Aron and throws him on top of his mother before fleeing the premises. After returning home, Cal confronts his father about Kate and proclaims that he will never again attempt to buy his father's love. The sheriff then arrives to inform the two men that a drunken Aron has enlisted in the army and is departing from the train station. An inebriated and despondent Aron refuses to listen to the pleas of his brother and father against deserting his pacifist principles and joining the war effort. Aron laughs hysterically and smashes a train window with his head. A distraught Adam then suffers a stroke and collapses in Cal's arms. Symbolically, Cal has destroyed Aron, following the biblical story of Adam's sons Cain and Abel. But the last scene of the film offers some hope for redemption.

East of Eden concludes with a dying Adam in his bedroom. Cal approaches the stricken man and apologizes for "the awful things" he has done, but Adam provides no response. After Cal exits the room, Abra begs Adam to reconcile with his son and provide Cal with some sign of affection and love. Abra then prevails upon Cal to return to the side of his paralyzed father, who in a mumble asks his son to get rid of the nurse, whom he cannot stand. The assumption is that Cal will now care for his father as the camera pulls back for a final, high-angle shot of Cal sitting at his father's bedside. For Kazan, the film's conclusion was obvious: "You have to forgive your father, finally. You have to say, 'Well, I don't like you for this, and I don't like you for that,' but if you continue to live in that hate, you don't grow up. I've always believed that hate destroys the hater. The thing to do is to have some compassion for everybody."[18] Asserting that he had to rid himself of hate and forgive his father in order to go on with his life, Kazan might also very well be referring to the compassion needed to deal with friends and associates impacted by his HUAC testimony.

In his autobiography, Kazan devotes considerable attention to the relationship with his father. The future filmmaker's initial reaction to his father was one of fear—and fear is a theme that occupies a strong place in the director's life. The basic fear and insecurity for Kazan appeared to be the need to alleviate his outsider status and find acceptance—whether the force threatening to control him was Turkish officials, Molly Thacher, the Group Theatre, the Communist Party, HUAC, studio officials, colleagues in the theater and film community, or his own father. Yet Kazan seemed to embrace an individualism that never allowed him to find the acceptance he sought. The director asserted that he always kept a suitcase fully packed in case he needed to flee from threatening authority figures. Kazan begins his autobiography with the comment that when he looks in the mirror as an old man, he perceives the image of his father, George, a man he feared for most of his life. As an immigrant rug merchant, Kazan's father is described as constantly compromising and avoiding conflict in his business environment. This lack of control in his everyday life led his father to compensate by exercising an almost dictatorial control over the household, including physical violence against his son, who rejected the commercial world of his father. The relationship between George Kazan and his wife, Athena, whom he brought from Turkey, was a rather cold and distant one according to the son. The father would spend most of his day at the store, then return home for a large evening meal, a nap, and an evening of cards with his friends. Athena's close friend, Lucy, initially accompanied the family from Turkey to America, but George eventually ordered her to leave the Kazan home. Increasingly alone and isolated, Athena bonded with her oldest son, supporting his educational and theatrical pursuits, which the father did not understand and opposed.[19]

While Kazan spent much of his youth in what he termed a conspiracy with his mother against his father, the onset of the Great Depression virtually destroyed George's business and led his son to finally experience a degree of empathy for the patriarch. Kazan writes that the depression finally allowed him to see his father "not as a household bully but as Yiorgos Kazanjioglou, who'd come to America a young man from the backcountry of Turkey in Asia, to find a place in the world, a man who'd worked his life away. Now here he was, sitting on the debris of his days, puzzled, soul-weary, a gray fifty-six, he the browbeaten one, not I, with no place to rest except on the battlefield of his disaster."[20] George Kazan never seemed to fully recover from the Depression, and suffering from Parkinson's disease, George Kazan died at a rest home in 1960. One of Kazan's greatest regrets was that he and his father were never able to adequately talk about their differences. Kazan would later describe his film *America America* as an effort to better understand his father and the immigrant experience.

And certainly *East of Eden* was an earlier attempt to address the troubled legacy through the characters of Adam and Cal Trask. At the core of both the Kazan and Trask families is a troubling examination of the American dream. George Kazan and Adam Trask believed in the dream that could be obtained through hard work in the land of opportunity. Despite their best efforts, however, both men experienced economic failure due to forces over which they exercised no control. The victims of impersonal market forces, neither man was able to achieve financial security, which seemed to translate into the inability to communicate with sons who wanted to forge their own plans and dreams. For George Kazan and Adam Trask, the American dream became the American nightmare. These themes were certainly apparent in Miller's *Death of a Salesman*, as Kazan acknowledged in his autobiography, but in 1955 the relationship between Miller and Kazan was considerably strained—perhaps best exemplified by Molly Thacher's reaction to *The Crucible* as she proclaimed there was no logical connection between the Second Red Scare and the Salem witchcraft hysteria because there were no witches or devils in Massachusetts, but there were plenty of Communists in the United States.[21]

Nevertheless, in his autobiography Kazan does explore the connections between George Kazan and Willy Loman—and indirectly Adam Trask as well. Reading the play again over thirty years after he directed *Death of a Salesman*, Kazan asserts that it still raised memories of his father and brought tears to his eyes. Kazan compared Willy Loman with his father and tried to forgive him. Kazan wrote: "George Kazan was a man full of violence that he dared release only at home, where it was safe to be angry. But the possibility that he might blow up at any time kept us all in terrible fear." Similar to Loman, George Kazan was also a salesman and depended on selling himself as well as goods—thus, both men were outer-directed males dependent upon the approval of others. Also, for one of the few times in his memoir, Kazan mentions his younger brothers, one of whom became a doctor and the other who for a while demonstrated an interest in the rug business. In this regard, Kazan's memories are similar to *East of Eden*; there is considerable development of Cal and Adam, but the brother, Aron, is often ignored and undeveloped. Like Loman, George Kazan was most disappointed in his eldest son, and both enjoyed the support of long-suffering spouses. In conclusion, Kazan perceived the tragedies of his father and Loman within the destructive aspects of the capitalist system, which he believed that Miller captured in a far more sophisticated fashion than the agitprop of Clifford Odets. Kazan asserted:

> The essence of our society, the capitalist system, is being destroyed not by rhetoric but by that unchallengeable vocabulary, action between people, which makes you believe that the terrible things that happen are true, are inevitable, and concern us all. Furthermore, the conflict we watch is between people who have every individual reason to love each other. Miller makes us reach out for the lesson, it is not thrust down our throats. The question remains: Why do we live by that law when we know—and Art shows us this—that the result is so humanly destructive. [22]

Despite these insights, Kazan was never able to completely reconcile with his father before George's death in 1960. Perhaps he could never quite get past the fear of his father, which is a major theme in the autobiography. Describing how he tried to work out his feelings for his father through psychoanalysis, Kazan proclaimed: "Ambivalence is the essential word. I'm still scared of my father and you can't be scared of someone and feel compassion for him. I have only one emotion when I think of him and it's not love." [23]

Despite the themes of revolution against the patriarchy and the questioning of the American dream and capitalist system, which highlight the progressive political agenda of *East of Eden*, public reaction to the film rarely mentioned these issues, which were submerged in the acclaim for and criticism of James Dean. The film did well at the box office, actually earning more than *On the Waterfront*. It was well received internationally at Cannes, and *East of Eden* earned Oscar nominations for Best Picture and Kazan as Best Director. Dean, Harris, and Jo Van Fleet also received Academy Award nominations, but only Van Fleet as Kate won an Oscar. Critical reactions to both Dean's acting and Kazan's direction were mixed. *Newsweek* termed *East of Eden* as one of finest movies of Kazan's career and praised Dean as "an exceptionally sensitive young actor."[24] In a similar vein, *Time* found that Kazan's direction of the film provided intelligence and control from a filmmaker who "is a man, above all, who knows exactly what he wants and exactly how to get it." The mainstream publication was also impressed with Dean. Although the *Time* review concluded that Dean seemed to sometimes try too hard, "no matter what he is doing, he has the presence of a young lion and the same sense of danger about him."[25]

Other reviews, however, were far less kind to the director and his young star. Lee Rogow in the *Saturday Review* chastised Kazan for attempting to graft Brando mannerisms upon Dean.[26] Robert Hatch in the *Nation* also found Dean to be a promising performer whose mimicry of Brando needed to be discouraged. Hatch, however, was much more critical of Kazan, arguing that the film "dragged" and did not benefit from CinemaScope. Hatch argued: "*East of Eden* deals with inner conflict, the entire story could be played out in a living room. Instead it sprawls all over the eye-filling landscape and the real action is padded or interrupted by a great deal of rushing to and fro that is inserted to justify all that expensive new machinery. The film looks like a Western, but it lacks that kind of excitement, and the very real excitement it does have is dulled by the giant sweep of Technicolor."[27] Writing in *Commonweal*, Philip T. Hartung was more positive about Kazan's direction, but did suggest that the cinematic artistry sometimes detracted from the story. Hartung was also enthusiastic about the performances in *East of Eden*; however, the critic found that Dean's acting was "patterned so closely after the style of Marlon Brando that at times the character is more like a parody than a straightforward portrait."[28]

Other reviews were even harsher in their appraisal of Dean. Bosley Crowther of the *New York Times* praised Kazan for his employment of CinemaScope and color, suggesting that the Salinas farmlands "sharply focused to the horizon in the sunshine, are fairly fragrant with atmosphere. The strain of troubled people against such backgrounds has a clear and enhanced irony." The *New York Times* critic also found the acting in *East of Eden* to be quite strong, with the notable exception of Dean, whom Crowther characterized as "a man of histrionic gingerbread." Describing Dean, Crowther wrote: "He scuffs his feet, he whirls, he pouts, he sputters, he leans against walls, he rolls his eyes, he swallows his words, he ambles slack-kneed—all like Marlon Brando used to do. Never have we seen a performer so clearly follow another's style. Mr. Kazan should be spanked for permitting him to do such a sophomoric thing. Whatever there might be of reasonable torment in this youngster is buried beneath the clumsy display." And John McCarten of the *New Yorker* was even more unforgiving in his assessment of Dean's performance, concluding: "He looks like a sort of miniature Gregory Peck, but he has obviously been going to a few movies featuring Marlon Brando. Or maybe he's just been going to the movies. At any rate, he represents a school of acting that might be described as unpredictable. There is no telling how he will react to any situation. Sometimes he jumps up and down like a kangaroo, sometimes he giggles like a lunatic, and sometimes he is surly and offended. He's a hard man to decipher."[29]

In response to such harsh criticism, Dean downplayed the comparisons with Brando, telling *Newsweek*: "I am not disturbed by the comparison, nor am I flattered. I have my own personal rebellion and don't have to rely upon Brando."[30] Kazan, who was often critical of the young actor, felt it necessary to come to the aid of Dean and the film. The director wrote to critic Helen Bower, who published a positive notice on Dean in the *Detroit Free Press*, that while Dean admired Brando, it was wrong for critics such as Crowther to suggest that he was simply imitating, with Kazan's encouragement, the star of *On the Waterfront*. Kazan concluded: "I actually don't think he's much like Brando. He's considerably more introverted, more drawn, more naked. Whatever he is, though, he's not an imitation of anybody. He's too proud to try to imitate anyone. He has too much difficulty—as does any decent worker in our craft—thinking about anything except playing the part as written. Critics who say he's imitating Brando just reveal a naiveté about acting, direction and production."[31]

What was lost on many established critics is that Kazan was tapping into a growing youth rebellion in the 1950s that would crest into the countercultural tsunami of the 1960s and the politics of the New Left, with which Kazan was more comfortable than the Communist Party of the tumultuous 1930s. Dean's biographer David Dalton credits Kazan with recognizing that Dean epitomized a new generation seeking to reclaim an America that was obsessed by a static and oppressive search for security following the Depression, two world wars, and the Cold War. Dalton writes, "At precisely this point, James Dean appeared as Cal Trask as Jim Stark as Jett Rink, the inevitable Cain in America's Garden of

Eden—the destroyer of illusion, the destructive adolescent, the violent agent of change and herald of a new era."[32] In his biography of Kazan, Richard Schickel also notes the degree to which Dean fit into the cultural zeitgeist of the 1950s in which a teenage culture was developing with its own music, movies, mores, and clothing in opposition to the dominant culture. Dean's Cal Trask fit perfectly into these sociological, historical, and generational conflicts; and "because he appeared in a historical context, in a work based on a novel by a seriously regarded writer and directed by a man who had never made anything like a cheap exploitation picture, people felt obliged to take the film with great seriousness."[33] Schickel, however, believed that *East of Eden* was more than just Kazan anticipating the cultural revolution in America. The film, as Kazan always suggested, was personal, and Schickel concludes that the director's politics moved from the larger societal context of a *Viva Zapata!* "into the family microcosm, with fathers representing a sort of emotional totalitarianism, sons the rebels with a cause, which might be defined as a need to make their own destinies."[34]

Kazan certainly recognized the progressive political implications for *East of Eden*. In his production notes for the film, the director noted that working with Dean was "gratifying because he always caught something of the spirit of the youth which considered itself disenfranchised by the preceding generation."[35] Dean seemed to embody the generational and patriarchal conflict for the 1950s, which Kazan had experienced with his father in an earlier era. Thus, in an interview with Jeff Young, Kazan acknowledged that he was increasingly placing the focus on political conflict within the family, which reflected the tyrannies of the larger society, but he asserted once again that the key to understanding his politics and cinema was the theme of ambivalence. Kazan observed: "The ambivalence of emotion. That's my specialty because that's what my life experience has been. I very rarely have a pure emotion. Even my feelings about America are ambivalent. In all my films, I knock it, and tear it down. I'm highly critical. I love Southerners, whom I criticize more than anyone else. I have great doubts about myself. I believe that that's the truth in my life. So I try to deal with that ambivalence."[36]

The commercial success of *On the Waterfront* and *East of Eden* allowed Kazan to become an independent producer with greater freedom to pursue these themes of ambivalence in politics and the human soul. In a letter to Darryl Zanuck, Kazan commented on his independence, noting that for *East of Eden*: "All the solutions were mine and for better or worse the picture is my picture. No one had a hand in editing, and I have the ultimate satisfaction of knowing that it's the way I really want it. I took a long time editing it and changing it around and scored it myself and dubbed it myself and for better or worse, I have the only important satisfaction: it's my own."[37] Kazan used this freedom to make a trilogy of films set in the South exploring dark themes of sexuality, demagoguery, and the impact of progressive change on a traditional way of life—all the while directly avoiding the civil rights movement, which was transforming the South. Nevertheless, the themes pursued by Kazan in the Southern trilogy again provide proof that the filmmaker's post-HUAC testimony films reflected his ambivalence regarding the promise of American democracy.

5

SEXUALITY AND THE NEW SOUTH

Baby Doll (1956)

In September 2015, the McCarter Theater in Princeton, New Jersey, premiered a stage version of the 1956 *Baby Doll* film collaboration between Elia Kazan and playwright Tennessee Williams, based on Williams's short plays *27 Wagons Full of Cotton* and *The Unsatisfactory Supper*. The 1950s production drew the ire of the Catholic Church, and the 2015 revival retains much of the original's sexual heat according to Bruce Chadwick, who reviewed the Princeton performance for the History News Network. Acknowledging the sexuality of Carroll Baker as Baby Doll in the film version, Chadwick, nevertheless, concludes, "The sex in this Princeton play is slow and subtle, but it is deep and it turns the heat up in the old theater to well over 100 degrees—in the shade."[1] Thus, Kazan's assault on American Puritanism, which commenced in *East of Eden*, was more visually and openly defined with the sexuality of *Baby Doll*.

Speaking of *East of Eden*, Kazan insisted that he wanted to "attack Puritanism; the absolute Puritanism of 'this is right and this is wrong.' I was trying to show that right and wrong get mixed up, and that there are values that have to be looked at more deeply than in that absolute approval-or-disapproval syndrome of my Left friends."[2] While many of his former comrades on the political left supported Kazan's questioning the legacy still exercised by puritanical and bourgeois perceptions of sexuality limiting individual expression, his Southern trilogy of *Baby Doll*

(1956), *A Face in the Crowd* (1957), and *Wild River* (1960) also raised troubling questions regarding Kazan's progressive attitudes toward women, black Americans, and the poor white farmers of the South. While recognizing the complexity of these film texts, biographers and scholars of the filmmaker argue that the Southern trilogy constitutes a progressive effort to address the problems of American democracy in the 1950s by turning toward rural and small-town America. Richard Schickel observes that beginning with *East of Eden*, Kazan made a series of six films over eight years "that would all deal with rural or small-town settings and figures, a definitive turning away from the largely urban environments and characters that had previously concerned him. One cannot believe that this was entirely accidental. There was something in the earth that he finally had to dig out."[3] In his study of Kazan's cinema, Brian Neve suggests that the director captures the transition from the Old South into the modern era, and the film scholar concludes, "The social aspects of Kazan's film—capturing something of the benighted American South of its time—have been neglected, yet it is also a much riskier, genuinely independent project, a chamber piece of convincingly human and semi-comic struggles for respect and survival."[4] Thus, the ambivalence of Kazan's post-HUAC cinema is certainly evident in the director's examination of sexuality and the American South in *Baby Doll*. Kazan's Southern trilogy was hardly a retreat into nostalgia, as the director continued to raise questions about American capitalism missing from his more simplistic congressional testimony.

Kazan based some of his best films on collaborations with leading American writers of the post–World War II era—John Steinbeck, Tennessee Williams, Budd Schulberg, and Arthur Miller—before pursuing his own career as a novelist and writer for his films. Of these writers, perhaps Kazan was most impressed with Williams, although the two often quarreled. Kazan directed both the stage and screen versions of Williams's classic *A Streetcar Named Desire*. In addition, he directed the acclaimed Broadway production of the playwright's *Cat on a Hot Tin Roof* (1955). However, the director's insistence on some revisions to the play and the return of the character Big Daddy to the third act antagonized Williams and contributed to a somewhat awkward collaboration on the ensuing *Baby Doll*. Although their backgrounds were certainly different, Kazan believed that the two friends were drawn toward one another by their outsider status in the 1950s. Williams was a gay man from the

American South in an era when homosexuality was still considered a mental disorder by the American Psychiatric Association. While the film-maker remained the Anatolian outsider immigrant whose acceptance into mainstream American society Kazan always questioned. In addition, while the Arthur Miller and Kazan friendship was considerably strained by the director's HUAC appearance, Williams remained loyal to his friend. Writing in his autobiography about Williams and the rejection he suffered from other friends following his testimony, Kazan asserted: "The big-shot had become an 'outsider.' Williams was always that. We both felt vulnerable to the depredations of an unsympathetic world, distrustful of the success we'd had, suspicious of those in favor, anticipating put-downs, expecting insufficient appreciation and reward. The most loyal and understanding friend I had through those black months was Tennessee Williams."[5]

This outsider theme is also one explored by John Lahr, whose 2014 biography of the playwright was a finalist for the National Book Award. Lahr argues that both men were insecure and afraid of their fathers. Both men sought to escape their outsider status through their success as artists, but awards and critical praise failed to fundamentally alter their insecurity, which was based on sexuality—in the case of Williams, his preference for same-sex relationships, while Kazan was plagued by a conviction that he was ugly and thus shunned by women in his youth. Lahr writes: "Kazan's appetite for vindictive triumph—which drove his compulsive ambition and unrepentant womanizing—was partly rooted in one inescapable fact: Kazan was unhandsome. 'Didn't you look in the mirror?,' his father asked him when he first announced that he was going to Yale Drama School. His gnarly mug, with its large, jugged nose, telegraphed both his foreignness and his ferocity, and it made a Hollywood film career a nonstarter."[6] Accordingly, despite the love of the attractive and patrician Molly Thacher, Kazan also needed to prove himself by having sex with as many young starlets as possible. Williams also followed a path of promiscuity, but Lahr argues that his impetuous nature was somewhat tamed by Kazan, who emerged as a father figure to the author. Lahr concludes: "Kazan's straight talk challenged Williams, it set for him both tasks and boundaries. Kazan organized Williams, and, figuratively speaking, forced him to clean up his mess. Like all sons of powerful fathers, Williams felt a certain ambivalence toward this authority. He needed Kazan's energy and inspiration; he also resented his instrusiveness."[7] On the other hand, Williams asserted that he was not a political person, and he refused to censure his father figure for cooperating with HUAC.

Thus, political differences did not interfere with the collaborative process, but there were plenty of artistic issues to make producing a film script for *Baby Doll* a challenging task. As early as 1952, Kazan was writing that he believed any censorship problems with the script could be resolved and Warner Bros. should plan on making the picture. Nevertheless, neither he nor Williams were as of yet satisfied with the screenplay, and much work remained to be done. Still, Kazan told Steven B. Trilling at Warner Bros. that Williams was beginning to show some real enthusiasm for the project: "I think from here on in he may be going to do his best writing. That's my hope and I certainly have no intention of going ahead with the project until we have something really wonderful—it is too important for me." Kazan, however, was overly optimistic in regard to both Williams and censorship issues that the film might encounter. Joseph Breen, in charge of enforcing the Production Code, found *Baby Doll*'s script problems far from being solved due to the film's "sordid tone" and absence of any character representing "decency and sanity." Meanwhile, a frustrated Williams proclaimed, "Help! Help! Send me a writer."[8]

Two years later, the rewriting was continuing, and Kazan sought to encourage Williams by suggesting Marlon Brando for the role of the Sicilian immigrant Silva Vacarro, who attempts to seduce Baby Doll in revenge for her husband's burning down of Vacarro's cotton gin. Kazan told Williams's agent, Audrey Wood, that Brando was quite interested in the role, for which the actor would be "perfect and invaluable."[9] In August 1955, Kazan was still touting Brando for the role of Vacarro, describing him as "just the right person."[10] Brando, however, passed on *Baby Doll* and moved directly from *Guys and Dolls* (1955) to *Teahouse of the August Moon* (1956). Kazan never seemed to accept that despite his admiration for the director's talents, Brando's disgust with Kazan's HUAC testimony made it impossible to ever work with the filmmaker again. For the role of Baby Doll, Kazan initially envisioned Marilyn Monroe, but changes in the script that made Baby Doll a young virgin bride rendered Monroe, at age thirty-one, too old for the part. In addition, there were personal reasons for not casting Monroe, such as Kazan's troubled relationship with Arthur Miller and Molly Thacher Kazan's knowledge of her husband's sexual escapades with the actress. Writing to his wife from Mississippi before his family joined him for the filming of *Baby Doll*, Kazan acknowledged his affair with Monroe, but he concluded that the actress really meant little to him. Kazan described Monroe as "talented, funny, vulnerable, helpless in awful pain, with no hope, and some worth and not a liar, not vicious, not catty, and with a history of orphanism that was killing to hear. She was like all Charlie Chaplin's heroines in one. I'm not ashamed at all, not a damn bit of having been attracted to her." The director apologized for hurting Molly, but he did not promise that he would remain faithful in the future. Apparently needing the reaffirmation of other women, the insecure director told his wife: "I'm sorry I hurt you. I do not look for anything like this. I do not want something like this. I am human though. It may happen again."[11]

With Monroe out of the picture, Kazan still had to cast the part of Baby Doll and denied to Williams that he was considering such prominent actresses as Grace Kelly or Deborah Kerr. In a correspondence that borders on misogyny, Williams said that such casting was inappropriate as Baby Doll was "touchingly comic, a grotesquely witless creature, almost as deep as kitty-cat's pee. Who the fuck gives a shit if she is, was, or ever will be 'fulfilled as a woman?'" In response, Kazan reassured Williams that they would "find some young piece of tail for Baby Doll."[12] For the sex-symbol role of Baby Doll, Kazan finally selected Carroll Baker from the Actors Studio, and her strong performance earned the young actress an Oscar nomination. Baker, who bore some physical resemblance to Monroe, appreciated the opportunity to portray Baby Doll, but she resented being typecast as a sex symbol.[13] Unable to lure Brando, Kazan cast newcomer Eli Wallach from the Actors Studio and Broadway as Vacarro. While he preferred Burl Ives to play the role of Archie Lee Meighan, Baby Doll's frustrated husband, Kazan was able to get his old friend Karl Malden, with whom the director worked on *A Streetcar Named Desire* and *On the Waterfront*, to accept the role when Ives was unavailable.

As casting for the film was completed, Kazan was still struggling with the film's conclusion. Failing to give the film project his full attention, Williams was sending the director bits and pieces of dialogue with the instruction to place the material wherever the director believed it worked best. Williams was still angry with Kazan over his direction of *Cat on a Hot Tin Roof* and was distracted with the film premiere of his *The Rose*

Tattoo, starring Italian actress Anna Magnani, and a production of *A Streetcar Named Desire*, featuring Tallulah Bankhead, playing at the Coconut Grove Playhouse in Miami. Kazan insisted that Williams join him for the filming of *Baby Doll* in the small town of Benoit, Mississippi, in November 1955. A reluctant Williams complained that he did not want to come to the rural South, where as a gay man he had been treated so poorly. The writer also insisted that he would need a swimming pool, which Kazan was able to secure in the nearby community of Greenville. But the playwright disappeared after only a few days, telling Kazan that he did not care for the way people were looking at him. Kazan asserted: "Now I was without an author, but I didn't mind. I was what I wanted to be, the source of everything."[14] Despite Kazan's claims of control, Williams was given full credit for the film's screenplay and received an Oscar nomination.

Williams and Kazan also argued over *Baby Doll*'s conclusion. Kazan's proposed ending antagonized the writer, who believed that the entire nature of the film was altered. Kazan suggested that the final confrontation between Archie Lee and Vacarro conclude with the Sicilian being pierced by a frog-sticking pole wielded by Archie Lee during a swamp battle. Then Archie Lee accidently shoots and kills a black man before being dragged off to jail by the sheriff. An incensed Williams proclaimed that Kazan's proposal was "false to the key and mood of the story." He insisted: "Killing a Negro is not a part of universal human behavior, witness all the universal Archie Lees' in this world who never killed a Negro and never quite would! They would commit arson, yes, they would lie and cheat and jerk off back of a peep-hole, but they wouldn't be likely to kill a Negro and slam the car door on his dying body and go on shooting and shouting, now, would they?" However, considering the level of violence in Mississippi during the 1950s and the murder of Emmett Till in 1955, Williams might be a bit naive regarding the racial aggression of white Southerners. Still smarting from the slight he believed Kazan inflicted on him in making changes in *Cat on a Hot Tin Roof*, Williams also took a swipe at Kazan the artist, writing: "You say that whenever I am in trouble I go poetic. I say whenever you are in trouble, you start building up a 'smash' finish—as if you didn't really trust the story that goes before. It is only this final burst of excess that mars your film—masterpieces such as *East of Eden*, and it is in these final fireworks that you descend (only then) to something expected or banal which all the preceding activity and sense of measure and poetry—yes, you are a poet, too no matter how much you hate it!—leads one not to expect."[15] In response, Kazan followed the suggestions of Williams and found the author's concluding line uttered by Baby Doll, "To wait for tomorrow and see if we're remembered—or forgotten," to provide a proper sense of closure for the film.

Baby Doll begins with Archie Lee Meighan (Karl Malden) repairing the roof of a dilapidated cotton plantation in Tiger Tail County, Mississippi. In a scene that drew the ire of censors and the Catholic Church, the middle-aged and balding Archie Lee pokes a hole in the plaster of a wall so that he might spy on his young wife, who is sleeping in the next room.[16] A seductive Baby Doll Meighan (Carroll Baker) is sleeping in the nursery inside an oversized baby crib while sucking her thumb in a provocative manner and clad in a white slip. She confronts Archie Lee for being a peeping tom, and during the course of their conversation the film audience learns that the marriage of two years has not been consummated. Archie Lee assured Baby Doll's father, who is now deceased, that he understood that the beautiful Baby Doll was really still a child, and he promised not to touch her physically until her twentieth birthday. As the film opens, it is only two days until Baby Doll's twentieth birthday, and an overeager Archie Lee attempts to rape his wife while she is bathing, but the young woman is able to elude him.

Baby Doll, to the amusement of Archie Lee's black sharecroppers, then keeps her husband waiting before she accompanies him to his doctor's appointment in town. While Archie Lee is with the doctor, Baby Doll flirts with a dentist who is looking for a receptionist. She explains that she is unable to type, but the dentist remains interested. The doctor prescribes some pills for Archie Lee, but the nurse looks at Baby Doll and suggests that medication will not cure what is bothering him. Archie Lee then purchases his wife an ice-cream cone, which she licks in a most provocative manner. An agitated Archie Lee is upset that everyone in town, both black and white, are watching them and seem to be poking fun of their relationship. And here Kazan makes excellent use of extras from the community of Benoit, whose company he enjoyed throughout the filming of *Baby Doll*.

Meanwhile, Archie Lee and Baby Doll notice a delivery truck passing with their repossessed furniture. They return home in time to witness the remainder of their furniture being removed from the crumbling mansion.

Archie Lee had promised his bride and her father that he would use the revenues from his cotton gin to restore the plantation to its former glory. However, he is unable to keep this promise and cannot even make the payments on the furniture as Archie Lee lacks the resources to compete with the larger and more efficient Syndicate cotton gin and plantation, which has the advantage of capital investment from outside the region. Archie Lee's American dreams of a status-symbol wife, successful enterprise, beautiful home, and community respect have collapsed.

That evening there is a party at the Syndicate plantation to celebrate the largest cotton crop in the history of the county. Yet this progress was achieved through the influx of outside capital, symbolized by the Syndicate's manager, Silva Vacarro (Eli Wallach), a Sicilian immigrant whose presence is resented by many in the community, such as Archie Lee, who have lost their jobs and been unable to compete with the larger enterprise. With Vacarro, we again see the theme of the Anatolian smile and outsider immigrant so prominent in Kazan's life and work. During the party, the Syndicate cotton gin catches fire and is destroyed. When a gasoline can is discovered near the origin of the fire, arson is suspected. Vacarro seeks to place blame on Archie Lee, as he is the only former competitor of the Syndicate not present at the party. The local authorities, however, are not eager to intervene when an outsider immigrant casts aspersions on a member of the local community.

The next morning Vacarro takes the Syndicate's cotton crop to Archie Lee's cotton gin. Excited about this business, Archie Lee asks Baby Doll to entertain their company while the cotton is being ginned. Left alone when Baby Doll's Aunt Rose (Mildred Dunnock) heads off to the hospital to satisfy her cravings by stealing chocolate from the patients, Vacarro and Baby Doll begin to engage in an erotic flirtation while the two talk. Vacarro learns from Baby Doll that Archie Lee was not home during the fire, as he originally told the Sicilian. Baby Doll also informs Vacarro about her unconsummated marriage and Archie Lee's financial difficulties. Vacarro appears to seize upon the opportunity to seduce Baby Doll in revenge for Archie's act of arson. As they sit together on a swing, Vacarro whispers into Baby Doll's ear, and the young woman grows quite flushed. During this scene, it is impossible to see Vacarro's hands, and many viewers perceived that Baby Doll was being aroused by Vacarro's riding crop placed underneath her dress.

Baby Doll attempts to flee Vacarro and runs to Archie Lee, who slaps her for being around the "niggers"—a word that is used numerous times in the film—and leaves her again with Vacarro as he goes to fetch a spare part for the cotton gin, which has broken down. Baby Doll and Vacarro return to the mansion, where they begin to engage in a flirtatious game of hide and seek that culminates in Vacarro getting the young woman to sign a paper stating that Archie Lee burned down the Syndicate's gin. Having garnered his evidence, Vacarro prepares to leave, but Baby Doll has not finished playing the game. She invites the Sicilian upstairs to take a nap in the nursery crib. Vacarro accepts, and after he climbs into the crib, Baby Doll places a shawl over him. When Archie Lee returns at the end of the day, he finds Baby Doll clad in a white slip. He orders her to put on some clothes, and he is shocked when Vacarro emerges from the nursery at the top of the stairs. He immediately assumes an act of infidelity, but Archie Lee agrees to Baby Doll's suggestion that the confident Sicilian stay for supper. The assumption that Baby Doll and Vacarro engaged in adultery opened the film to charges of immorality and demands that the film be censored. Kazan, however, insisted that the exhausted Vacarro simply took a nap, as with the affidavit that Archie Lee was guilty of arson he already had what he needed from Baby Doll. On the other hand, the maturity that Baby Doll exhibits at the supper table after her afternoon with Vacarro suggests that Baby Doll has undergone a major transformation from a childlike nymph to a mature woman. Kazan's rather modest reading of the relationship between Baby Doll and Vacarro seems more directed toward addressing the concerns of the Catholic Church than following the logic of the screenplay.

Baby Doll comes to the supper table wearing a more modest black dress and displaying a sense of self-confidence lacking earlier in the film. An increasingly distraught Archie Lee becomes upset with Aunt Rose and her cooking, insisting that she has overstayed her welcome and ordering her to leave the premises. Vacarro interjects that he could use a cook and offers Aunt Rose a position, which she accepts. Archie Lee then asks the Sicilian if there is anything else—meaning Baby Doll—that he wants to take with him. Before he receives a reply, Archie Lee grabs his shotgun and begins to chase Vacarro, who calmly finds refuge in a large tree, where he is joined by Baby Doll. Meanwhile, Archie Lee discharges his shotgun into the darkness before collapsing, and sobbing with despair he calls out Baby Doll's name. The local authorities arrive and take Archie

Lee into custody, telling their friend that they will not be able to protect him due to the affidavit Vacarro possesses implicating Archie Lee in the arson of the Syndicate cotton gin. As a clock chimes twelve, signaling Baby Doll's twentieth birthday, Archie Lee is taken away in a police car, while Vacarro, having exacted his revenge against Archie Lee, leaves without Baby Doll, but he promises to return the next day. He also forgets Aunt Rose, who is waiting on the porch with her packed bags. Baby Doll gently ushers her aunt back into the dilapidated mansion, telling her they will have to "wait for tomorrow and see if we're remembered—or forgotten."

While there is considerable room to argue about what the film is attempting to say regarding poor whites, race relations, and the changing nature of the South, almost all of the immediate attention surrounding *Baby Doll* was focused on sexuality and allegations that the film was obscene. Obviously, a great deal of this was due to Kazan's promotion of the film. He arranged for a 15,600 square foot billboard, featuring a provocative Baker as Baby Doll, to be constructed above the Victoria Theatre on Broadway, where the film debuted. John Lahr proclaimed, "The behemoth image of Carroll Baker, sprawled the length of a city block in her short nightie, sucking her thumb, and reclining in a crib, became as iconic an erotic emblem of the era as Marilyn Monroe holding down her billowing white skirt in *The Seven Year Itch*."[17] The controversy over *Baby Doll*, however, was well under way before the sensationalized billboard. In a November 15, 1955, letter to Jack Warner, Kazan defended the film against the changes presented by Geoffrey Shurlock of the Production Code office that the film promoted adultery. Kazan vehemently disagreed. The director insisted that Archie Lee was the center of the film and "a pathetic misguided, confused, desperate man. Sin and violence and so forth come out of fear and desperation. Archie Lee should be pathetic. And he will be. And amusingly so." In other words, it is possible to perceive elements of Willy Loman and the failed American dream in Archie Lee, only this time the theme is portrayed through farce rather than tragedy. Furthermore, Kazan denied the assumption of adultery between Vacarro and Baby Doll, asserting that the Sicilian was interested in obtaining justice rather than a sexual liaison with Baby Doll. He believed that Vacarro's rejection of Baby Doll at the film's end "will make the adultery issue quite clear. There wasn't any, and actually while Silva has aroused her, he isn't particularly interested in her, once Archie

Lee has been taken away." Kazan concluded that the sexual frustration of Archie Lee was essential to the film and could not be removed. It was imperative for the Production Code office to recognize that for the film industry to differentiate itself from the growth of television, it was crucial that Hollywood pictures be allowed to engage in more adult examinations of topics such as sexuality. Whether this last argument carried any weight is uncertain, but the Production Code office did approve Kazan's film, with Archie Lee's sexual frustration at its core.[18]

The Catholic Church, however, was not convinced by Kazan's arguments. The Catholic Legion of Decency issued a condemned rating for the film, terming it an obvious violation of the Production Code; but it was Francis Cardinal Spellman, archbishop of New York, who succeeded in making the censorship of *Baby Doll* a national issue. After returning from a Thanksgiving trip to visit American troops in Korea, the Catholic leader, noted for his patriotism and fervent anti-Communism, felt it incumbent on him to denounce the moral decay of American culture represented by *Baby Doll*. On the morning of December 16, 1956, while celebrating mass in St. Patrick's Cathedral, he mounted the pulpit, something he had not done since February 1949 when he spoke out against the Communist Hungarian government's persecution of Joseph Cardinal Mindszenty, to denounce Kazan's film. Spellman proclaimed that the revolting sexual themes of *Baby Doll* "and the brazen advertising promoting it constitutes a contemptuous defiance of the natural law, the observance of which has been the source of strength in our national life. It is astonishing and deplorable that such an immoral motion picture should have received a certificate of approval under the so-called self-regulatory system of the Motion Picture Association." The church leader concluded that any Catholic patronizing the film would be unable to receive Communion.[19] Spellman insisted that he was speaking as a loyal citizen as well as a religious leader. It is interesting here to note that Spellman and Kazan shared similar views of the Communist Party as a criminal conspiracy, but the persistence of progressive ideas in Kazan's cinema, such as questioning capitalism, the American dream, and sexual standards, led to a parting of the ways between the two anti-Communists.

In response, Kazan challenged the archbishop, observing that Spellman condemned the film without screening it—a charge that seems accurate. He also believed that the clergyman was responding to the *Baby Doll* billboard of which Kazan remained quite proud. Proclaiming himself a modern-day P. T. Barnum, Kazan told Jack Warner:

> That half-sleeping, day-dreaming, thumb-sucking, long-legged chick, astride one-block long with only Warner Bros. (small type of course), Tennessee Williams, and yours truly's name on the sign, and a big arrow pointing down to the Victoria Theatre will be the talk not only of Broadway, but of the show world, of café society, of the literati, of the lowbrows, and of everybody else. I really don't see how anybody could avoid going to the picture if we put that sign up there. What's wrong with show business is that its balls have been cut off and it is no longer show business.[20]

With the sexualized billboard and controversy generated by Cardinal Spellman, *Baby Doll* opened to solid business in New York City. In addition, reviews of the film were generally positive, but critics were unsure how to respond to the sexuality of *Baby Doll*. The critical commentary, however, rarely touched upon how blacks were represented and women objectified. Joseph McCarten in the *New Yorker* praised the film for its direction, writing, and performances that captured Southern decadence. McCarten concluded, "Mr. Kazan's decision to make the picture in the cotton belt has paid off beautifully in photography that really conveys the look of a section lost in ignorance, poverty, and despair."[21] In a somewhat similar fashion, Arthur Knight of *Saturday Review* credits Kazan with highlighting the major sexual issues dealing with lust, abnormal sexual appetites, and calculated revenge that fascinated Tennessee Williams. Knight described *Baby Doll* as Kazan's best film, but he expressed concern that neither Kazan nor Williams offered any positive characters—providing the film with a disturbing moral ambiguity. The critic argued, "Kazan seems not unlike the Negroes in this film, watching everything with a quiet smile but personally disengaged. If he has any strong personal convictions about these people, any private resentment or objection to their way of life, it is kept well hidden behind the smile."[22] Although Kazan demonstrated empathy for poor Southern whites when working on *People of the Cumberland* for Frontier Films in 1930 and expressed how he enjoyed the fellowship of Mississippi locals during the filming of *Baby Doll*, in the final analysis the completed picture furthers negative stereotypes of poor white trash, which were embraced by the patronizing attitudes of film critics for elite newspapers and magazines.

Thus, Bosley Crowther of the *New York Times* found parallels between Williams and Kazan's *Baby Doll* and Erskine Caldwell's *Tobacco Road* in exposing the depredation of Southern white trash. The film critic found the characters to be without redeeming social value, and he concluded, "Mr. Kazan's pictorial compositions, shot in stark black-and-white and framed for the most part against the background of an old Mississippi mansion, are by far the most artful and respectable feature of *Baby Doll*."[23] Robert Hatch in the *Nation* was less patronizing than Crowther, noting that Williams was telling a sex tale in the nature of Balzac, but in reality, despite the strenuous objections of Cardinal Spellman, not that much really happened in *Baby Doll*. Hatch argues that Williams displays an infantile interest in sexuality, but "he cannot work it out to a satisfactory consummation." The reviewer, however, has nothing but praise for Kazan, proclaiming, "He produces an atmosphere of hunger and heat, danger, revulsion and futility which must be precisely what Williams intended."[24]

On the other hand, *Time* discovered the sex in *Baby Doll* to be a little more interesting, asserting in its lead that the film was "the dirtiest American-made motion picture that has ever been legally exhibited." Nevertheless, the mainstream publication did not necessarily believe that the "carnality" of *Baby Doll* made it unfit for adult audiences. *Time* found that the film did have a moral center, and concluded that "as the script continues, long after it has made its moral point, to fondle a variety of sexual symbols and to finger the anatomical aspects of its subject, the moviegoer can hardly help wondering if the sociological study has not degenerated into the prurient peep."[25] The magazine's prose seems to emulate the charges lodged by the review's introduction—perhaps offering some proof that *Baby Doll* did succeed in generating some sexual intensity.

The film opened to decent audiences in New York City and Los Angeles, but the censure and fury unleashed by Cardinal Spellman seemed to have a significant impact. A screening in Hartford, Connecticut, was disrupted by a bomb threat, and fifteen hundred moviegoers were forced to evacuate the theater where *Baby Doll* was playing. Police censors in Providence, Rhode Island, cut material from half a dozen scenes before allowing the film to be exhibited, while in the Southern cities of Memphis, Tennessee, and Atlanta, Georgia, the film was simply banned. In an exhibition of his solidarity with the Catholic Church, Joseph P. Kennedy, the father of Massachusetts senator John F. Kennedy, announced that his chain of twenty-three theaters in Maine and New Hampshire would not show *Baby Doll*. Meanwhile, the Joint Services Committee in Washington decided that Kazan's film was not suitable for exhibition in theaters on American military bases. In a *Life* magazine feature on the controversy, Kazan displayed his frustration, defending *Baby Doll* as a truthful piece of art. Kazan argued: "Life is not lived as politely as Hollywood suggests. Life is gross. These people are selfish and mean. But glints of poetry come out. It is depressing to see a defeated, middle-aged man trying to hold on to a young girl, but it happens." The director concluded that he was disappointed with the fuss made by Cardinal Spellman, lamenting: "Now my picture looks like a sexy, dirty, sneaky film. And this isn't what I had in mind when I made it."[26]

Continuing the Catholic offensive against the film, Father James Fenton Finley censured Americans and especially members of the Catholic faith who insisted on viewing *Baby Doll*. Writing in the *Catholic World*, Finley complained, "Despite a general critical opinion that the picture has a mired and depressing theme, despite moral advice that pointed up the degeneracy of the story's treatment, too many people have supported *Baby Doll*." To explain this phenomenon, Finley argued that a general sense of "childishness" had descended upon American culture. Describing the juvenile mentality of Americans who were losing the cultural Cold War, Finley arrogantly proclaimed: "Like so many spoiled brats, they manifested childish curiosity about sex, displaying willfulness when given any intelligent advice and point their way through a life of wanting to do as they please. Interesting to think that a *Baby Doll* fascinated them—but, I suppose, it's to be expected, where children are concerned."[27] Despite Finley's jeremiad, *Baby Doll* did not enjoy the commercial success expected by Kazan, who initially seemed to believe the film would benefit from the controversy it had generated. Whether it was the Catholic boycott, which reportedly included priests in the lobby recording the names of parishioners who purchased tickets, or the lack of admirable characters in Williams's screenplay that accounted for the failure of *Baby Doll* is difficult to determine.

Years after the film, however, Kazan was still bitter regarding the reaction of Cardinal Spellman. He told interviewer Michel Ciment that the condemnation of the film by someone who never admitted to seeing *Baby Doll* was ridiculous. Nevertheless, Kazan conceded that the Catholic Church campaign was "an effective piece of censorship," yet when one screens the picture, "it's so mild that you wonder what in the hell all the fuss was about."[28] In the 1990s, when he was interviewed by journalist and biographer Richard Schickel, Kazan was still angry with Spellman, remarking: "That old priest was a fool. God almighty, how foolish can you be? There's nothing in the movie except sweetness and humor." Schickel begged to differ with the filmmaker, arguing that *Baby Doll* promoted childhood eroticism. According to Schickel, this interpretation had not occurred to Kazan, who concentrated on plot and character. Kazan reportedly acknowledged Schickel's point, observing: "I never thought of that, but that's what it is. What could be more dangerous to conventional morality than childish eroticism. Someone who's in a crib and thirsting for it and hungry for it and not ready for marriage. How are you going to beat that?"[29] Despite Spellman's and Kazan's identification with the anti-Communist movement, *Baby Doll* provides further evidence of the ambivalence found in Kazan's post-HUAC testimony films as he challenged the Catholic Church and traditional manifestations of morality.

But what of the film's depiction of capitalism and the American dream, the South in the mid-twentieth century, black Americans in the South, and poor Southern whites? Most of the commentary on *Baby Doll* seemed to ignore these issues. For example, the black characters in the background elicit little attention, and the controversy surrounding the film did not extend to the use of derogatory language such as "nigger" and "wop." Critics, of course, did focus on the central Southern white characters of Archie Lee, Baby Doll, and Aunt Rose, but they were usually described with little sympathy and perceived as reflective of the region's uneducated poor white trash. However, a closer reading of *Baby Doll*, along with Kazan's comments on the film, suggests a more progressive orientation for the film text.

Baby Doll was made as the civil rights movement was beginning to gain steam in the South, but there is certainly no direct reference to the growing protest in the segregated community featured in the film. Nevertheless, Kazan employed his black characters in *Baby Doll* as a Greek chorus to comment and poke some humor at the expense of the white characters, leading University of Southern Mississippi scholar Philip C. Kolin to conclude that *Baby Doll* was an "attack on racism at a crucial junction in American racial history."[30] The film begins with the blacks on

Archie Lee's plantation laughing at the man as he is clearly unable to exercise any control over his young wife, who makes him late for his doctor's appointment. No wonder that the black man working to repair the mansion roof pays little attention to the instructions of Archie Lee. Thus, Brian Neve argues that despite segregation and disenfranchisement, the blacks in *Baby Doll* are able to articulate their feelings. Neve writes, "It soon becomes clear that the black characters who watch and comment on the action at regular intervals—lurking like plantation ghosts—find Archie Lee to be a man completely without status, social or otherwise, and to be deserving only of laughter and derision."[31]

This black voice was included in the film text just as there was violence and intimidation being employed to silence the emerging civil rights movement. In 1954, the Supreme Court in the *Brown* decision outlawed de jure segregation in the schools, and the South commenced a campaign of massive resistance to school integration. In August 1955, as Kazan was preparing to commence location shooting, Emmett Till, a young black teenager from Chicago who was visiting relatives in the Mississippi delta, was brutally beaten, murdered, and his body thrown into the Tallahatchie River with a cotton gin fan attached to his neck with barbed wire. His crime was that he allegedly whistled at a white woman, whose husband later admitted to murdering Till after he was acquitted by an all-white jury. There appears to be a reference to the murder in *Baby Doll* as a group of workers, who seem to be white, whistle at Baby Doll, angering Archie Lee, who yells at the men to be quiet. Also in December 1955, as *Baby Doll* was opening in American theaters, Rosa Parks in Montgomery, Alabama, refused to surrender her seat on the city segregated buses to a white customer, setting in motion the Montgomery Bus Boycott and the emergence of Martin Luther King Jr. as a significant civil rights leader.

Baby Doll does not directly address the tumultuous historical and cultural context in which the picture was made, but the black characters in the film display restlessness and an unwillingness to silently accept and acknowledge white superiority. While Kazan was quite fond of the white residents in Benoit, Mississippi, he was also certainly cognizant of the racial crisis in the American South during the mid-1950s. Tending to define the South through whiteness, Kazan argued:

The film expressed a great deal of affection for the South. They're very hospitable to you. They send you presents, you give them presents, like the Greeks in Europe. But I abominate what their tradition is with the blacks. We had several episodes of protecting blacks from the police there. Once I hid a black man all night in one of our trailers; the police were chasing him, they were going to put him back in jail and we helped him get away. All these whites, they really despise the blacks. But I found them in other ways the most loveable, generous people.[32]

Kazan, thus, believed that *Baby Doll* exhibited a degree of sympathy for both its black and white characters, which were either ignored or despised by most film critics. The director described Archie Lee as the hero of his film, but Kazan approached the subject through the humor of Tennessee Williams rather than the agitprop tradition of Clifford Odets or the stark realism contained in the classic James Agee study of Southern sharecroppers, *Now Let Us Praise Famous Men* (1941).[33] Nevertheless, Archie Lee is a tragic figure, similar to Willy Loman, who hopes to attain the American dream but ends up frustrated with a young, independent wife, a crumbling mansion, and a declining cotton gin business. The characters of Archie Lee and Vacarro may also be interpreted as symbols of the Old and New South. In this reading, Archie Lee may be perceived as representative of the failures of the Old South, while Vacarro, as the knowledgeable immigrant businessman, is reflective of the New South, which is relying on capital from the North and large corporations such as the Syndicate to transform the Southern economy. But the question is whether this new wealth will trickle down and change the lives of common people. Accordingly, Aunt Rose and Baby Doll are waiting to see whether Vacarro will honor his pledge and return or if they will be forgotten again. As a progressive, Kazan questions whether the capitalist development of the New South will actually transform the lives of common Southerners. And this doubt is even more apparent in Kazan's second film of his Southern trilogy, *A Face in the Crowd* (1957), in which Andy Griffith portrays a Southern demagogue in bed with capitalists and the mass media, who constitute a clear and present danger to American democracy.

6

A RETURN TO PROGRESSIVE PRINCIPLES AND THE SHAPE OF THINGS TO COME

A Face in the Crowd (1957)

While disappointed that *Baby Doll* failed at the box office amid accusations of sexual deviance—a controversy for which the director was partly responsible in the film's marketing campaign—Kazan was still committed to employing the South to examine the challenges confronting American democracy. Explaining to interviewer Jeff Young that he was quite fond of *Baby Doll*, Kazan described the film as "a microcosm of the changing South as I know it and like it. . . . I like everything in the South except its ideas, standards and beliefs. But the way the people are has always impressed me. It's part of my own maverick anarchism. I find them very funny and cute and human, very Chekhovian."[1] While *A Face in the Crowd* places the changing South in a broader perspective by examining the influence of modern advertising and the emerging industry of television on a Southern populist/demagogue whose story raises serious questions about contemporary American democracy and capitalism, Kazan's South and America remain an essentially white society. The protagonist, Larry "Lonesome" Rhodes, is no Southern race baiter, and race remains a subsidiary theme in *A Face in the Crowd* even as the civil rights movement was gaining steam. Nevertheless, the important issues raised by the film regarding the influence of big business and media on American politics, which some credit with anticipating the rise of Ronald

Reagan, again highlight the progressive strain in Kazan's post-HUAC cinema.

For *A Face in the Crowd*, Kazan turned to another collaboration with Budd Schulberg, with whom he shared a close personal and professional relationship based on their work with *On the Waterfront* and a common experience of both progressive politics and informing. The inspiration for the film was the short story "Our Arkansas Traveler" from Schulberg's collection of short stories, *Some Faces in the Crowd* (1953). According to the author, the story originated from an inebriated conversation he enjoyed with Will Rogers Jr., the son of the beloved Oklahoman humorist who died tragically in a plane crash. The son told Schulberg that his father was actually a hypocrite who only pretended to champion the common people. The young Rogers asserted, "My father was so full of shit, because he pretends he's just one of the people, just one of the guys . . . but in our house the only people that ever came as guests were the richest people in town, the bankers and the powerbrokers of Los Angeles and those were his friends and that's where his heart is and he was really a goddamned reactionary."[2] The son, however, was certainly able to use his father's name to win election to Congress from California.

Regardless of the inspiration for Lonesome Rhodes, Kazan was delighted to once again be working with Schulberg. After reading the short story, Kazan committed to the project, and the Schulberg family moved to Connecticut, where the two men could work closely and the families might enjoy social time together. Kazan emphasized that the two men carefully researched the film with trips to Arkansas, New York City, and Washington, DC. The director said he approached the topic the way a scholar would carefully examine a historical subject. Describing the collaborative process as ideal, Kazan commented: "Theoretically, I think one man should make a picture. But in the rare case when an author and a director have had the same kinds of experience, have the same kind of taste, the same historical and social point of view, and are as compatible as Budd and I are, it works out perfectly."[3]

Indicative of how simpatico the two men were, Kazan agreed to write the preface for the published version of the screenplay. Somewhat undercutting his own status as a director and challenging the auteur theory of film criticism, gaining vogue in both Europe and the United States, that the director was the most creative force in filmmaking, Kazan celebrated that Hollywood was becoming more cognizant of the essential role played by writers in cinema. Kazan extolled the values of his travels and conversations with Schulberg on the power of television and how it was employed by Richard Nixon and Joseph McCarthy. Anticipating some of the same ideas later developed by Joe McGinniss in his classic investigation into Nixon's 1968 presidential campaign, Kazan and Schulberg speculated about "the power of television to sell synthetic personalities as it sells the soup and the soap" and "the way public figures are now coached for their broadcasts and how the medium can make a performer or politician overnight—or break a man that fast, too." Referring to Schulberg as the "original source and perhaps the conscience for the film," Kazan concluded, "I have never worked more closely with an author in the theatre. And as for the lunch hour, we eat together."[4]

Preparing for location shooting, Kazan and Schulberg visited Piggott, Arkansas, in the fall of 1955. In a letter to Molly Day Thacher, the filmmaker expressed his joy in spending time with plain folk, although he still seems to display a somewhat patronizing tone in his admiration for these white Southerners. Kazan described his experience while spending an afternoon loafing on a courthouse square with locals. He occupied a couple of hours with whittling alongside two men, one of whom sold him a knife marked "for flesh only" that was to be used for castrating animals. Kazan also visited a small radio station that would play an important part in the early story of Lonesome Rhodes. Baton twirling also assumes a significant role in the story line, and Kazan visited a local high school to watch a drum majorette rehearsal as well as touring Arkansas State College, which gave credit for their classes on baton twirling and sponsored a summer class for drum majorettes. The director told his wife that he would love to stay in Arkansas longer, but it was important to scout locations in Memphis, Tennessee. Kazan concluded: "I could stay here for a month. I like Arkansas. All virgin territory. We had been with a guy age 56 and tough who elaborately explained to us why they had to hang three niggers once. Have you ever heard this elaborately and heavily explained? But even down here they don't think those two fellas should have killed that fourteen year old."[5] In this last comment, Kazan is making reference to the case of Emmett Till, who was murdered in Mississippi on August 28, 1955. At this point, of course, Kazan would have no idea how significant the murder of Till would become for the civil rights movement, but his observation seems a little too nonchalant. Kazan was not a racist, but his sympathy for Southern whites seemed to limit his expressed indignation for racial injustice.

His visit to Arkansas also convinced Kazan that Jackie Gleason was not the right choice to play Lonesome Rhodes. In October, Kazan informed Gleason that a native Southerner was required for the part, and the comedian agreed with the relieved director. Gleason appreciated Kazan being honest with him. Reporting to Schulberg on the conversation, Kazan wrote, "Feeling that his mood was good, I also told him that we would probably want to use ideas that he had given to us and he said go ahead and help yourself to everything and anything, that we were free and clear to do whatever we wished with what we had gotten from him. I really fell for the guy all over again, but this time as I watched him I felt we were really right in not casting him as Rhodes."[6] Instead, Kazan decided to go with newcomer Andy Griffith from North Carolina, who was appearing on Broadway in *No Time for Sergeants* and whose best-selling comedy record "What It Was, Was Football" (1953) impressed Kazan and Schulberg.

While Griffith would later gain considerable fame as laid-back Sheriff Andy Taylor in the popular *The Andy Griffith Show* (1960–1968), he had little experience with the type of acting expected by Kazan. Accordingly, the director often had to initially act out the scenes so that Griffith would understand the type of performance for which Kazan was searching. Nevertheless, Griffith was often too soft spoken for the larger-than-life character Kazan envisioned. Therefore, for the dramatic conclusion to the film when Lonesome's television empire comes crashing down, Kazan made sure that the actor was intoxicated so that the director could elicit the bombastic reaction that the scene required. Kazan was complimentary of Griffith's performance and believed that as a newcomer to film acting, he did not resent the intrusion of the director. The filmmaker asserted that he was gentle with the actor and "made a big favorite of him." Griffith, according to Kazan, did not perceive him as controlling, for "he didn't know anything about directing, so he took it as if it were the normal way to work."[7]

For the female lead of Marcia Jeffries, who discovers Rhodes and loves him despite his betrayal of her and his television audience, Kazan selected experienced actress Patricia Neal to work with the novice Griffith. Jeffries is a proper Southern aristocratic woman, educated at Sarah Lawrence University, who is, nevertheless, drawn to the crude but appealing populist demagogue. In some ways, she is similar to Molly Day Thacher and her love for the talented but womanizing outsider immigrant with the Anatolian smile. Kazan noticed this connection and commented on it in his autobiography. Despite a turbulent relationship due to the director's dalliances with other women, Kazan wrote:

> For many years, I'd clung to Molly because she was my talisman of success and my measure of merit. She was the reassurance that the very heart of America, which my family had come here to find, had accepted me. That is why we never divorced, never could or would or did. Behind my bluster, I was still a person uncertain of his final worth. If there was anyone who represented conventional, decent, historic America, it was Molly Day of the New Haven Thachers. [8]

As for Molly, he believed that he was her creation just as "Lonesome Rhodes was the creation of Marcia in our film. And that's the realest story in *A Face in the Crowd*." Despite these insights into his relationship with Molly, Kazan, similar to Rhodes, could not seem to control his libido. During the filming of *A Face in the Crowd*, Kazan met a young actress named Barbara Loden, who would become his second wife following the death of Molly. Although the affair began in a more casual manner, Kazan was attracted to Loden as she was the opposite of the respectable Molly. Kazan recalled: "Conceived in a field of daisies, Barbara Loden was born anti-respectable: she observed none of the conventional middle-class boundaries, the perimeter walls within which Molly lived. A roulette wheel that didn't stop turning, Barbara would keep me wondering when it would, and where. Life with Molly, to continue the figure, was a safe-deposit vault."[9]

While Kazan seemed to identify with Lonesome Rhodes in his Southern, folksy ways and the desire to not be controlled by one woman who was more than his social equal, he also shared the character's fascination with and contempt for Madison Avenue advertising. *A Face in the Crowd* critiques an industry that created built-in obsolescence and fostered a conformist consumer culture in the suburbs, providing an opportunity for Kazan and Schulberg to embrace their progressive values. And they were certainly not alone in calling into question the liberal consensus of Cold War America for encouraging an outer-directed corporate culture in which inner-directed individuals were suspect. Thus, *A Face in the Crowd* should be examined within the context of such works as William

H. Whyte Jr., *The Organization Man* (1956); David Riesman, *The Lonely Crowd* (1950); C. Wright Mills, *White Collar: The American Middle Classes* (1951); Sloan Wilson, *The Man in the Gray Flannel Suit* (1956); Vance Packard, *The Hidden Persuaders* (1957); and even the Clifford Odets screenplay for *The Sweet Smell of Success* (1957).[10] Film scholar Brian Neve concludes that the director agreed with these intellectual critics that power in America was flowing to "wealthy figures whose only culture is Las Vegas and the *Saturday Evening Post* and the *Readers Digest*." Serious journalism such as that produced by Edward R. Murrow was being replaced by the cultural wasteland of celebrity and entertainment features—a new version of the Romans' bread and circuses.[11]

That Kazan's film was part of a broader social criticism, however, should not discredit the hard work of the director and his collaborator in researching and producing a film that was far ahead of its time and of most film audiences in the late 1950s. Kazan relates that he and Schulberg "went to Madison Avenue like explorers going into a strange country. We talked with performers and account executives and writers. We had interviews with big shots and lunch with medium-sized shots and drinks with little shots. We are indebted to all of them—not least for permission to sit in on a conference about the photography of a ketchup bottle."[12] While poking fun at advertising, just as Lonesome Rhodes does in the film, Kazan did concede that no matter how ridiculous the product under consideration was for the advertising men, "you could feel the intense, neurotic pressure they all worked under."[13]

Kazan and Schulberg also made a contribution through their depiction of how television was beginning to impact American politics, where candidates were packaged and sold in similar fashion as brands of detergent, dog food, or underarm deodorant. Kazan mentions that the filmmakers were able to meet Lyndon Johnson, who in the 1950s was the powerful Democratic Senate majority leader. Johnson, Kazan reported, seemed pleased that Hollywood people were asking questions and speaking with him. And Johnson certainly knew a thing or two about media, power, and politics for the media empire of his wife, "Lady Bird" Johnson, played a big role in the rise of the Texas politician.[14] Kazan and Schulberg also found inspiration for their depiction of the connection between entertainment and politics within the Republican Party. Hollywood stars Robert Montgomery and George Murphy were avid Republicans who in 1952 wanted to wrest the presidency from twenty years of Democratic control.

The actors considered Dwight Eisenhower to be a candidate who came across as "wooden" on television, and they assumed the responsibility for his media campaign, similar to the way Lonesome Rhodes crafted the image of Senator Fuller in *A Face in the Crowd*. Describing the activities of Murphy and Montgomery, film historian Steven J. Ross writes: "The pair taught the general how to sell himself on the screen. Murphy understood that messages would not matter unless voters found the messages appealing. Under their tutelage, Ike became a more relaxed and confident speaker. People who saw him on TV and voted Republican told pollsters the general appeared 'good-natured, sincere, honest, cheerful, and clear headed,' qualities one might also attribute to Murphy."[15] Following Eisenhower's electoral success, the general-turned-politician became good friends with Murphy, who in 1964 was elected to the Senate from California. Murphy also exerted considerable influence over his friend Ronald Reagan to enter politics and run for the governorship of California. The elevation of the former president of the Screen Actors Guild to the governor's mansion and White House cemented the alliance of business, media, and politics, which Kazan and Schulberg anticipated with Lonesome Rhodes.

While predicting the rise of Reagan, Kazan also perceived the character of Rhodes to be based on the career of the ukulele-strumming and folksy Arthur Godfrey, whose radio program in Washington gained national attention for his tearful coverage of Franklin Roosevelt's funeral. The entertainer was able to parlay this moment of fame into a national CBS radio show and eventually a popular television variety program. Other similarities between Godfrey and Rhodes included a tendency to poke some fun at the sponsors while ignoring their scripted material and a growing intolerance for subordinates. Godfrey also became increasingly vocal regarding his right-wing politics and aligned with conservative military and business figures. However, the event that brought about his decline was the humiliating public firing of his show's popular singer Julius Rosa in 1953. The parallels between Rhodes and Godfrey did concern Kazan, and he got permission from Godfrey to use the entertainer's name one time in the film. When Rhodes has to be away from his show, he asks an assistant to get Godfrey to fill in for him and he will return the favor someday. Writing to his lawyer, H. William Fitelson, Kazan commented: "This puts Lonesome on the same basis as Godfrey and also makes clear that Lonesome is not Godfrey. Is my legal brain okay or am I off? I can't see how Godfrey can object. He does exist and is a public figure, does work in the TV business and there is no derogatory reference in the phrase."[16]

While Kazan was able to deflect litigation from Godfrey, he still had to deal with censorship issues, which left a bad taste in his mouth after the confrontation with Cardinal Spellman over *Baby Doll*. While the intersection among entertainment, advertising, business, and politics was at the core of *A Face in the Crowd*, the character of Lonesome Rhodes was very much a sexual animal and raised concern among censors. In his correspondence with Ben Kalmenson of Warner Bros., Kazan made it clear that he was prepared to make few changes in his film to gain approval from the Production Code and the Legion of Decency. The director refused to omit the shot of Lonesome's suitcase outside of Marcia's hotel room in Memphis, suggesting that he had spent the night with her. Kazan also found it ludicrous to delete a scene of Lonesome Rhodes chasing attractive girls from the advertising agency, as such fare was standard for Harpo Marx. Nor would Kazan change Marcia's attraction to Lonesome when he comes to her apartment after sending his young wife back to Arkansas, as this physical desire was crucial to establishing the conflict she experiences when exposing his true nature. He did, however, agree to make some alterations with the somewhat over-the-top and sexualized Vitajex commercial. In the original script, a sultry blond in bed is apparently waiting for her lover to take his Vitajex, and she purrs, "I'll be waiting for you when you do." Instead, the blond delivers the replacement line, "I bought my boyfriend a ten year's supply." The Vitajex scene was certainly sexually provocative, but it appears that no one wanted a repeat of the *Baby Doll* controversy. Kazan described *A Face in the Crowd* as containing little sex and "deeply moral in conception and execution," and the film received approval from the Production Code and the Legion of Decency.[17]

The rise of Larry "Lonesome" Rhodes begins inside a jail cell in the small town of Piggott, Arkansas. Marcia Jeffries (Patricia Neal) is looking for subjects to appear on her local radio program, "A Face in the Crowd," and as an educated woman with a degree from Sarah Lawrence University, she decides to go slumming in the jail, offering a get-out-of-jail-free card to anyone willing to appear on her radio show. She is drawn to a man named Larry Rhodes (Andy Griffith), who is sleeping off a drinking spree but maintains a hold on his guitar. Angry about being awakened, Rhodes does not want to be on her show, but Marcia secretly records him singing "Free Man in the Morning." Marcia plays the recording on her uncle's radio station, and they are besieged with telephone calls expressing interest in learning more about the singer. Marcia and her uncle return to the jail, only to discover that Rhodes was released. They find him hitchhiking outside of town and offer Rhodes a job, which he accepts temporarily, in part because of his attraction to Marcia. [18]

Rhodes quickly becomes a local favorite and begins calling himself "Lonesome." The townspeople, especially the women, are drawn to his singing and folksy anecdotes. The entertainer also projects a sense of animal magnetism, and young women are shown leaving his hotel room in the early morning hours. Marcia's interest in him draws the ire of her beau, Sheriff Big Jeff Bess (playing himself), who gives Lonesome a black eye. For revenge, Lonesome takes to the airwaves and points out that Big Jeff is running for mayor but that he is more qualified to be dog catcher. Lonesome suggests that everyone should deposit their dogs at his home, which they obediently do. In another example of his newly discovered media power, on a hot afternoon he invites everyone in town to go swimming at his employer's home. The story of Lonesome's appeal soon begins to spread throughout the South, and he is offered a job with a Memphis television station. But he insists that "his girl Friday," Marcia, be allowed to accompany him. The town throws a huge farewell party for Lonesome, although Marcia is somewhat taken aback when Lonesome tells her that he cannot wait to get out of the hick town.

In Memphis, he meets his writer, Mel Miller (Walter Matthau), a Vanderbilt graduate whom Lonesome insists on calling "Vanderbilt '44" after his year of graduation. Lonesome does not quite trust this member of the intellectual elite, who exhibits a rather patronizing attitude toward the entertainer and also appears to be a rival for Marcia's affections. Some critics detected a note of anti-intellectualism in the way Mel was depicted. Kazan insisted that he had no problem with intellectuals; however, he does provide Vanderbilt '44 with a degree of smugness. He told Jeff Young: "If Mel hadn't been so absolutely sure of himself and his values and, thus, a bit pompous, we might only have felt disgust for Lonesome. We might not have seen that something good went down with Lonesome Rhodes. Without that ambivalence the whole film wouldn't be worthwhile." [19]

Rhodes refused to depend on writers, trusting in his own instinct for what the masses wanted to hear. For example, he will not follow the copy supplied by his sponsoring mattress company. Instead, he spontaneously provides his own material, which the sponsor finds offensive, and there is an effort to remove Lonesome from the show. In response, crowds, mostly women, begin to burn the company's mattresses in the streets—again demonstrating the power of Lonesome. While behaving as a demagogue, Rhodes refused to play the race card. When he finds a hard working black woman who lost her home in a fire, he wants to bring her on the show and help her family. Asking for small contributions from his largely white working-class audience, Lonesome is able to raise wheelbarrows full of quarters. This is one of the few scenes from the film that includes black characters, for Kazan's South remains primarily populated by poor Southern whites. While living in a segregated society, these poor whites were willing to help out a black person who shared their economic misfortune. In this regard, they are somewhat similar to the followers of the Depression era Louisiana governor and senator Huey P. Long, whose solution to the economic crisis was to share the wealth and denounce organizations such as the Ku Klux Klan. Long was assassinated before he could attain national power, but Kazan described him as one of the models for the character of Lonesome Rhodes. Kazan observed: "But Huey Long did a lot of good in Louisiana. He was basically a tyrant, but he got many, many reforms, and he was genuinely interested, at the beginning, in the problems of the poor. Lonesome Rhodes should have been more like him, more genuinely interested in the poor."[20] Rhodes demonstrates little additional concern for the poor, but he does not play the race card, as blacks essentially disappear from the film in a way they never did in *Baby Doll*.

Observing Lonesome's increasing power and influence, an ambitious office boy from the mattress company, Joey Kieley (Anthony Franciosa), contacts a New York City advertising company, and posing as Lonesome's agent, he gets them to sign on as a sponsor for a national variety show featuring Lonesome Rhodes. He then gets Rhodes to sign a document making Joey officially his agent, a decision that Rhodes will later regret—an example of other forces controlling Rhodes and raising the question of whether the entertainer may also be considered a victim of his own success and far more powerful sources of capitalist exploitation.

Nevertheless, a confident Rhodes with Joey and Marcia, who is now Lonesome's lover, head to New York City. Lonesome is introduced to his sponsor Vitajex, an energy supplement perhaps based on Geritol and Carter's Liver Pills. Advertising executive Mr. Macy (Paul McGrath) wants a dignified campaign for the product, which appears harmless, for company scientists point out that it has no impact on those taking the pill. Lonesome, however, has other ideas. He is immediately energized by popping a couple of Vitajex tablets, and he begins to chase a couple of attractive secretaries around the room. This scene is followed by a montage of advertisements marketing Vitajex as a sexual supplement for males, accompanied by charts showing the increasing sales of the product. The advertisements featuring a laughing Lonesome Rhodes, scantily clad models, and a sultry blond crawling into bed with a supersized Vitajex bottle are incredibly suggestive for the 1950s while anticipating such twenty-first-century products as Viagra.

The success of the Vitajex campaign earns Lonesome Rhodes an invitation to the mansion of the company's owner, General Hainesworth (Percy Waram), where he is also introduced to Senator Fuller (Marshall Neilan). It is obvious that Hainesworth and Fuller are interested in more than selling energy supplements; they impress upon Lonesome the importance of grooming strong national leaders, and there is a subtext of Fascism here. Brian Neve writes that Kazan and Schulberg reflected contemporary liberal concerns with the mass political right-wing populist movement personified by Joseph McCarthy. Kazan also drew on his own experience with the James Dean cult of personality in which Dean was corrupted by power and his admiring fans. Neve concludes, "Yet the film shows some sympathy towards the populism of the Lonesome Rhodes character at the beginning—the grass roots tradition—and only later, when he becomes a vehicle for big business and right wing politicians, is he presented as a political threat."[21]

Meanwhile, with this power behind him, Rhodes becomes a national icon with battleships and mountains named for him, while he appears on the covers of such mass circulation periodicals as *Life* and *Look*. His headquarters are concentrated in the two top stories of a New York City skyscraper. Marcia is Lonesome's business manager and lover, although Rhodes is obviously seeing other women. Lonesome is both attracted to and afraid of his growing power and tells Marcia that she is his "lifeline to truth" before proposing marriage to her. These plans, however, were threatened by a woman claiming to be Lonesome's wife, demanding $3,000 a month to assure her silence. Marcia confronts Lonesome, who acknowledges the marriage but reassures Marcia that he is headed to Mexico, where he will be able to quickly obtain a divorce.

On the way to Mexico, Lonesome stops off in Arkansas to judge a state baton-twirling competition. His wandering eye finds seventeen-year-old drum majorette Betty Lou Fleckman (Lee Remick), who wins both the contest and Lonesome. She agrees to accompany Lonesome to Mexico, where he is granted a divorce and immediately marries Betty Lou. They return to New York, and Marcia is present at the airport to welcome her lover, unaware that Lonesome has gained a young bride. A distraught Marcia now insists that she be given a partnership in his enterprise as she was the "creator" of her own Frankenstein monster in Lonesome Rhodes, and he reluctantly agrees to the partnership. Meanwhile, Rhodes employs his show to highlight Betty Lou in a skimpy outfit twirling flaming batons. In this scene, there is again considerable sexual objectification for a mainstream film of the 1950s.

As Lonesome deals with his personal issues, the political goals of his sponsors and handlers become more apparent. The entertainer was invited by General Hainesworth to groom the presidential candidacy of the reactionary but dull Senator Fuller. Rhodes explains that the candidate must be sold just as one would market a product. To develop a little sense of humor for the stodgy Fuller, Rhodes coins the nickname "Curly" for the balding senator. Lonesome also demands that Hainesworth provide him with a new show called *Lonesome Rhodes on the Cracker Barrel*, which would provide an environment for Rhodes to feature political commentary and guests such as Senator Fuller. Hainesworth reluctantly agrees to the new programming, but the wealthy patron is beginning to perceive Rhodes as showing signs of being difficult to control in pursuance of the larger and vaguely Fascist purposes the general seems to have in mind. Fuller appears on the new show and is packaged as a man of the people who enjoys such pursuits as duck hunting. While munching peanuts and sitting atop a cracker barrel, Fuller demonstrates his brand of reactionary politics by attacking Social Security and asserting that the American people must be self-reliant and vigilant against government programs that might endanger their independence. Kazan and Schulberg were concerned about the threat of Fascism in America, as exhibited by the support of the Fuller campaign by the charismatic Rhodes. Kazan explained:

"It was about a phenomenon that was happening in America at that time. We were always talking about looking out for native, grassroots Fascism. One thing that a lot of people overlooked is that Fascism always had attractive elements of populism in it. Hitler's followers initially, the members of the National Socialist Party, were guys who were on the outs, who had no power or even jobs."[22]

However, there were elements of overreach and opposition that would limit Lonesome's ambitions but not dismantle the continuing threat of an American Fascism. Mel and Marcia meet for a drink, and Vanderbilt '44 informs her that he no longer works for Lonesome and is about to publish a book titled *Demagogue in Denim*, exposing the truth about the manipulative entertainer. Marcia, however, is still in love with Lonesome and attempts to defend him. Meanwhile, Lonesome returns home to discover Betty Lou having an affair with business manager Joey Kieley. Infuriated, Lonesome places Betty Lou on the next train back to Arkansas, but Kieley proves somewhat more difficult to handle. Lonesome announces that he is fired, but Joey counters that Lonesome lacks the power to terminate him as the business agent is a majority stockholder in Lonesome Rhodes Enterprises—an indication that Lonesome does not enjoy the control he assumes. Lonesome heads to Marcia's home, where he begins to undress and climbs into bed with Marcia, who is clad in a black slip. He informs her that after the next broadcast he will be hosting a dinner with Hainesworth, Fuller, and influential sponsors of the campaign. At the gathering, Fuller is to announce that when he is elected president, one of his first actions will be to appoint Lonesome to head the newly created cabinet post for public morale. Although she is still attracted to Lonesome, Marcia realizes that power is making him a dangerous man. She grabs a coat and flees into a rainy night.

The next day, an inebriated and angry Lonesome prepares for his broadcast, but Marcia fails to report to work. On the air, Lonesome is as charming as ever, but behind the scenes he is constantly making derisive remarks about his audience and the stupidity of Senator Fuller. Marcia enters the control room as the credits are rolling. Knowing that his remarks cannot be heard, a smiling Lonesome continues to ridicule his audience. Marcia, realizing that she must destroy the monster she has created, turns on the sound switch, and the entire country hears Lonesome's insulting dialogue. As Lonesome returns home to his headquarters for the banquet unaware of Marcia's actions, television switchboards are swamped by calls from viewers denouncing Rhodes. Senator Fuller and his financial backers cancel their reservations for Lonesome's dinner, and General Hainesworth discusses with Joey a new populist host to take the place of Lonesome. Only Marcia and Mel show up to confront Lonesome, who is incredulous when Marcia tells him that she was responsible for pulling the switch and exposing him. Mel tells Lonesome that, unfortunately, the entertainer is not finished but will never again enjoy such power and fame. Lonesome will be replaced by a similar figure, and someday he will probably be given a second chance in a smaller market. As a distraught Lonesome screams her name, Marcia hesitates, but she finally leaves with Mel in a taxi. The last shot of the film is a neon advertisement for Coca-Cola, demonstrating that the power of the media and advertising to create and destroy remains intact.

Schulberg and Kazan struggled with how to end their film. They had considered having Lonesome commit suicide but eventually concluded that might arouse too much sympathy for the entertainer. Nevertheless, they still end up with a rather pessimistic statement about American democracy. Similar problems confronted director Frank Capra in *Meet John Doe* (1941), which also examines the possibility of an indigenous Fascism.[23] The people in Capra's film turn on John Doe (Gary Cooper), who is also contemplating suicide. Before he can leap to his death, the common people, who had abandoned him, ask John Doe for forgiveness and the opportunity to forge a real people's movement. The effort to force-fit an optimistic conclusion onto *Meet John Doe* rang hollow, and Kazan and Schulberg were determined to avoid such a simplistic and unconvincing solution. The filmmakers do have the people rise up against Lonesome in righteous indignation, but the common folk are only able to perceive these truths when they are provided by the elite Vanderbilt '44 and Marcia Jeffries. Hainesworth also assumes that the fickle populace will fall back into line and follow the next country philosopher whom he brings aboard his show. It is similar to the longshoremen in *On the Waterfront* moving from following Johnny Friendly to Terry, for the corruption and exploitation of Mr. Upstairs and General Hainesworth are still in place. The manipulative influence of the capitalist media, as the neon Coke bottle reminds us, is still calling the shots. The ambivalence of Kazan's cinema is most apparent in *A Face in the Crowd*, but perhaps it was simply ahead of its time for film audiences in the 1950s who did not want to think about the implications of their consumer culture.

Kazan was proud of the film and anticipated solid box office receipts. But the early showings of *A Face in the Crowd* failed to find an audience. A disappointed Kazan wrote Schulberg: "In five days, in two theaters in Boston, we did $8,700. This is, you realize, disastrously bad. It is just not bad, it is a rejection. There is no other way to look at it I'm afraid. We should have done that much business in one theatre in one day." The film opened on Memorial Day weekend and faced stiff competition from *The Ten Commandments*, *Around the World in Eighty Days*, and *Gunfight at the O. K. Corral*. Kazan confided that he was pleased with the initial promotional efforts from Warner Bros., but now they would need to alter their approach in order to attract a younger audience. The director despaired that these new endeavors would not find success, and he told Schulberg that he was currently too depressed to even think about why the film had fared so poorly.[24]

Kazan, however, would get around to a serious postmortem on the film several months later in his production notes. The main problem with *A Face in the Crowd*, Kazan believed, was that he and Schulberg were trying to teach their audience a lesson—something that art should never do. The director argued that real art "has many meanings, all as complex and mixed up as life itself, contradictory, unfathomable, mysterious." The film text should have meaning, but it is up to individual audience members to figure this out for themselves rather than have the filmmakers spell out everything. Instead, Kazan wrote: "We conceived *Face in the Crowd* as a 'warning to the American people.' This was the complete give away. The movie was conceived, written and directed, and acted to show, to teach. Therefore, it was oversimplified. It was mental. The complexity that we know was left out. Above all, we were out to show what a son of a bitch LR (Lonesome Rhodes) was—where we should have been showing that LR was us." Kazan concluded his memo by observing that a better story would have Lonesome recognizing that he was becoming "a shit" and the tool of others, but he cannot figure out how to escape his predicament. Thus, Rhodes, with both his positive and negative characteristics, would reflect the complexity of American life.[25]

Reviews of the film were mixed, with many quite critical. Robert Hatch of the *Nation* found Lonesome Rhodes to be, "L'il Abner Come to life, simple, lovable, drunken, lecherous, half-crazed and as trustworthy as a moron with a meat cleaver." While Lonesome was the "voice of the mob," Hatch argues that it was difficult for an audience not to discover itself "slipping under his spell." Concluding that the film was a "monstrous fable," Hatch, nevertheless, praised *A Face in the Crowd* for providing "a kind of realism that Hollywood seldom attains."[26] Other critics disagreed, arguing that Kazan and Schulberg fell short in achieving their goals for the film. Writing in the *New Yorker*, Joseph McCarten termed *A Face in the Crowd* "an entertaining piece of work" and praised Griffith's performance. The critic, however, claimed that the end of the film degenerated into "second-rate melodrama" as Lonesome's career destructed. McCarten also believed that the fixation on Rhodes led the filmmakers to never quite get "around to establishing the fact that he and his kind could not become fat and sassy if a lot of lame-brained citizens weren't out to prove Mencken's dictum that nobody ever got poor underestimating the intelligence of the American people."[27] Bosley Crowther in the *New York Times* expressed similar sentiments. While praising the work of Griffith, Schulberg, and Kazan on the picture, Crowther concluded that by focusing so much on Rhodes, the film failed to adequately develop the forces that created this monster. Crowther writes, "Lonesome Rhodes builds up so quickly that it is never made properly clear that he is a creature of the television mechanism and the public's own gullibility."[28]

Mainstream publications were far more critical of the picture. *Life* described Griffith as a "powerful film personality," but the review concluded that the film was "much too long for its own good."[29] *Newsweek* complained that *A Face in the Crowd* was "satire gone haywire" and was certainly not to be confused with the Kazan-Schulberg collaboration for *On the Waterfront*. The review found Griffith's acting to be tiresome and the plot line to be derivative of previous Hollywood film treatments of "hillbilly political dictators as well as Madison Avenue megalomaniacs."[30] *Time* characterized Griffith as "uneven and never quite convincing" while complaining that Kazan simply did not know the first thing about handling a satire, as the film was too over the top to foster realistic considerations of its themes. The review concluded, "Instead of keeping the menace down to life size, the script permits its corn-fed psychopath to sphacelate through the U. S. social body like some malignant growth until he actually threatens to take over the Federal Government."[31]

The film also provoked commentary on the politics of Kazan and Schulberg. In the 1950s, the two men were lionized by many on the political right for their courageous break with the Communist Party and denunciation of Stalinism. However, *A Face in the Crowd*'s concentration on the dangers of an indigenous American Fascism did not sit well with many conservatives, who seemed to still harbor doubts about Kazan's Americanism. Despite naming names before HUAC, the progressive principles espoused by Kazan in his post-HUAC films made him suspect among many anti-Communists. Thus, Henry Hart, in a piece for *Films in Review*, lamented that Schulberg and Kazan were "not depicting truths they have perceived but a synthetic untruth reminiscent of the Marxist delusions of the 30s, and of no intellectual, cultural, or political value, save to those who seek to confuse the American people about themselves, or to those who desire to denigrate the American people before the world." Hart concluded that the filmmakers were talented, but, "it is too bad they have not in their work progressed to an understanding of American life, but have doomed themselves to repetitive sniping at it."[32] This right-wing critique of Kazan was repeated in the pages of *Counterattack*—a publication that endorsed the Hollywood blacklist. An editorial in *Counterattack* referred to Kazan and Schulberg as commercial liberals who "rave about conformity and thought-control" because they have nothing else in a positive sense to offer the American people. The piece concluded: "Still commercial liberalism rules the communications roost today, as it has for a long time. All that effort to beat a straw man into the dust—a straw man of a theory that isolationists, reactionaries and anticommunists are ready to seize power in the United States and throw everybody who voted for Henry Wallace into a concentration camp. It's bunk but it's profitable bunk and Messrs. Schulberg and Kazan are masters of the art of dispersing it."[33]

On the other hand, the *People's Daily World*, the West Coast publication of the Communist Party, praised *A Face in the Crowd* for its depiction of how public opinion was manipulated in the United States and how the country was susceptible to a Fascist assumption of power. The *People's Daily World* editorialized, "Whether it is the residual understanding Schulberg and Kazan retain from their days in the progressive movement, or whether it is a guilty conscience (or both) that has prompted them to give us this picture, we should be grateful for what they have done."[34] Kazan seemed almost embarrassed that former comrades on the left were embracing *A Face in the Crowd*. In his autobiography, Kazan proclaims his unyielding and vehement opposition to the Communist Party, which he claims continued to harass him and his family. According to Kazan: "My response was silence. I knew that I was the official target of a well-organized campaign that had marshaled lefties everywhere and provided their dialogue. I knew their tactics well, and many of their people. So I went my way, didn't worry about lost friends, and lived it out. Was there some guilt in my silence, as many of my critics alleged? Yes, at first, some. But there was also a growing belief in what I'd done. I could take it now and damn well did."[35]

Thus, there was considerable discrepancy between the progressive principles and anti-Fascist message of *A Face in the Crowd* and Kazan's anti-Communism and pride he continued to publicly express for his HUAC testimony. While many progressives praised his film, which was often denounced by conservatives, Kazan remained proud of *A Face in the Crowd*, but he was disappointed with the film's poor public reception. He blamed himself and Schulberg for taking the wrong approach to the serious issues raised by the film, leading the director to consider a remake of *A Face in the Crowd*. As late as 1982, Kazan and Schulberg were discussing updating the project to make Lonesome a disgruntled Vietnam veteran. Kazan envisioned a more sympathetic treatment of Rhodes but not of the forces seeking to manipulate him. Kazan eventually withdrew from the project, and the film was never remade.[36] The interest in a remake reflects the growing reputation of *A Face in the Crowd* among film scholars and critics as a harbinger of things to come. For example, during the 2000 election, Howard Rosenberg, the film critic of the *Los Angeles Times*, noted that *A Face in the Crowd* never got the credit it deserved for its commentary on media, which in some ways was as visionary as *Network* (1976) about what lay ahead for broadcasting.[37] In a similar vein, J. Hoberman of the *Village Voice*, lauding a 2008 New York City screening of the picture, argued that *A Face in the Crowd* anticipated politicians such as Ronald Reagan, Ross Perot, and Bill Clinton, as well as the influence of political operatives such as Lee Atwater. Hoberman concluded: "As political rhetoric, *A Face in the Crowd* has never ceased to be relevant. Darkly alluded to during the 1960 campaign (decided, so people thought, by a television debate), it was quasi\remade as *Wild in the Streets*, American International's contribution to the madness of 1968, re-released (with a nod to George Wallace) in 1972, invoked to explain Watergate in 1974, and reconfigured as *Nashville* in 1975."[38]

Kazan was disappointed that *A Face in the Crowd* and its warnings about the dangers of an indigenous Fascism failed to resonate with the American people, who seemed already lulled to sleep by the commercialism and consumerism of popular culture, which exerted a major influence over American politics. Accordingly, Kazan biographer Richard Schickel argues that *A Face in the Crowd* marked "a significant passage in Kazan's development, for it openly acknowledges, as never before, his fear of the American mass, his sense that its fundamental good nature, its lack of historical sense, its feckless need for idle amusement, always leaves it open to some form of baronical (mis)leadership, to some form of benignly presented fascism. It was, for Kazan, the true end of his 1930s idealism, his implicit belief in the sturdy common sense of the American yeomanry."[39]

Schickel's conclusion, however, seems a bit too pessimistic and premature. After the failures of *Baby Doll* and *A Face in the Crowd*, it was three years before Kazan released another film. With *Wild River* (1960), the director completed his Southern trilogy, and the film that he was contemplating since the 1930s exemplifies Kazan's ambivalence regarding the conflict between progressive ideas and tradition. The fundamental antagonism in *Wild River* is between Tennessee Valley Authority (TVA) representative Chuck Glover and the elderly Ella Garth, who refuses to leave her land so that the TVA may construct dams to prevent flooding and provide hydroelectricity for the Tennessee valley. Kazan initially envisioned the film as sympathetic to Glover and the programs of the New Deal bringing economic relief and reform to the American people. In the completed film, however, Kazan demonstrates a great deal of understanding for Garth, as a way of life is being destroyed to make way for progress. Thus, Kazan had not given up on American progressivism and democracy, but as *Wild River* demonstrates, he was ambivalent as he made his final cinematic sojourn into the American South.

7

LOOKING BACKWARD AND THE COST OF PROGRESS

Wild River (1960)

Wild River was the final film in Kazan's Southern trilogy and the least commercial of the three films, which struggled to find an audience. Nevertheless, *Wild River* was one of Kazan's favorites, and he bemoaned the lack of attention paid to the film. He told Michel Ciment: "This film, like some others that I particularly favor, was a box office disaster. It is never shown in the United States and except for certain discerning and sensitive critics in Europe might have been completely forgotten. I'm particularly proud of this neglected work."[1] This interest, in part, was due to what Kazan considered to be the autobiographical aspects of the film text. The self-confident government agent from the Tennessee Valley Authority (TVA) represents the younger Kazan, who was assured that the progressive policies of the New Deal would improve the quality of life for the common people of the American South. By the time he finally got around to making the film, Kazan was less certain that government bureaucrats necessarily knew what was best for the people, and his sympathies tend to be with an elderly white woman who refuses to sell her land and abandon tradition so that the TVA might construct a dam. Thus, Kazan was again drawn to the theme of political ambivalence that characterized his post-HUAC appearance films. In his autobiography, the director concludes that the ambivalence of *Wild River* is what made him so proud of the film, for both sides were right—also reflecting the ambiguity and complexity of Kazan's film texts in contrast to the political rigidity he displayed in his HUAC statements. [2]

The civil rights movement was continuing to gain impetus in 1960, yet Kazan again focuses on Southern whites and looks to the past rather than the future. Blacks in *Wild River* do play a larger role than in *Baby Doll* or *A Face in the Crowd*, yet this ambivalent film raises questions as to whether the efforts of an outsider reformer really improve the conditions of black sharecroppers and laborers. Considering the timing of this film, *Wild River* and Kazan hardly seem to embrace the civil rights movement, although there is general sympathy toward the black characters. Nevertheless, there is a considerable tolerance in *Wild River* for Southern traditions opposed to social change. In addition, 1960 was the year in which John Kennedy narrowly defeated Richard Nixon, and the new president talked a great deal about reform, change, and passing the torch to a new generation. Yet *Wild River*, in its examination of change and progress, looks back to the New Deal rather than forward to the Kennedy promise of a new frontier. These factors sometimes give *Wild River* almost a reactionary feel, but in the final analysis the last shots of the film concentrate on the constructed dam, which provides a degree of security in contrast to the picture's opening shots of chaotic flooding in the region. There has been progress but not without some cost.

Kazan struggled with the drafting of his script for his reimagined TVA film. While working to finish *A Face in the Crowd*, Kazan inquired as to whether Robert Ardrey would be interested in writing the screenplay for *Wild River*. Kazan directed Ardrey's plays *Casey Jones* (1936) and *Thunder Rock* (1939), but both closed after brief runs. In the post–World War II period, Ardrey turned his writing toward the venues of film and television, and he was looking forward to a collaboration with Kazan on *Wild River*. In March 1957, Kazan made it clear to Ardrey that he would not be subject to the degree of independence the author originally anticipated. Kazan asserted that Ardrey would not be able to write the screenplay while in Europe, as the director wanted more personal involvement in the writing process. The filmmaker insisted:

> I feel now that I want to be equally involved with the author in the evolution of the story line. I have done this now with the last four and the results have been critically mixed, but personally they were satisfying. I not only like to do it. I think the only way I will get better at it is to keep on doing it. What worries me about us being apart is the fear

that it may put a time limit on this collaborative aspect. I don't want to write a line of dialogue, but I do want to be creatively involved in the choice, shape, and telling of any stories I do from now on in.[3]

In addition to Kazan's insistence on control of the script, Ardrey was disappointed that Kazan would be doing *Wild River* for Twentieth Century Fox rather than as an independent producer.

Ardrey withdrew from the project, and Kazan pursued his own drafts—a process discouraged by his wife Molly, who was not particularly supportive of her husband as a writer. Eventually dissatisfied with his own drafts, Kazan elicited input from writers Ben Maddow and Calder Willingham before turning the script over to Paul Osborn, with whom the director collaborated in the adaptation of John Steinbeck's *East of Eden*. In his final draft before surrendering the project to Osborn, Kazan tried to become the TVA bureaucrat, whom he then called Dave, asserting, "If I could tap something in unconscious memory, so that Dave will flow out of me it would be so much truer and better." But Kazan believed that he had failed to achieve this goal. Twentieth Century Fox, however, was willing to move forward with *Wild River* based on the Kazan drafts. Kazan told Osborn that his first thought was an affectionate look back at the enthusiasm of his youth. Kazan proclaimed:

> I remember the days of the New Deal with a special feeling. I was in some of it, and very much interested in all of it. It was a period of my life when I liked my fellow Americans and my fellow humans best. It was a time when we felt we could do anything. We were bumptious and cocky, but were all daring too. What we were doing in the Theatre, paralleled in spirit what was going on in Washington. . . . I was ridiculous in some ways, as were all of us "world changers"—but there was something effervescent and marvelous in the air that is sadly lacking in this sodden era. This all—and more—is what I should have captured in the character of Dave—which I didn't.[4]

In describing Dave to Osborn, Kazan was positive and nostalgic in recalling the promise of his youthful progressivism with the New Deal and, yes, even the Communist Party. Many of Kazan's later comments, however, were more critical of his commitment to progressive reform during the 1930s and further demonstrate the ambiguity of his politics.

Kazan also made it clear to Osborn that *Wild River* was not to mirror Soviet socialist realism, celebrating the development of a government construction project that would enhance living conditions for the masses. Instead, Dave's certainty is tested by Ella Garth and her granddaughter Carol, with whom Dave falls in love. The focal point of the story is the conflict between opposites. Ella embraces her traditions and has what she wants in life. Kazan envisioned Carol as existing between these two opposites, recognizing that what Dave represents is inevitable and positive, but on the other hand, she respects tradition. The film acknowledges that progress comes with considerable pain, and by the end of the film Dave is somewhat bewildered but humanized and is a better person. Kazan summarized the film to Osborn by concluding: "Dave comes down absolutely sure of every conviction (you might say prejudice). He meets up against some people who are from a certain point of view (his) crazy. And wrong. And worthless. He is there to act towards them for the greater good in an official capacity. He slowly begins to feel towards them an unaccustomed emotion. And he finally realizes that he is in love with them, and by this, deprived of his absolute convictions, and of his ability to act."[5]

Osborn accepted the assignment and received credit for the *Wild River* screenplay, which was also loosely based on the novels *Mud on the Stars*, by William Bradford Huie, and *Dunbar's Cave*, by Borden Deal. A major change made by Osborn was to erase Dave's Jewish background and turn the character into a Gentile by the name of Chuck Glover. Initially, Kazan was reluctant to make the change, complaining that Osborn always wanted to create a regular guy, a "Henry Fonda type," with whom the author was comfortable. After further thought, however, Kazan believed Osborn was on to something. Having Jews and Gentiles not get along was a cliché and as Kazan put it, "bullshit." In addition, Kazan had already explored the subject of anti-Semitism in his 1947 Academy Award–winning film *Gentleman's Agreement*. The director concluded that dropping the Jewish identity of Chuck Glover allowed the film to "make the conflicts on the basis of city vs. country, intellectuals vs. uneducated, bureaucrat vs. emotionally committed peasants. And that's much deeper and much more real, and it's the conflict of the story—not New York City Jew vs. a country person."[6]

Kazan also perceived the character of Chuck as reflective of the confidence he and Clifford Odets once displayed regarding the transformative nature of the Communist Party to create a better world. In a production note for the film, Kazan asserted that during his youth he was the character Dave/Chuck Glover. At age twenty-five, Kazan was directing and teaching at the New Theatre League. The director perceived himself as "the hero of the young insurgent working class art movement" and "the first of the communist intellectuals in the dramatic arts." His young ego seemed to know no bounds, and even after he left the Communist Party, Kazan writes: "I was even superior to the Communists. And when they didn't go along with me, I quit them. Finding all the inhibitions of the party insufferable, I went on my own. I was the future."[7] But the reality of the world finally caught up with Kazan, and like Chuck Glover he had to mature and forego his narcissism—although Kazan always maintained a surface air of confidence, he was actually beset by many insecurities for which he sometimes appeared to overcompensate.

In conversing with Jeff Young about the making of *Wild River*, Kazan remarked how Chuck Glover reminded him of the smug New Dealers he met while working briefly with the Department of Agriculture during the 1930s. While acknowledging that these young men of the New Deal contributed to recovery and reform, Kazan concluded, "At the same time there was something of a know-it-all quality in them that I found very false." Young observed that Kazan was more sympathetic to country people, many of whom in the film could be characterized as rednecks. In response, Kazan conceded that he was probably guilty of romanticizing the country people, but he nevertheless found many of their values quite admirable. The director acknowledged that Ella Garth was a reactionary, yet her dedication to tradition and her home was a tribute to her individualism and way of life. She would rather die than surrender to the "progress" represented by Glover, and Kazan found this quality admirable in many white Southerners. Thus, Kazan told Young that he sympathized with Ella Garth as "she had to make a difficult choice. There's something good going down. I felt that all through about civilization, about improvement. I think our cities are monstrous. I think our civilization, which has been improved and improved and improved, has been dehumanized. In many ways I don't think it's as good as the way it used to be. I made Miss Ella as reactionary as possible. She is against all progress. She considers blacks chattal."[8]

Kazan's biographer Richard Schickel does not believe that Kazan originally intended to embrace the reactionary Ella Garth, but this is what evolved through the course of the filmmaking. According to Schickel, Kazan even believed that the idealism of the 1930s and New Deal might contribute to the reform of contemporary society and culture, about which the director often complained. Fed up with the narcissism of consumer culture, Schickel argues that Kazan expressed hope that the hero in *Wild River* "could be a sort of answer to Brando and Dean—whose salient quality, their childish rebelliousness, he had himself done so much to create."[9] Although Kazan wanted to recapture the idealism of his earlier self with Chuck Glover, this task proved impossible for the older director, and he was increasingly drawn to the character of Ella Garth, who refuses to compromise her principles. This direction of the film, however, may be due less to ideology than the acting performances of *Wild River*.

Jo Van Fleet, who played the mother of James Dean in *East of Eden*, was cast as Ella Garth, and Kazan was drawn to her performance, describing Van Fleet as "formidable and unyielding as the rock-ribbed country where we were working."[10] At age thirty-seven, Van Fleet successfully portrayed a woman in her eighties. Even on days when she was not before the camera, the actress still spent hours applying makeup on her hands to accentuate the liver spots of an elderly woman. She wanted to remain in character for every day of the shoot. The problem for the film was that the contest of wills between Glover and Ella Garth proved to be quite unequal, with Van Fleet as Ella dominating Montgomery Clift, who was cast as Chuck Glover.[11]

Brando, of course, was Kazan's first choice for the role, but as usual he refused to work with the director. Kazan relates that he finally agreed to accept Clift at the insistence of Twentieth Century Fox president Spyros Skouras. The director was well acquainted with Clift, having worked with him on the stage in *The Skin of Our Teeth*, and he described the sensitive young actor as a frequent houseguest for whom Molly Kazan often seemed to function as a surrogate mother. The director was also aware of Clift's problems with alcohol and drugs following his serious 1956 automobile accident, and Kazan asserts that he made Clift promise that he would not drink during the filming of *Wild River*—an agreement that the actor essentially kept. In his autobiography, Kazan went on to describe Clift as "balding, no longer handsome, and unsure of himself." Kazan wrote: "As far as my story went, he'd be no match for the country people whom he'd have to convince of the greater good; and certainly no physical match for any of them if it came to violence. Pictorially, the story would be the weak against the strong—in reverse. I accepted that readily and reinforced the pattern with every bit of my casting."[12]

Thus, Ella Garth tends to dominate Chuck Glover, but an even bigger problem was the love story. For Ella's granddaughter Carol, who falls in love with Glover, Kazan cast Lee Remick, who played the young bride of Lonesome Rhodes in *A Face in the Crowd*. According to Kazan, Remick was simply a stronger actor than Clift was at this point in his career. Clift projected weakness and sexual ambivalence, which Kazan attributed to Clift's "homosexuality," although the actor's sexual orientation was more complex than Kazan was willing to acknowledge. Accordingly, the director encouraged Remick to be the sexual aggressor in the relationship between Chuck and Carol, while off the screen Remick played a nurturing role to the troubled actor. Thus, the widow Carol abandons a safe relationship with a local man to aggressively pursue the neurotic Chuck, whom she decides to marry. Revealing many of his own sexist assumptions and stereotypes, Kazan commented on Carol's assertiveness by observing: "Sexually, I find that girls who have strength, who are nice girls, 'proper' girls—when they find a man, they go to bed with him quicker, because there's not calculation; that's it, they don't hold anything back. In other words, she is much more uninhibited, she's natural. She's a fifties girl living in the thirties."[13]

Kazan's penchant for the Southern Garth women was probably also influenced by his growing relationship with Barbara Loden, who for appearance's sake was given a small part in the production. Describing Loden during the making of *Wild River*, Kazan asserted: "A 'hillbilly' from the back country of North Carolina, Barbara had a side to her character—to go with her great sensitivity—that was defiantly tough. She feared no man—feared only what she might, in some instant of desperation, do to herself. Barbara was as wild as the river I was making a film about."[14]

After working out the casting for *Wild River*, Kazan was generally pleased with the film's progress. He began shooting *Wild River* in southeastern Tennessee, near the small community of Cleveland, in October 1959 and did not wrap until January 1960. He was distressed that Twentieth Century Fox wanted him to rush the production and editing so that the studio might release the film in March and avoid a tax penalty. Kazan attempted to explain to studio executives that *Wild River* was not the type of picture that one rushed to completion. The director asserted that *Wild*

River had the potential to be an outstanding film, but he was not there yet. Perhaps Kazan was remembering the criticism of his friend Tennessee Williams—a relationship that would be forever strained in 1960 by Kazan's refusal to direct the playwright's *Period of Adjustment*—that the TVA was no longer a topic with which a mass audience could identify. Williams told Kazan that the proposed picture reminded him of a 1930s Federal Theater project and included "a connotation of the pedantic." Thus, Kazan told the Twentieth Century Fox executives that *Wild River* contained the popular elements of romance, humor, violence, and pathos, but the more important element was the larger themes to provide the film text with the meaning that Williams found missing.[15] Kazan wrote: "First, whatever 'big' theme you choose, it has to be transmitted into personal terms. It's the impact on the individual that counts. And secondly, the more difficult and less usual the theme, the more perfect the treatment of it must be. When you're traveling off the beaten road, you cannot afford any mistakes. The first requirement I think I have met. The second I have still to meet."[16] The studio eventually surrendered to Kazan's argument; the film was not released until after March, and the studio evidently paid the tax penalty. Nevertheless, Kazan would later blame Twentieth Century Fox for not promoting *Wild River*, which failed at the box office.

Wild River begins with a documentary look that one might associate with the New Deal documentaries of the 1930s, such as *The River* and *The Plow That Broke the Plains*, directed by Pare Lorentz. The footage highlights the destructive power of the floodwaters from the Tennessee River, while a voice-of-God narrator explains that the TVA was created by the Roosevelt administration to control this destructive power. The narrator notes, however, that some people refused to sell their land to the government so that dams could be constructed and living conditions improved.[17]

After the opening documentary homage to the New Deal, viewers are introduced to Chuck Glover (Montgomery Clift), the third TVA representative dispatched from Washington to convince Ella Garth (Jo Van Fleet) to give up her land located on an island in the Tennessee River. Glover is confident that he can succeed where others have failed because he respects Ella's "rugged individualism" as reflective of "the American way of life." Nevertheless, she must move and sell her land to make way for progress, but Glover is convinced that he will be able to achieve this goal without applying force. This self-assurance, however, is tested when Chuck boards a raft and propels himself to the island, passing a sign proclaiming, "TVA KEEP OFF." He finds Ella and four generations of Garth women seated on the front porch of the family home. As Chuck explains his mission, he is ignored by the women, who follow Ella's lead and one by one retreat into the house. Chuck then attempts to speak with Ella's sons, who are working in the yard. The arrogance of Chuck is apparent when he refers to Ella as senile, and Joe John Garth deposits him in the river. Encouraged by another Garth brother who visits his hotel room and urges him to try again, Chuck makes another trip to the Garth property.

When Chuck arrives, Ella is lecturing to her black sharecroppers about the threat of the New Deal to the Southern way of life. Implicit here is the argument made by white Southerners during the civil rights movement that blacks in the region were satisfied with segregation and their lot in life until discontent was fostered by the federal government and outside agitators from the North. Although blacks are included in his films and treated with a degree of respect, Kazan does little to challenge this mythology. Instead, he has Ella employ one of the black laborers, Sam Johnson (Robert Carl Jones), to make her point as to why she will not sell her land. Ella offers to purchase Sam's dog for a fair price. Sam tells her that the dog is not for sale, but Ella is insistent, and Sam is clearly uncomfortable resisting his white landlord. She finally relents after having made her point, telling Chuck, "Sam don't sell his dog, and I don't sell my land." Chuck attempts to counter her argument by describing the progress that the TVA will bring to the region. Ella is suspicious of this government-sponsored improvement and asserts that she prefers nature "running wild," and only force will move her from the island.

After this exchange, Ella, accompanied by her granddaughter Carol (Lee Remick), takes Chuck on a tour of the family cemetery located on the island, sharing the traditions and history of the Garth family, which are intertwined with the land. Ella returns to the house, leaving Chuck with Carol, and viewers begin to understand the strength of her character. A widow with two children by her nineteenth birthday, Carol came back to the island, where she buried her husband in the family cemetery. Carol informs Chuck that she is engaged to a nice man with whom she is not in love. Chuck counsels her against such a marriage, but he makes no moves toward a woman to whom he seems attracted. It will be necessary for

Carol to take matters into her own hands. As Chuck prepares to navigate the raft back to the shore, Carol jumps aboard and decides to show the man from Washington the home along the shore that she abandoned following the death of her husband. Taking the initiative, Carol invites Chuck to spend the night with her.

Upon returning to the office, Chuck begins to pursue a racial agenda in defiance of Southern Jim Crow traditions. He hires the blacks living on the Garth family island to work for the TVA clearing trees for the dam project. To make the job offer attractive, Chuck promises government housing with electricity and that blacks and whites would work together while drawing equal wages. A committee of white community leaders complains to Chuck about the problems caused by challenging the Southern way of life. Chuck compromises by agreeing to maintain segregated work gangs, but he maintains his commitment to equal pay for both blacks and whites. Chuck, however, learns that his racial reforms do not come without a cost when he is informed that some black sharecroppers were beaten for accepting TVA jobs. Of course, some New Deal reforms did have unanticipated consequences. Plantation owners receiving cash payment for reducing production under the Agricultural Adjustment Administration no longer required as many black sharecroppers and forced them off the land. Considering the historical context in which *Wild River* was made, Kazan seems to be raising some concerns about the cost of the civil rights movement to the black community. Many sacrifices were certainly made in the grassroots struggle against Jim Crow, but, similar to the improved living conditions under the TVA, they were well worth the effort. In his treatment of blacks in the film, Kazan seems less certain regarding the benefits of integration, and his position is only mildly progressive while reflecting on an earlier segregated America. [18]

Chuck goes to see Carol, who has moved back into her former house on the shore, and this seems symbolic of her commitment to a more progressive future while putting the traditions of her mother behind her. Key to this change in her life is Carol's love for Chuck, who remains uncertain about his future plans. Nevertheless, Carol has the strength to convince the rather weak Chuck to spend the night with her. The next morning, Chuck and Carol witness the black families departing the island. That is, all except Sam Johnson, who remains with Ella Garth, similar to one of the loyal slaves in *Gone With the Wind* who will not desert Scarlett O'Hara. Carol attempts to convince her grandmother to join the exodus, but the two end up quarreling. Carol departs with Chuck, signifying her reluctant commitment to the New Deal and TVA.

Meanwhile, Carol's local boyfriend, Walter Clark (Frank Overton), is alarmed by the threat Chuck poses to his future with Carol. Walter arranges for a meeting between R. J. Bailey (Albert Salmi) and Chuck in his hotel room. Bailey is a local farmer and bigot who demands that Chuck pay him four dollars for a white cotton picker he had to hire because one of his black laborers was planning to work for the TVA. After Bailey administered a beating, the black man was unable to work awhile for anyone. The bigot then takes out his anger on Chuck, striking him and taking the money he demanded for compensation. Essentially a good person, Walter goes to check on Chuck, and the two men pursue an evening of comradeship and drinking. As the evening winds down, they end up at the island, where an inebriated Chuck informs Ella Garth that he now understands that she is fighting for her "dignity." He then passes out, and Ella assumes a more nurturing stance toward the fallen bureaucrat.

This level of understanding, however, does not alter the fact that Ella Garth has only two weeks left before the government releases water that will submerge the island. Facing the inevitable, the Garth brothers approach Chuck about having their mother declared mentally incompetent so then they could sell the land. Chuck, who has undergone somewhat of a political transformation through his dealings with Ella Garth, is incensed by their level of betrayal. He refuses to cooperate with this scheme, telling the sons, "I'd rather have her put off at the point of a gun." Nevertheless, Chuck still has a job to perform, and he spends the night before Ella's eviction with Carol in her home on the shore. That evening a local mob led by Bailey attacks them, ramming a car into Carol's home and pushing Chuck's TVA government vehicle down a ravine. Chuck initially makes no effort to resist the assault, while Carol grabs a club and goes after Bailey. She is knocked down, and finally Chuck makes an effort to fight back. The bullies leave Carol and Chuck beaten and lying in the mud, but Chuck takes this opportunity to finally agree that he will marry Carol. It is a rather strange scene, as one might wonder why Carol would be so willing to marry a man who has refused to defend her. But Chuck obviously needs Carol's strength, while she has made a decision to embrace the future by wedding Chuck. In many ways, she represents both her grandmother and new husband. Kazan suggests:

"She's smart enough to stay in the middle and not take sides. She knows there is something valuable in what he's trying to do, and still her affection for her grandmother is basic and human. She's a very plain, straightforward, affectionate woman, like the picture itself."[19] Recognizing that her traditions provide her with strength as they transition to the future, Carol tells Chuck, "You're not easy to love, but you need someone."

The next day Ella Garth is removed from the island by federal marshals. Chuck and Carol watch as she silently climbs into the police boat sent to fetch her. Meanwhile, Chuck has found her a home in town with a large front porch. But her traditional dignity is dependent upon much more than a front porch. Cut off from her family roots, Ella dies, and before the island is flooded, she is buried in the Garth family cemetery beside her husband. The film concludes with a shot of Chuck, Carol, and her two young children on a small plane flying over the river. They look out the window of the plane, and we see a shot of the new federal dam and the calm flow of the Tennessee River in contrast to the raging and destructive wild river of the film's opening sequence. The wild river has been tamed, but Kazan raises questions regarding the cost of this progress.

Wild River was a film of which the director was quite proud, and Kazan was most critical of Twentieth Century Fox for not giving the picture a wider release. It was, however, embraced by a number of French critics, and today *Wild River* enjoys considerable respect among film scholars. When the film was released, most reviews—and the limited exhibition means that there were few contemporary critical commentaries on the picture—unfortunately did not know what to make of the film. For example, A. H. Weiler of the *New York Times* found *Wild River* "an interesting but strongly disturbing drama rather than a smashing study of a historic aspect of the changing American scene." The reviewer was complimentary of Kazan's colorful on-location filming of a beautiful area—and *Wild River* was only the director's second picture made in color. The performances of both Van Fleet and Clift were praised, but Weiler recognized that Ella Garth was the focal point of the movie. The critic noted that Ella Garth was not some "cantankerous old fuddy-duddy." Instead, "She is well aware of the benefits of this proposed change—the electricity that will make life easier and bulwarks against the constant floods that took their toll of the population and land regularly. But this is her home and farm—'good bottom land'—that she helped her husband clear and in which her family has been buried for generations." The review concluded that the drama contained in the confrontation between Chuck Glover and Ella Garth, however, was negated by the intrusion of a love story between Glover and Garth's granddaughter. Weiler failed to notice the symbolic aspects of Carol Garth's character in which she attempts to embody the strengths and possibilities of both her idealistic lover and traditionalist grandmother. [20]

While not focusing on symbolism, Arthur Knight's critique for the *Saturday Review* was quite positive. Knight described Kazan's work on *Wild River* as "craftsmanship of a high order" while dealing with such themes as "the latent violence of a wild near-lynching, seamy love scenes of incredible intimacy, and withal a fundamental respect for human dignity and human decency." [21] Henry Hart of *Films in Review* tended to echo these sentiments, describing *Wild River* as "very good indeed" and extolling themes of conflict between old and new, the individual and the state, and humanity and technology. Hart, however, believed that in the vigilante scene, Kazan denigrated the South. Hart also accused Kazan of distorting both Southern and black attitudes, but it is not quite clear what he means by this. It is interesting to note that the word *Southerner* here seems reserved for whites only and does not apply to the large black population of that region. Nevertheless, this commentary seems to suggest that Kazan's rather modest examination of race relations was too progressive for some observers. Hart concluded his positive review by praising the work of Remick and Van Fleet, but he was less kind to Clift, asserting, "Clift is no longer capable of acting, and his tense form and visage devitalize every scene he is in." [22]

Other reviews were far more critical. John McCarten of the *New Yorker* found the film old-fashioned in its stereotypical treatment of rural life. While claiming to examine significant social and political issues, *Wild River*, argues McCarten, "never gets into any chancy waters; in fact; it skims along like one of those old movie resurrections that glaze one's eyes on television's *Late, Late Show*." [23] Robert Hatch of the *Nation* agreed, concluding: "The conflict between private independence and government welfare is certainly vexing, but there seems little point to raising the issue if all you care to say is that a stubborn old lady is a splendid spectacle and so is the TVA; and isn't it too bad we can't have both." [24] *Time* was a bit more generous to *Wild River*, although the review proclaimed that the film was "an epic in search of a poet," but Kazan was certainly not that poet. Nevertheless, *Time* concluded that *Wild River* deserved praise for the film's embrace of moderation for dealing with difficult social issues. An advocate for the consensus, *Time* argued, "Kazan comes down firmly on the side of eminent domain and the commonweal, but also takes time to recognize with a kind of puzzled honesty, that what is good for the greatest number is often bad for the soul."[25]

While the critique in *Time* did somewhat capture Kazan's ending for *Wild River*, none of the reviews recognize to what extent the film was a personal experience for the director, recalling how the certitude of his younger years embracing the Communist Party as well as the New Deal were tested by the realities of post–World War II America. The director perceived the film in terms of ambiguity and ambivalence, telling Jeff Young: "Both sides are right. There's a need to do things for the good of the majority, which in this case is to establish inexpensive electric power and to control the erratic, devastating flooding of the Tennessee River. It's obviously important. But when you do that, some individuals are just ruled out, and I think that's a loss. It's necessary. I'm not saying it's not. But it is a real loss and should not be ignored."[26] Kazan was certainly empathetic with Ella Garth, but the fact that in the final analysis, despite the sense of loss, the director comes down on the side of Chuck and the TVA makes the film politically progressive. According to film historians Wilson McLachian and M. Dawson, *Wild River* is a mature film to note that progress comes with a price; however, "the brilliance of it is that it never condemns the progress or the price as being too high. It is not polemic or a diatribe, but rather a reasoned conclusion. It is a politically intelligent film made by a filmmaker whose politics seem to matter more than his art in retrospect."[27]

While more conservative in his political orientation, Kazan biographer Richard Schickel concurs that *Wild River* was one of Kazan's best pictures and rather progressive in its politics. He describes Chuck Glover as somewhat of a Kazan clone: "A man who knows that the good he intends to do is not unambiguous. He persists because, by the narrowest of margins, he judges the engineering, both hydraulic and social, that he intends to do will likely be more useful than the harm he must also do."[28] According to Schickel, Glover was a man committed to changing the world for the better rather than simply complaining about conditions. Thus, as suggested earlier, Glover was in some ways an antidote to the rebellious generational attitudes fostered by Brando and Dean. The fact that Chuck

Glover does not come across as a greater champion of reform is perhaps also due to the performance of Montgomery Clift, who failed to provide the TVA bureaucrat with a sense of energy, strength, and vitality.

The executives of Twentieth Century Fox, however, did not concur with Schickel's assessment. In agreement with Tennessee Williams, who found the TVA a dated topic, they feared that *Wild River* would not appeal to younger film audiences, who flocked to the pictures of Dean and Brando in the 1950s. Accordingly, the film was given only a limited art house release in the United States, and Kazan had to lobby the studio to exhibit *Wild River* in Europe, where it was better received. Kazan considered *Wild River* to be one of his best and favorite films, but as he observed in his memoir, "Money makes the rules of the market, and by this rule, the film was a disaster."[29]

Wild River was the last of Kazan's so-called Southern trilogy, and none of the films were particularly successful at the box office. At a time when the civil rights movement was calling Southern traditions of Jim Crow into question, Kazan directed a series of films that he perceived as sympathetic to the plight of poor white Southerners. Yet characters such as Archie Lee Meighan, Lonesome Rhodes, and Ella Garth hardly represent a progressive image for the South, and despite his frequent expressions of how much he loved the people of the South, Kazan remained the outsider, and it is difficult to not read his tone as patronizing. Archie Lee is unable to compete with modernizing forces embodied in the character of the Sicilian immigrant Silva Vacarro; Rhodes is a country demagogue who is no match for the reactionary financial interests who dump him in favor of another country bumpkin whom they can bring under their control; and Ella Garth is unable to hold back the progress of electrification. As for black Southerners, they remain in the background even when the civil rights movement was bringing black Americans out of the shadows. Kazan does not resort to the broad racial stereotyping of an earlier Hollywood cinema. His black characters are treated with a quiet dignity, but they are not empowered with a sense of agency. In fact, in *Wild River* there is also the suggestion that progress for blacks may come with some of the social costs we see in Ella Garth being forced to abandon her traditions to create a better future. The possibilities for a New South are perhaps best explored with the characters of Baby Doll Meighan, who, having achieved a degree of maturity following her encounter with Vacarro, is waiting to see if she and Aunt Rose will be remembered or forgotten, and Carol Garth, who refuses to wait passively. She recognizes that the future lies with the progressive forces of change represented, however ineptly, by Chuck Glover. It is time for the South to embrace change.

On the other hand, Kazan sought to embrace the future by once again looking to the past. Young people were an important audience for Kazan in his films with Brando and Dean, but this generation failed to identify with the director's Southern characters. The filmmaker had reservations regarding the youth cult that formed around Dean; however, Kazan needed this audience, and in the problems he had dealing with his own father, which were certainly incorporated into *East of Eden*, the outsider still identified with youthful rebellion. Thus, he wrote Budd Schulberg in 1960 about the death of his father, who had passed away in a rest home. Kazan informed Schulberg that his father resented being moved from his home in New Rochelle, New York. Describing George Kazan's final days, Kazan wrote: "Sort of the old woman in *Wild River* come real. His last days in the hospital with his lost strength were spent planning how he could get out and go back to New Rochelle. He thought of a hospital as a place you go to die. . . . He was mean but honest. At the end I liked him. That's enough. I've never written anyone about him."[30]

Despite some reconciliation with his father, whom he no longer needed to fear, the difficult relationship with the parent was still of paramount concern to the filmmaker in his next three films, *Splendor in the Grass* (1961), *America America* (1963), and *The Arrangement* (1969). Working with playwright William Inge, Kazan set *Splendor in the Grass* in Kansas during the late 1920s as America transitioned into the Great Depression. The future plans of two young lovers, played by Natalie Wood and Warren Beatty, are foiled by their controlling and materialistic parents. While some critics asserted that the film was a shameless manipulation of the youth market, the film certainly reflected Kazan's own conflict with his father, in addition to resonating with audiences and providing Kazan with his first solid box office hit since *East of Eden*. *Splendor in the Grass* seems to anticipate the youth rebellion with which the 1960s would later become associated in American history.

8

ANTICIPATING THE YOUTH REBELLION OF THE 1960s

Splendor in the Grass (1961)

The ambivalence of Elia Kazan's Southern trilogy was apparently confusing to film audiences, who largely avoided the films. Kazan also expressed a strong degree of ambiguity regarding the youth culture and its identification with Marlon Brando and James Dean, who starred in the director's most successful films. He was especially uncomfortable with the cult status Dean gained following his tragic and deadly automobile accident. Nevertheless, Kazan had cast Dean in one of his most personal films, *East of Eden*. The director identified with Dean's struggle as Cal Trask to please his father, but in 1960 the man Kazan feared in his youth died. *East of Eden* had not exhausted Kazan's examination of the complex relationship he shared with George Kazan. In fact, he addressed the topic in his next two films, with *America America* (1963) providing an opportunity to try to understand his father's immigrant experience. *Splendor in the Grass* (1961), however, embraced the rebellion of young people against parental authority, resonating well with a younger generation on the eve of a revolution against the patriarchy and consensus values of the 1950s. Set during the 1920s and the onset of the Depression, *Splendor in the Grass* also appealed to young people who would come to question consumer culture and the values of American capitalism.

The film owes its origins to Kazan's direction of playwright William Inge's *The Darkness at the Top of the Stairs* (1957). Kazan enjoyed working with Inge and casually asked the writer if he had any material that would make a good screenplay. Inge responded with a draft for *Splendor in the Grass*, based on the story of some high school classmates in Kansas, and the script earned Inge an Academy Award. Set in Kansas during the late 1920s, *Splendor in the Grass* tells the story of high school sweethearts Bud Stamper and Deanie Loomis, who are struggling to control their sexual desire. Bud comes from a more affluent family, and Deanie's mother warns her daughter not to surrender her virginity to Bud before marriage. The mother's advice is based less upon conventional moral standards than marrying into the Stamper family's wealth. Meanwhile, Bud's father, a self-made man from the oilfields, is afraid that Bud will impregnate Deanie and be forced into an early marriage. The father plans for Bud to attend Yale and attain the status denied to the nouveau riche patriarch. Thus, the parents intervene, and the couple separate with tragic results. Deanie ends up in a mental institution, while Bud hates Yale. His father commits suicide after losing the family fortune during the stock market crash, and Bud marries an Italian waitress. Bud and Deanie briefly meet after her release from the hospital, but they are unable to recapture the splendor in the grass that they once enjoyed.

Kazan attributed the appeal of the film to the "subtle and unobtrusive story-telling of Inge and his humanity." He said that the story was quintessential Inge, as "it starts with an engaging and deceptive innocence, seems bland and conventional, then begins to go deeper and finally to hurt."[1] In his autobiography, Kazan, however, was less enthusiastic about Inge's contributions to the film, commenting: "He's done some fussing with the scenes, and some of the dialogue he added was good and some not necessary, photographed action would tell most of it. His story had the one essential, an excellent flow of incident to a true conclusion. Bill was an accomplished story-teller, it's a special talent. But I also knew how much I'd contributed, and this gave me the confidence in writing that I'd lacked up until then. I was ready to try my own story."[2]

Kazan would do this with *America America*, but Inge's story also forced the director to again confront the troubled relationship with his own father. The director observed that Bud, unlike Cal Trask, did not rebel against the patriarch. Instead, Kazan concluded that Bud was more like the filmmaker, who concealed his antagonism. Kazan told Michel Ciment: "If my father had given me a chance, I would have tried to live up to his hopes for me, to a certain extent. I did try, I tried to be a good boy, do what he said, run his errands. He always wanted me to cut my hair and shine my shoes; I tried all that. But then after a while I just broke loose."3 When his father finally died in September 1960 after an extended illness, Kazan wrote Budd Schulberg that his father was mean but honest, and that when the parent died, the son finally "liked him." Whether George Kazan felt the same way is unclear, but the son no longer had to fear the patriarch's wrath.

Kazan insists that his father's death left him more contemplative and less angry, but a few months earlier in a production note for *Splendor in the Grass*, Kazan was anything but contemplative as he railed against parents who embraced the materialistic values of a consumer culture and ignored the wishes of their children. It is a devastating critique of Eisenhower's America and sounds nothing like the informant who named names before HUAC. Leftist principles certainly influenced Kazan, as he asserts that he decided to make *Splendor in the Grass* because of the parents who meant well but in reality were murderers and the destroyers of a precious commodity: romantic love. He argues that Mrs. Loomis and Ace Stamper embody the values of the Eisenhower era. They deny their children happiness while maintaining that their sacrifices are for the good of the children. Kazan proclaims that the parents reflect "the great American middle class. They are absolutely perfect in the middle of this tradition. They are the killers. All their rules are business rules, what is practical, and what will make the most money. They are the dominators and castrators. And you'd never know it to look at them; to look at them they are the image, the perfect image, of paternal and maternal concern and love, right down the middle of the tradition."4

Kazan goes on to say that the parents represent the American bourgeoisie, who are running the country and destroying the dreams of a younger generation. Obviously thinking about his own father, Kazan denounces the parents for not listening to their children while forcing the values of an older generation upon them and insisting they live a fake existence. He concludes that tragic things happen to Bud and Deanie because "they love their parents and follow the moral rules of a materialistic and business-corrupted Midwestern culture."5 But Kazan insists that at the end of the film Bud and Deanie do prevail, as the younger generation will in the future, for the couple are still spiritually together and conduct themselves with honor.

Kazan also perceives Bud's older sister, Ginny, played by Kazan's lover Barbara Loden, as heroic in her rebellion against the patriarchy. Ace Stamper was disappointed that his eldest child was not a son upon whom he could bestow his hopes and dreams. After the birth of Bud, he ignores Ginny, who rebels in order to gain her father's attention. She refuses to play the role of "a young lady," partying, drinking, and flaunting her promiscuity. Kazan described Ginny as a "destructive force. She wants to break up her society. She is a revolutionist without knowledge, without a theory, without any technique; she has no goal; and no antagonist." The director also pointed out that Ginny defied social conventions by being aggressive, but that is what Kazan liked about the character. He asserted: "I think it's wonderful when a woman goes after a man. I like it for myself, and I also like to show it."[6] Nevertheless, Ginny pays a price for her rebellion and dies young in a car accident, similar to that iconic rebel James Dean.

Kazan's enthusiasm for Ginny's flaunting of social conventions may also relate to his increasingly public sexual relationship with Barbara Loden, who portrayed Ginny. In his autobiography, the filmmaker asserted that he felt no guilt during the filming of *Splendor in the Grass*, describing himself as "out of control. I didn't care if I was found out. During every lunch break, I enjoyed my lover in her dressing room."[7] After a day of filming in New York City, the director returned home to his wife and children and a traditional bourgeois existence. Thus, Kazan seemed to be living the very hypocritical lifestyle that angered him so much in his critique of middle-class culture, which *Splendor in the Grass* was supposedly exposing. And while Kazan and Molly were in Europe promoting *Splendor in the Grass*, Loden gave birth to the couple's child.

Regardless of whether there is a degree of unconscious self-loathing in this analysis, in his comments on *Splendor in the Grass*, Kazan consistently reflected a criticism of capitalism, materialism, and the middle class more aligned with an earlier progressivism than the opinions expressed before HUAC. In an interview with Michel Ciment, Kazan emphasized the role played by the Great Depression in the film and in shaping American culture. He describes how the crash devastated his father, and Kazan claims that he saw people jumping out of windows and committing suicide, just as Ace Stamper did in *Splendor in the Grass*. Kazan concluded: "I think the crash still haunts this country. When they talk about inflation, what they all remember is that moment when the banks were closed, when you couldn't get money, when you couldn't buy anything with a dollar."[8] In his description of the Great Depression, Kazan sounds like the young radical of the 1930s who questioned capitalism and identified with the goals of Communism. During the post–World War II period, many Americans experienced a greater degree of financial security and the middle class grew, but Kazan did not necessarily perceive this as a positive development. Interrogating American materialism and puritanism, Kazan remarked: "You know what American puritanism is: a man who has a good business and makes a lot of money is somehow good. And a man who doesn't make money and is a failure in business has something wrong in his character." The struggle for the legal tender forced Americans to commit violent and shameful acts simply to survive. Kazan praised his own films for capturing this struggle, concluding: "I think you could see the spiritual history of the goddamn country."[9]

Although Kazan claimed to respect the people of the Midwest and Kansas, just as he did Southerners (and the reference always seems to mean white people), his comments on the region do not seem to reflect a similar degree of empathy. Kazan made numerous trips to Kansas to research the film, although he ended up photographing most of the picture in New York City. After a trip to Kansas City, Kazan wrote: "Kansas City, an unvarying materialistic civilization. No illumination in people's faces. There is no spirituality, inner light, or humanity, on any of their faces. Nor are there marks or evidence of living for pleasure. No sensuality, the faces are dumpy, drab, and plain." He concluded his note with a rather sexist observation: "The middle-aged women are terribly unattractive, it's hard to believe the men do it to them. But the women don't want these men to do it to anyone else. They'd prefer them dead."[10] One detects in this commentary some anxiety regarding his personal problems with marital infidelity.

Kazan described Midwesterners as staid, reactionary, and in terrible trouble, reflecting that the region was similar to the South as "there's an appearance of courtesy, chivalry, hospitality, gifts, and drinks—but underneath it there's this terrific violence."[11] The director, however, made it clear to Jeff Young that he did not perceive middle-class hypocrisy limited to the South or the Midwest. Instead, Kazan insisted that middle America was about business values that could be found in every section of the country. Materialism and profit trumped morality and individual freedom. The filmmaker proclaimed: "One of the things I've harped on all my life is that we live in a business civilization, and that the business orientation determines every value. Every time there's a conflict between values, what's good for business is what resolves it."[12] While his HUAC testimony suggested that internal subversion and the criminal conspiracy represented by the Communist Party were the greatest danger to America, in his comments regarding *Splendor in the Grass* the director strongly asserts that the violence and corresponding lack of moral direction in the nation were the product of business and capitalism.

Kazan's biographer Richard Schickel acknowledges that the progressive Kazan was certainly on display with *Splendor in the Grass*. According to Schickel, *Splendor in the Grass* was the film in which the director most directly criticized American puritanism and business practices, seemingly anticipating "many of the attitudes that would yet be more screechingly stated by the rebellious youth culture of the sixties." Perhaps some of this anger was due to Kazan again entering psychoanalysis as he attempted to deal with the death of his father and conflicts within his marriage as he maintained his love for Molly while pursuing a sexual relationship with Barbara Loden. In his interviews with Kazan, Schickel nevertheless noted a political perspective to the director's mounting discontent with America's middle class, which the filmmaker described as spoiled. On the other hand, Kazan expressed his admiration for the nation's working class, telling Schickel: "I do believe in honest effort in an honest cause. I do feel that there's a dignity in honest labor. I like work. I like workers. I like people that work. And I don't like the spoiled and I think almost everybody in the middle class is spoiled, so there you are. Make of it what you will. Maybe some is a hangover from the Communists. But I thought they were spoiled, too." In conclusion, Kazan remarked that the American upper and middle classes needed to be humbled as they had never been bombed like the Europeans in World War II.[13]

While Kazan had clearly split with the Communist Party, his ideas regarding capitalism and class continue to have a Marxist orientation, making his post-HUAC filmography more complex than many leftist critics seem to appreciate. For the victims of the capitalist and class oppression symbolized by the parents in *Splendor in the Grass*, Kazan cast Natalie Wood and Warren Beatty, in his first starring role. Wood was a child star, perhaps best known for the Christmas classic *Miracle on 34th Street* (1947), and she transitioned into more adult roles as James Dean's love interest in *Rebel Without a Cause* (1955). By the late 1950s, her career was lagging, but 1961 proved to be a comeback year for the actress, with major roles in *West Side Story*—which won the Oscar for Best Picture—and *Splendor in the Grass*, for which Wood garnered an Academy Award nomination as Best Actress.[14]

While Beatty was initially dismissed by some critics as just another imitation of Brando and Dean, the actor moved on to an outstanding film career and became good friends with Kazan. Their relationship got off to a somewhat rocky start when Beatty confronted the veteran director about naming names in his HUAC testimony. The director responded by taking the young actor's arm and guiding him to a nearby dressing room, where Kazan spent nearly three hours explaining his actions. This is not the response one might have expected from an experienced director toward a young performer cast in his first major role. Certainly Kazan must have perceived this investment of time important to establishing his connection with Beatty early in the production of *Splendor in the Grass*. It would also seem to indicate that Kazan wanted to convey the complexity of his decision to the young actor—it was never really as simple as the criminal conspiracy explanation he often proclaimed as a defense mechanism. Beatty was impressed with Kazan's willingness to explain himself, rewarding the director with an outstanding performance. Although often better known for his Don Juan image and the conclusion of one biographer that the actor slept with thousands of women, Beatty is a political activist who played an important role in the 1972 presidential campaign of George McGovern and considered running for political office. In 1980, Beatty won an Oscar for directing *Reds*, a sympathetic treatment of American Communist John Reed.[15] And in 1999, the actor known for his leftist politics supported Kazan's nomination for a Lifetime Achievement Award.

While pleased with Inge, Beatty, Wood, and the rest of his cast—especially Barbara Loden—Kazan was once again frustrated by demands that he make changes to the film in order to receive Production Code approval and avoid the censure of the Catholic Legion of Decency. Much of the controversy centered on the gang rape of an inebriated Ginny Stamper in a parking lot outside of a dance. In a letter to Jack Warner, Kazan argued that the scene was essential for providing greater explanation as to why Bud cuts off his relationship with Deanie. According to Kazan, the boy is so shocked by what happened to his sister that "he is frightened to give expression to his own sexual impulses." The director proclaimed that the rape scene did not succumb to sensationalism, insisting, "It is wrong—in anticipation of criticism—to ruin one of the best and potentially one of the most talked about sequences in the film." [16]

Nevertheless, the studio continued to push for alterations to the film, and in February 1961 Kazan angrily responded to Jack Warner, after screening the Oscar-winning performance of Elizabeth Taylor in *Butterfield Eight*. In the film, Taylor plays a prostitute, and it is interesting to note that the director of *Baby Doll* termed the film "vulgar." He could not understand why *Butterfield Eight* received the approval of the Production Code while his film portraying the beauty of young love was encountering difficulty with the censors. He considered it immoral that Taylor's character described her initiation to sex as a thirteen-year-old with her mother's lover by proclaiming that she loved "every minute of it." A rather excited Kazan compared *Butterfield Eight* with a stag film, complaining: "Elizabeth Taylor is shown in a slip which is too small for her. With a lot of cleavage showing. Her breasts are so compressed that they squash out on the sides." The man who often glorified in his sexual conquests concluded that *Butterfield Eight* was glorifying infidelity. On the other hand, the character portrayed by Natalie Wood in *Splendor in the Grass* "never has sexual intercourse with anybody through the course of the film." Kazan concluded that the whole point of the picture was "these two young people should have been allowed by their parents to get married since their love is a pure one and a genuine one involving both physical attraction and spiritual depth of feeling for each other." [17]

In the final analysis, changes were made to the film, with the rape of Ginny becoming an attempted sexual assault. Nevertheless, Kazan told his friend Clifford Odets that the cuts in the film were minor and he had triumphed over cowardly studio executives and "the capons in the black frocks." He also confessed to Odets that he really did not like the film enough to make a "cause" about the "inconsequential" cuts. [18] Regardless of whether he was entirely satisfied with *Splendor in the Grass*, Kazan pushed Warner Bros. to promote the film, something he believed that Twentieth Century Fox had failed to do with *Wild River*. He urged the studio to publicize positive reviews and promote the film for Academy Awards. After praising the performances of Beatty and Wood, he noted: "Barbara Loden gives a performance that's one of the showiest and flashiest in years. It's an attraction in itself. As far as advertising was concerned, the film should be marketed at a broad audience and not simply the younger crowd." Kazan concluded, "The word of mouth, as I hear it, is immense."[19] And *Splendor in the Grass* proved to be the director's first significant commercial film hit since *East of Eden*.

Set in southeastern Kansas in 1928, *Splendor in the Grass* begins with Deanie Loomis (Natalie Wood) and Bud Stamper (Warren Beatty) engaged in a heavy petting session while in Bud's car.[20] Deanie begs Bud to stop, and he reluctantly takes her home. Mrs. Loomis (Audrey Christie) is waiting up for her daughter, whom she cautions about premarital sex with Bud. The Loomis family is not affluent as are the Stampers, and Mrs. Loomis wants her daughter to preserve her virginity. If able to engage in premarital sex with Deanie, Bud might not marry her, and she would lose out on "the catch of a lifetime." Her father (Fred Stewart), a small-town pharmacist, seems more sympathetic to Deanie, but he is a weak man who defers to his wife.

Meanwhile, Ace Stamper (Pat Hingle) is having a somewhat similar conversation with his son. Ace is an uneducated man who earned a small fortune in the oilfields, but his pursuit of the American dream has come at a price. He is crippled from an oilfield accident, but Ace wants his son to enjoy all the advantages he never had. The father has his heart set on Bud attending Yale and attaining social respectability for the nouveau riche Stamper family. Bud is less keen on going to Yale, but the father does not listen to the boy. Instead, Ace is concerned that his plans for Bud might get derailed if Deanie were to become pregnant and the couple forced to marry. Instead, Ace suggests that Bud see "another type of girl" for sexual purposes. After listening to their respective parents, Bud and Deanie retire to their bedrooms sexually frustrated. Both Kazan and Inge were engaged in psychoanalysis, and the film certainly emphasizes a Freudian approach to the neurosis that Bud and Deanie suffer as they are prevented by the older generation from consummating their love and sexuality.

As Bud begins his senior year as the star football player on his local high school team, he tries to tell his father he really does not want to attend Yale. He would prefer to marry Deanie and enroll at the local agricultural college. His mother (Joanna Roos) is sympathetic to Bud, but, similar to Mr. Loomis, she will not stand up to her spouse. Bud reluctantly agrees to follow his father's wishes as he does not want to challenge the patriarch and follow the example of his older sister, Ginny

(Barbara Loden). Disappointed that his first child was not a male, Ace essentially ignored his daughter, who gained attention by rebelling against her father and middle-class conventions. Ginny was expelled from school and had an abortion while she was in the East. Upon returning to her Kansas home, Ginny antagonizes her father by smoking, drinking, playing her jazz music loudly, and dating an older bootlegger. For the Prohibition era, she is the quintessential flapper. To please his father, Bud agrees that he will go to Yale, and he tries to get Ginny to tone down her behavior.

Ginny refuses to change her conduct, and she is punished for her rebellion. At a New Year's Eve party sponsored by the Stamper family, Ginny drinks heavily and flirts with every young man in attendance. While Kazan insisted that he admired sexually aggressive women, she earns little respect from the small-town young men, who believe that she must be punished for flaunting their social mores. She is taken to the parking lot, where there is an attempted gang rape that is foiled by Bud's intervention. Ginny survives that evening, but she perishes shortly thereafter in an automobile accident, seemingly brought on by driving while intoxicated. Meanwhile, Bud is shocked by the violent sexuality that he witnessed with his sister in the parking lot. An innocent Bud takes Deanie home and tells his girlfriend that they should end their relationship before things go too far.

Following the breakup, things do not go well for either Bud or Deanie, who, due to parental pressures, are not following their young love that would bring them happiness. Bud begins to do poorly in school and his health declines, culminating in his collapse during a high school basketball game. After a short stay in the hospital, his doctor tells Bud to take better care of himself and, similar to Ace Stamper and in the best Freudian tradition, urges the young man to find a proper outlet for this pent-up sexuality. In response, Bud begins to date a girl with a reputation for sexual promiscuity. The relationship drives Deanie into more neurotic behavior, such as cutting herself off from friends and engaging in emotional outbursts both at home and in school. This erratic behavior reaches its crescendo on the night of the senior prom.

Deanie attends the prom with one of Bud's friends, Toots (Gary Lockwood). She is dressed provocatively in a low-cut red dress, sporting the image of a "fast" girl. Deanie abandons Toots at the dance and goes outside with Bud to his car. Telling Bud that she is no longer a nice girl,

Deanie attempts to initiate a sexual encounter. Bud, still in love with Deanie and apparently remembering what his sister suffered for her sexual aggression, tells Deanie to maintain her pride, and he refuses to have sex with her. A distraught Deanie then departs with Toots. When the couple park, Toots assumes that he will be able to have sex with Deanie. Instead, Deanie leaps out of the car and jumps into a lake, where she attempts to drown herself, but she is rescued before taking her life. Deanie's doctor informs Bud that he must not see Deanie as it would only upset her. Deanie is shipped off to a sanatorium, while Budd leaves for Yale. The lake scene was a difficult one for Kazan to stage due to Wood's fear of water. The director was going to film the scene at the studio in a large water tank, but Wood worked up the courage to shoot the scene in a lake. Kazan remarked how ironic it was that Wood apparently drowned while on a yacht with her husband Robert Wagner and actor Christopher Walken, who was rumored to be romantically involved with the actress. The yacht was named *The Splendor*, and her death led to a criminal investigation, although no charges were filed. [21]

Bud is unhappy at Yale, and his studies suffer. He begins to date a young Italian waitress named Angelina (Zohra Lampert). Concerned that Bud may flunk out of Yale and marry someone beneath his station, Ace Stamper travels to New Haven. While he is attempting to use his wealth to get Bud reinstated, Ace receives an urgent phone call that he is immediately needed in New York City due to problems with his investments. Ace decides to take Bud with him, and that evening they attend a nightclub. One of the chorus line dancers bears a physical resemblance to Deanie, and Ace procures her to spend the night with Bud—perhaps trying to compensate in some fashion for his intervention that separated his son from Deanie. Meanwhile, Ace returns to his hotel room and jumps out the window. His suicide comes after he learns that he has lost the family fortune in the stock market crash. Ace's pursuit of the American dream has brought only tragedy to himself and the Stamper family. Mrs. Stamper goes to live with her aging parents, while Bud marries Angelina and moves onto what is left of the Stamper property to earn his living as a farmer.

Deanie is institutionalized for almost three years before being sent home. While hospitalized, she met another patient, who is being released to pursue his medical practice in Cincinnati. Deanie has agreed to marry him, but first she goes back home to visit her parents. As her mother helps her unpack, Mrs. Loomis asks if the doctors blamed her for Deanie's problems. Although considerable fault could be attributed to Mrs. Loomis, Deanie decides that it is time for reconciliation and forgiveness, and she does not chastise her mother. This is somewhat similar to the evolving feelings of Kazan toward his deceased father. Deanie does ask her mother about Bud, and Mrs. Loomis lies, stating that Bud had moved to Tulsa. For once, her father demonstrates some initiative and tells Deanie that Bud lives just outside of town at the old Stamper place.

Accompanied by several girlfriends, she goes to see Bud. He is a working farmer and married to Angelina. The couple has one child and another is on the way. Bud appears happy but is still in love with Deanie. The former lovers have a quiet conversation, and Deanie informs Bud of her marriage plans. They part as friends, and as Deanie drives back to town with her girlfriends, they ask her if she is still in love with Bud. In response, she recalls a William Wordsworth poem she once studied in high school.

> Though nothing can bring back the hour
> of splendor in the grass, of glory in the flower;
> We will grieve not, rather find
> Strength in what remains behind[22]

Kazan was quite proud of the film's conclusion, calling the last reel of *Splendor in the Grass* his favorite conclusion—although overall he liked films such as *Wild River* better. Perhaps recalling his own troubled personal relationships at the time with his wife and Barbara Loden, Kazan also considered the ending of *Splendor in the Grass* to be rather bittersweet. He asserted that after Deanie came out of the institution, she was too complicated for Bud, who was settled into a simpler farming and family lifestyle. Kazan believed that "the American notion that love is the solution to all of life's problems is only true for an inhibited society. Even if you get the right woman you still have the same problems: you have to solve them within yourself."[23]

Whether the average filmgoer perceived the conclusion this way or not, audiences loved the film, and Kazan had a hit on his hands for a change. The commercial success of the picture, however, did lead to a strained relationship between Kazan and Inge, who expected a greater share of the film's profits. An exasperated Kazan argued that Inge had received a better deal than other Kazan writing collaborators, such as Tennessee Williams and Budd Schulberg. Irritated, Kazan wrote:

> Have you any way, in your self-indulgent mood, to compare the amount of work I put into *Splendor* and what you did? Bill, I put more time into that movie after I go through shooting than you did the entire time. I did every single step, dubbing, cutting, re-cutting, re-recutting, fighting with the Legion of Decency, fighting with Warners, scoring, re-scoring, previewing it to the Warner people, going to California to preview it there for the festival, fighting out the advertising step by step for months. Then I went to Europe and toured there ahead of the picture. The big grosses in the countries where there were big grosses came from the work I did "ahead of our movie."

In conclusion, Kazan responded to Inge's complaint by proclaiming, "I think your letter is utter shit."[24] Inge eventually received approximately $250,000 for his work on *Splendor in the Grass*, and the relationship between the two men was somewhat mended.

While audiences seemed to love the film, critical commentary on *Splendor in the Grass* was bitterly divided. Bosley Crowther of the *New York Times* asserted that Inge and Kazan "hurled upon the screen a frank and ferocious social drama that makes the eyes pop and the modest cheek burn." Crowther found the sex scenes to be rough but not sensationalized due to the social context the filmmakers provided in their critique of small-town America and the vulgar pursuit of materialism and acceptance. The critic concluded: "For the turmoil of sex-starving youngsters is set within the socially isolated frame of a Kansas town in the late 1920s— a town raw, sick, and redolent with oil, with the arrogance of sweaty money grubbers and the platitudes of corn-belt puritans. The torment of two late adolescents, yearning yet not daring to love, is played against the harsh backdrop of cheapness, obtuseness, and hypocrisy." Crowther lauded the performances but panned Barbara Loden's acting as "all fireworks and whirling razor blades" and urged Beatty to purge himself of the Brando and Dean mannerisms.[25]

Although failing to note Kazan's critique of the price paid by the children for the parents' pursuit of the American dream, *Newsweek* also praised the film, calling it "one of the richest American movies in years." The review described Kazan's direction as "swift, strong, and, at moments, as plain and clear as a painting by Grant Wood."[26] Writing in the *Saturday Review*, Arthur Knight lauded *Splendor in the Grass* for its honesty. He also noted the film's critique of the pursuit of wealth in the 1920s that culminated in the Great Depression. In conclusion, Knight asserted that *Splendor in the Grass* was "not an easy picture, nor is its suggestion that growing up may mean settling for second best likely to make it a popular one. But the combination of detached writing and impassioned direction make it constantly fascinating to watch, and its obvious integrity can earn it only respect."[27]

Other critics, however, found the film to be extremely dishonest, and *Splendor in the Grass* earned Kazan some of his most negative film reviews. The critiques paid little attention to the film's questioning of the American dream and puritanism. Instead, they accused Kazan and Inge of preying upon prurient interest in adolescent sexuality to sell movie tickets. Robert Hatch of the *Nation* described *Splendor in the Grass* as lacking a sense of realism, concluding: "Sentimentality is contempt for the human spirit, the willingness to use emotion, not as catharsis, but as a laxative. It is often very popular, as I expect *Splendor in the Grass* to be."[28] *Time* also criticized the film for its commercial exploitation of youthful sexuality and Freudian psychology. The publication did praise Wood as "quietly adroit and appealing," while predicting that Beatty "has that certain something Hollywood calls star quality." Their performances, however, could not rescue a weak script, which *Time* attributed to Kazan's influence, as Inge abhorred art that told an audience what to think. *Time* concluded, "The show, of course, is slick, exciting, professional in every detail—trust crony old Kazan for that every time."[29]

Perhaps the most negative assessment of *Splendor in the Grass* was provided by Brendan Gill in the *New Yorker*. Gill proclaimed that Kazan's film was "as phony a picture as I can remember seeing," with the adolescents of the film bearing no resemblance to young people in real life. Rather than a sensitive portrayal of young people in love, *Splendor in the Grass* was "a prolonged act of voyeurism, which we as adults are invited to become parties to on the pretext that it will provide us with fresh insight into the sexual anguish of teen-agers." Gill concludes his review with an indictment of Kazan for commercially exploiting fascination with adolescent sexuality, but the critic lets the parents of the film and the American middle-class values condemned by Kazan off the hook. Gill proclaims: "One has no choice but to suppose that this unwholesome sally into adolescent sexology was devised neither to interest our minds nor to move our hearts but to arouse a prurient interest and provide a box-office smasheroo. I can't help hoping that they have overplayed their hand."[30]

This critical response to *Splendor in the Grass* seems to anticipate the cultural division regarding the youth rebellion and counterculture of the late 1960s, and despite the assertion of Gill that Deanie and Bud bore little resemblance to contemporary teens, young people flocked to the film. In his study of Kazan's cinema, Brian Neve notes that the filmmaker reflected the changes underway in American society during the early 1960s, writing of *Splendor in the Grass*:

> Its social resonance owes something to the passage towards maturity of the baby boom generation and the "generation gap" that was becoming apparent between the views and experiences of contemporary adolescents and traditional fifties' notions of the family. At the same time the cinema was also in transition from a medium directed at an adult or broad family audience to one in which the young and their concerns were central. For teenagers in the early sixties, and indeed for their parents, issues of youth identity were of growing significance as alternative "youth cultures" and lifestyles emerged as options.[31]

By the time *Splendor in the Grass* was in theaters, however, Kazan was beginning to look more toward the past and, with the death of his father, was coming to grips with the immigrant experience of early twentieth-century America. In his production notes before the filming of *Splendor in the Grass*, Kazan describes the parents as the great American middle class of the 1920s or 1950s out to destroy, kill, and castrate the dreams of the youth, all in the name of business and its support of wealth. Yet in the conclusion to the film, Kazan strikes a less Marxist pose as he has Deanie forgive her mother after she returns home from the mental institution. Kazan told Jeff Young that he was proud of that scene, and, similar to Deanie, it was important to strike a note of reconciliation and forgive our parents for their transgressions.[32]

Based on his success with *Splendor in the Grass*, Kazan might have continued to mine the growing youth film market. Instead, the film director was turning inward in a desire to understand his father and the immigrant experience of which he was a product. Responding to a letter from Clifford Odets, now diagnosed with cancer, in which the playwright discussed problems with his father that almost drove him to suicide, Kazan conceded that his father was "the big problem of my life, so it's appearing, so it's turning out."[33] While the director had dealt with his father indirectly in films such as *East of Eden* and *Splendor in the Grass*, he hoped that by making *America America* about his uncle's travails on his immigrant journey from Turkey to the United States, he would be able to purge many of the unaddressed issues with his family and deceased father. As Kazan informed Michel Ciment, "If you embrace your parents and forgive them, you can step past them and forget them."[34] The director envisioned *America America* as the first film in a trilogy examining the history of his immigrant family in the United States. Plowing considerable love and labor into *America America*, Kazan produced his favorite film. It earned a number of favorable reviews, along with Academy Award nominations for Best Director and Best Picture, but this personal film looking backward into the immigrant past of Southern and Eastern Europeans failed to resonate with audiences—a problem that many critics attributed to the film's epic length of nearly three hours. *America America*'s limited appeal at the box office precluded the trilogy planned by Kazan. However, he returned to autobiographical themes with his bestselling novel *The Arrangement* (1967) and film adaptation of the book, which Kazan directed in 1969. The youth rebellion of the 1960s, which Kazan commercially anticipated with *Splendor in the Grass*, represents a lucrative path that the director chose not to follow in favor of the personal examination of his family's struggles with pursuing the American dream.

9

THE ANATOLIAN SMILE AND THE IMMIGRANT EXPERIENCE

America America (1963)

Elia Kazan initially titled his family history project "The Anatolian Smile," again referring to the enigmatic expression of the outsider immigrant who must find his or her way in a different culture and place. Wanting to emphasize the United States as a place of hope for the oppressed people of the world, Kazan changed the title to *America America*—a significant repetition of longing for a better life that Kazan often heard on his travels. *America America* is the story of Kazan's uncle Avraam Kazanjioglou, who became known in the United States as Joe Kazan, and his journey from Turkey to the United States, establishing the path that would eventually bring Elia Kazan and his family to America. The many compromises, tragedies, and degradations he experienced on this odyssey, however, leads one to wonder whether reaching the shores of America was really worth the sacrifice. The film is also ambivalent about exactly what America represents. In the case of Kazan's family, they are fleeing the tyranny of the Turkish government, and America seems to offer the hope of freedom from fear. *America America*, however, somewhat negates this idealistic optimism with a focus on materialism and capitalism contributing to the destruction of tradition in pursuit of the almighty dollar. Fear of authority and concerns about financial security were prevalent throughout Kazan's life and certainly a part of his decision to name names before HUAC. Thus, the theme of ambivalence best describes *America America*, placing the film firmly within the themes of Kazan's post-HUAC cinema. *America America* is not really the celebration of the American experience with which Kazan sometimes tried to sell his film. Rather, it better reflects the enigma of the Anatolian smile.

Although long in the planning stages, when Kazan sat down to write *America America* in 1961, he was going through a series of personal issues that certainly impacted his perception of what America meant. In addition to informing, which always cast a large shadow over the filmmaker, he was dealing with the death of his father, as well as juggling his love affair with Barbara Loden while maintaining his marriage to Molly Day Thacher Kazan. He was also struggling as director of the Repertory Theatre of Lincoln Center in New York City, a position that frustrated him, although it eventually led to a reconciliation with Arthur Miller and the production of *After the Fall* (1964), in which Kazan cast Loden in what most observers, despite Miller's objections, considered to be the Marilyn Monroe role. In his professional life, Kazan increasingly sought an independence that repertory theater and the Lincoln Center failed to provide. Although he collaborated with renowned authors such as Miller, Steinbeck, Williams, Schulberg, and Inge, the director wanted to write his own material. Thus, he described *America America* as his favorite film "not because it's my best film but because I wrote it and made it and because it's about the subject I spent years contemplating: how my family came to America."[1] As Kazan acknowledged, however, the financial failure of *America America* actually reduced his independence as a filmmaker, and his future writing was to be concentrated on novels rather than the cinema.

As early as 1955, Kazan was contemplating a film about his family origins and was vacationing in Greece and Turkey while scouting potential locations. Encouraging his friend Tennessee Williams to visit the region and spend some time in Athens, Kazan wrote: "It is an extraordinary city. I have no idea what the hunting will be like there, but everything that I did to get in touch with the air, the food, the sites, the light, the liquor, the museums, the music, I found most congenial and all of it was tied together by an extraordinary independence and dignity of just about every Greek you meet." On the other hand, Kazan had a far less positive view of Turkey, telling Williams: "Istanbul is full of every kind of vice and pleasure. Full of poverty and license, has the veiled life and the most brutal daily life of the streets. You immediately feel that you're in Asia even though the city itself is mostly in Europe."[2] Kazan's comments reflected the experience of his family as well as the historical conflict between Greece and Turkey. Thus, it is not too surprising that the Greek director would later have trouble with Turkish officials when filming *America America.*

Kazan's desires to shed the Anatolian smile, confront his family history, do his own writing, and establish a sense of independence was evident in a 1960 letter to John Steinbeck, who was about to embark on a pilgrimage that would form the basis for *Travels with Charley* (1962). The director wanted to rid himself of the nickname "Gadg," short for "Gadget," which he earned during the 1930s performing any task necessary for the Group Theatre and with which Steinbeck greeted Kazan in his letter. Kazan proclaimed: "My nickname has taken on a particularly disgusting meaning for me. It marks the abdication of a true identity and the assumption of a false one. False because the mask: GADJ suggests over-ready compliance, subservient, scattershot friendliness and an adaptability that made it possible for me to be the 'necessary' thing to any man. A most successful mask!"[3]

Asserting his independence, Kazan began writing *America America*, which was initially somewhat of a hybrid between a screenplay and novel. Molly was impressed with the manuscript's potential, and after some editing she convinced her friend Sol Stein, who was establishing the publishing company Stein and Day, to issue the book as his company's first title. *America America* traces the journey of Stavros Topouzoglou, based on Kazan's uncle Avraam, from Turkey to the promised land of America. In his preface to the novel, playwright S. N. Behrman praises Kazan's vision, noting that by focusing on the immigrant experience, Kazan was getting at the heart of America. He wrote: "The boy Stavros is rent by homesickness; for the home he has abandoned, for the home he seeks. It is the pain at the heart of every migration. But here is a high exaltation, too. Stavros makes it."[4] Nevertheless, in his commentary Behrman perpetuates one of the problems that plagued both Kazan's novel and film. It was clear that Stavros and other migrants from Southern and Eastern Europe wanted to escape the pogroms, prejudice, and ethnic violence that threatened their existence, and in America they would be far more secure. But does not America mean something more than safety? Kazan was better able to describe what the immigrants were fleeing rather than the ideas of the new land they were entering. Ambivalence over last traditions, a theme so important to *Wild River*, and the exploitive aspects of American capitalism rendered Kazan uncertain about the immigrant experience. Stavros knows what he is against, but what does he actually want?

While this dilemma would haunt his film, the modest success of the novel and some positive reviews convinced Kazan that there was reason enough to pursue the family project. While Molly supported the film, Kazan's family was opposed to placing the family history on the screen. The director attributed this opposition to a continuing fear of the Turks. His mother thought it wonderful to film in Greece, but she feared for her son's safety in Istanbul.[5] Kazan dismissed these concerns and persisted with his film plans, traveling to Greece and Turkey in 1961 accompanied by Barbara Loden, who was three months pregnant with the couple's child. Throwing caution to the wind, the director traveled openly with Loden, whom he introduced to Greek and Turkish officials as a friend and professional colleague. The filmmaker recognized that he was placing his marriage in jeopardy, but he believed that it was more important to have no regrets. He described Loden as resembling all the beautiful young women at Williams College who would not even look in his direction.[6] This confession in Kazan's autobiography certainly reveals that the filmmaker was still plagued by insecurity. As for Molly, Kazan confessed that the couple no longer enjoyed a sexual relationship. Yet he maintained: "In every other essential, I was faithful to Molly; I'd devoted my energies without reserve to supporting and, when she needed it, protecting her. I was her husband truly, and my thoughts and energies were always with her. Friendship, at the end, was our truest bond."[7]

Thus, while traveling with Loden, Kazan wrote Molly about his plans and negotiations for filming *America America*. He confided that the Communist Yugoslav government had made a pitch for the film, but he had decided that most of the project would be filmed in Greece, which would assure that costs were held to a minimum. Nevertheless, it would be essential to film some scenes in Turkey, especially those involving the *hamals*, or human beasts of burden, who labored on the Istanbul waterfront. He also confessed to Molly the difficulties he was encountering finding someone to play the role of Stavros, who in order to secure his passage to America was forced to commit numerous sordid acts. Yet film audiences would still need to maintain a degree of sympathy for him.[8]

For the role of Stavros, Kazan asserted: "The actor should be (or seem) Greek 'with eyes like moist olives,' but of course he had to speak English. He should be home-spun, back-country, conscientious, dutiful, hungry, intense, unswerving. As always, I noted which was the most important of the needed qualities. It was the last. He had to be unswerving."[9] The director began his search in the New York theater for a newcomer who might meet his requirements. He then expanded his net to include California and England, where he encountered many rebel figures in the mold of Brando and Dean. But he was looking for something else. One actor who displayed the persistence Kazan was looking for in the role was Warren Beatty, who sought to work with the director again after he learned so much about his craft during the filming of *Splendor in the Grass*. Beatty even went so far as to suggest he was willing to don a prosthetic nose or undergo some cosmetic surgery if it were necessary to attain the part. Kazan told Beatty that he would very much enjoy working with the actor again, but the role of Stavros was not right for Beatty. Instead, Kazan concluded:

> Let me put it plainly. I am going to find a Latin boy, a Greek or an Italian, some sort of Mediterranean for this role. It is not—at least for film—a matter of a nose, or a speech pattern. It is built in. It's a matter of temperament and kind of behavior that a kid takes in with his mother's milk. Anything synthetic in this particular film would ruin it—perhaps in ways that would not be apparent, but in some distinctive way. My kid is a Greek—and I am setting out to find him. I can't believe that he doesn't exist.[10]

Accordingly, the director issued a casting call while in Athens. Among the more than 150 who responded, Kazan was drawn to Stathis Giallelis, who looked perfect for the part. However, his difficulty with English led Kazan to dismiss the young man. When Kazan returned to Athens a few months later, he was accosted at his hotel by Stathis, who insisted that he had learned English. In conversation with the young Greek, Kazan found out that Stathis's father was a Communist who had been beaten to death and died in the boy's arms during the bloody Greek civil war following the nation's liberation from Nazi occupation. At age twenty-one, Stathis had to care for his widowed mother, three sisters, and younger brother. Kazan was impressed but told the young man that his English was simply not good enough to feature him in the film. Three months later, Stathis showed up unannounced at Kazan's New York City office. Kazan was uncertain how Stathis was able to reach New York, but his airline ticket was supposedly obtained through the sale of some land, a loan from a friend, and the assistance of an attractive airline stewardess. While his English was still far from perfect, Kazan found in Stathis the perseverance he was seeking for the character of Stavros.[11] Of Stathis, Kazan later remarked: "He was the real thing. *America America* is my favorite film both despite the performance in its central role and because of it."[12]

With an unknown Greek in the title role and an international cast supplemented by Greek extras, Kazan might be able to keep production costs down, but financial backers usually preferred a more bankable cast. Recognizing the financial challenges of *America America*, Kazan wrote his attorney, H. William Fitelson, that he could make the film in Greece on a modest budget and that Fitelson should not worry about getting the director a half million dollar dividend spread over ten years. *America America* was going to be a film for the art houses in the United States, and Kazan did not care if he was not going to make a great deal of money on the film. He did not want financial guarantees to interfere with the artistic statement he wanted to make with *America America*. Kazan concluded, "I have enough money now—if I don't waste it or spend it or take to gambling or women and so on."[13]

While perhaps a little more interested in the dollar sign than this statement suggests, Kazan was on target that the major studios did not find *America America* a particularly commercial venture, perceiving Stavros to be an unattractive hero upon whom to hang the picture. Thus, United Artists, Columbia, Twentieth Century Fox, and Warner Bros. turned the film down. Seven Arts finally agreed to produce *America America* for roughly $1.5 million. The company usually focused on more commercial material, such as film adaptations of Broadway shows. Ray Stark, a former agent who presided over Seven Arts, wanted to expand the studio's reputation and establish a relationship with Kazan. However, Seven Arts and Stark got cold feet at the last minute and pulled the plug on the project. The biggest problem for Kazan was that when he received the phone call from his lawyer, William Fitelson, with the news that Stark was withdrawing from *America America*, the director and his crew were already in Istanbul. According to Kazan, the crew was in the hotel bar running up a significant tab, but he did not want to share the misfortune, so he ordered another round of drinks. Kazan got together with his assistant director, Charlie Maguire, and they were able to come up with enough cash and travelers' checks to cover the bar bill. The director, however, was uncertain about being able to pay for the hotel rooms. The situation was saved by William Fitelson, who reapproached Warner Bros., arguing that considering some of the fine pictures that Kazan had made for the company, they had an obligation to bail out their friend in this crisis. The studio reluctantly agreed, and *America America* was back in production. Kazan concluded: "Against their better judgment, they backed the picture, and of course their opinion was right. They lost a million and a half dollars on it!"[14]

In addition to his problems with financing for *America America*, Kazan was encountering problems with the Turkish officials. Kazan had to submit his script for approval by the Turkish Central Film Control Commission, and the director balked when they asked for changes in the film. The Turks were clearly concerned about their international image, especially regarding the early-twentieth-century genocide of Armenians, which the Turkish government continues to deny.[15] And the opening scenes of *America America* include the burning of an Armenian church, which the Turkish authorities wanted removed from the picture. Kazan complained that he could make the film in Greece and Yugoslavia without governmental interference. He also resented that as an artist he was being forced to answer to a committee, lamenting: "Can a committee paint a picture, chisel a piece of sculpture? The greatest sculptor of our day, Vigeland, offended his own country. Was Shakespeare a committee? Did someone tell Beethoven what theme to use? Or not to use a chorus at the end of the Ninth Symphony? Russia has killed its art, this way. Poor Pasternak!" Kazan denied that his film was political but pointed out that good art often offended someone. He concluded: "Is Turkey so small, so weak that a motion picture with a few critical views of the Turkey of 1896 can hurt it?"[16] It is interesting to note here that Kazan made no mention of censorship battles he waged in the United States over such films as *A Streetcar Named Desire* and *Baby Doll*. In addition, Kazan completely ignores the legacy of HUAC and the impact of the blacklist on Hollywood filmmaking.

Kazan essentially dealt with the Turkish objections by promising to make alterations that he would then conveniently ignore when shooting. However, Turkish surveillance of the filmmaking was more intrusive than the director anticipated. The government assigned a bureaucrat to supervise all shooting in the streets of Istanbul in order to assure that there was no departure from the script or negative depictions of Turkish daily life. For example, Kazan complained in a letter to Molly that the bureaucrat insisted that all costumes must be kept clean, even when filming some of the squalor in which the *hamals* at the port worked and lived. Nevertheless, Kazan believed that he was beginning to charm the terrified bureaucrat, who was scared of his superiors. On the fifth day of shooting in Istanbul, Kazan and his crew were filming scenes of haggling in the bazaar when the secret police showed up and terminated the shoot while removing the censor with whom Kazan had formed a relationship. At this point, Kazan determined that the situation in Istanbul was becoming untenable and perhaps even dangerous.[17]

Nevertheless, Kazan was still somewhat reluctant to depart Istanbul, but he was prevailed upon by Charlie Maguire, who argued that it was essential to leave Istanbul and commence filming in Greece. Maguire said that it would be possible to smuggle the Turkish footage out of the country by placing the completed reels in boxes marked "raw stock." The plan worked, but Kazan still believed something was lost in the abrupt departure from Turkey. Speaking of Istanbul, Kazan wrote in his autobiography:

> In that extraordinary city, I had before my camera the rotting hulk of the civilization from which my hero was to escape and from which my father had freed me. We'd never find its like again—not the harbor, not the streets, not the mosques, not the people's faces. Where would I find extras like these again? And quite as important was the effect of the place upon me; as it was a source of fear, it was a source of inspiration. The very force that drove my hero west was the one I experienced every day as I walked the streets; I was a foreigner who feared his surroundings. I still felt what my hero felt: I've got to get out of here alive.[18]

Kazan's biographer Richard Schickel believed that the director's fears regarding the Turkish authorities were crucial to understanding the filmmaker, who told Schickel that *America America* "tells more about me than I care to say." The biographer speculated that the insecurity of an outsider perhaps also revealed "something about what motivated his HUAC testimony."[19]

After relocating to Greece, Kazan was free from government censorship, but problems with *America America* continued to plague the director, as he acknowledged in letters to Molly. On October 22, 1962, Kazan complained that he was not enjoying making *America America* as the script was too long and it was difficult working with an amateur in the title role. He confided to Molly: "I'm not the innocent, confident, cocky boy of 35 that I was during *Gentleman's Agreement* and *Boomerang*. I know too much to be simply and purely happy about anything. And I always have the feeling that I'm somehow falling a little short of what I should be doing."[20] He promised his wife that he would produce a better film and script with his next project. On November 15, he followed up with another letter to Molly explaining that the filming was taking longer than expected and he would not be home before Thanksgiving. He complained about the cameraman and crew, but he acknowledged that he accepted primary blame for the delays, writing: "The script, as I have explained, is deceptive. It's much much longer than it seems. And much longer to shoot, with constant locale moves, which are the things that take the time." In addition, he was "always covering for Stathis's inadequacies. Remember the days when I had real good actors. Today I'm hitting the bottom of the barrel." And money was also a consideration. Kazan observed that he still needed to shoot the important Ellis Island footage of Stavros's arrival in America. It would be far cheaper to prepare the scenes with four hundred extras at a Greek customs house. In the United States, the extras would cost $15,000 a day, while in Greece the expense would be approximately $2,000 per day and they would have a look of desperation that one could not get in America. Accordingly, Kazan would not be home for Thanksgiving dinner, but he asked Molly to save him some "plain white meat of turkey, chestnut stuffing, cranberry sauce, and white dry wine," for he was tired of "olive oil, butter, and greasy meat."[21]

Before the end of November, Kazan was back in the United States and quarreling with his cameraman Haskell "Pete" Wexler, who as a member of the political left remained critical of Kazan's HUAC testimony. Nevertheless, Wexler admired Kazan's artistry and hoped to learn from the filmmaker. But as filming for *America America* was concluding, Wexler angered the director by telling him that he never liked the script. An angry Kazan exploded:

> Apparently you don't feel that it's odd for a cameraman to accept an
> assignment to photograph a script that he doesn't like. I think it is
> unethical. It's beyond my understanding that one sensitive man would
> do that to another. There are few professional relationships as intimate
> as that between a cameraman and director. I had to walk on my set for
> four months and face a cameraman who didn't like the script he was
> photographing and who was artistically scornful of my work in gener-
> al.[22]

Kazan cooled off a bit after reviewing Wexler's work, conceding that in
most cases the cameraman's material was excellent and captured Kazan's
vision. The director also acknowledged that he learned how to employ the
handheld camera from Wexler. As for Wexler, who would later earn
Academy Awards for his cinematography and direct his own films, he
told Richard Schickel that *America America* was "one of the highest
points of my life" due to the intensity that Kazan brought to this family
history project. Wexler described Kazan as "possessed," concluding:
"Nothing would stop him. You say, 'Jesus Christ, the guy's over the top.'
But he gave off a kind of electricity, an excitement about the story. And
when someone stays in that mood consistently you say, 'Well, he believes.'"[23]

Despite all the tribulations with the making of *America America*, Kazan was proud of the film but disappointed that Molly found fault with
the finished product. After screening a rough cut of the film, she prepared
a five-page, single-spaced critique that Kazan compared to a Supreme
Court ruling. According to Kazan, she found the film difficult to follow
and urged changes that could no longer be incorporated into the picture.
Molly told her husband that the film did not live up to the promise of the
novel, in which she had some proprietary interest with revising and publishing. Kazan responded by saying he would think about her suggestions. However, he probably displayed more honesty in his autobiography, admitting: "I'd admired her critical candor when it was directed at
others, but when I was the target, it made me furious and alienated. I
wasn't allowed to forget her points; however, she constantly worried me
about them—she loved the book that much, she said. So I crawled into
my cave of silence and never again showed her the film."[24]

Nevertheless, Kazan still believed in *America America*, and in a note
written before the film's release, he proclaimed his faith in the American
dream. He wrote:

> Like it or not we are a dream. People hate us as well as love us. They point to our shortcomings and to the limitations of our "gadget culture," scoff and scorn, often with weight and some reason. But we are still a dream. We were in 1896 when my family came here looking for something. And we are now. Thousands and thousands still leave the stone mountains of Greece and the hot plateaus of Turkey in Asia. They go to Australia and they go to Germany. But if they are lucky, they manage to get here. This is still the dream they choose if they can choose.[25]

Film audiences, however, appeared to agree with Molly's evaluation of *America America*. The picture fared poorly at the box office, and many critics, in agreement with studio heads who turned down the film, believed that filmgoers could not perceive Stavros as a hero due to the crimes and compromises he committed to reach his destination of America. And in retrospect, Kazan became more critical of an American culture and capitalism that destroyed the morals and traditions of so many striving to achieve the American dream.

America America begins with a brief narration from Kazan, asserting, "I am a Greek by blood, a Turk by birth, and an American because my uncle made a journey."[26] The film then flashes back to 1896 and introduces us to a young Greek man, Stavros Topouzoglou (Stathis Giallelis), who works with his Armenian friend, Vartan Damadian (Frank Wolff), delivering ice. The two young men share a common dream of moving to America, where they will become wealthy. Their desire to migrate is also fostered by oppression from the Turkish authorities in Anatolia, where the Greeks and Armenians live as subject populations. Stavros's family fears the Turks and do not want their son associating with Vartan. Stavros, however, goes out with his friend for an evening on the town, during which the Turkish forces attack the Armenians. In a scene that certainly offended the Turks, who continue to deny the Armenian genocide, Vartan is killed while the young Armenian's friends and family are burned alive inside a church. When Stavros attempts to recover the body of Vartan, he is arrested by the Turkish authorities.

The next day, Stavros's father, Isaac (Harry Davis), a local merchant, pleads for his son's release, pledging his loyalty and kissing the ring of the Turkish governor. This act of submission angers Stavros, who flees into the mountains after his release. He visits his grandmother and begs her for money that would allow him an escape to Constantinople, where he could work and earn money for a voyage to the promised land of America. The grandmother complains about the cowardice of the Greeks and provides him with a knife, reminding Stavros that "no sheep ever saved its neck by bleating." However, she will not provide him with the money hidden beneath her clothes. He considers killing the old woman for the treasure, but Stavros is not yet that desperate. After fleeing his grandmother, Stavros encounters a young Armenian boy, Hohanness Gardashian (Gregory Rozakis), who also shares the American dream. Remembering what happened to his Armenian friend, Vartan, Stavros gives the barefoot refugee his shoes. It is an act of charity that will later be repaid with great sacrifice.

Stavros reluctantly returns home, where his father has a plan to save the family. Isaac knows that Stavros is disappointed with him for cooperating with the Turks, but it was a strategy for survival, as the father explained, "I've always kept my honor safe inside me." This was the tactic of the Anatolian smile that Kazan often assumed. Yet with Turkish oppression growing, Isaac is convinced that it is time to demonstrate greater initiative. The family has money and valuables buried under the floor of their dwelling. The family fortune is entrusted to the eldest son, Stavros, who takes everything of value with him to Constantinople, where he will meet a cousin, Odysseus (Salem Ludwig), who is a rug merchant.

As Stavros travels, leading a donkey with the family fortune attached, he is befriended by a Turkish man named Abdul (Lou Antonio), who claims that he wants to help Stavros protect his possessions. However, Abdul asserts that it is only proper that Stavros share his food and money with his "brother." Abdul is a confident man who tends to remind one of the King and Duke in *The Adventures of Huckleberry Finn* who prey upon the innocent Huck and Jim. When Stavros decides to abandon Abdul, the unscrupulous man denounces Stavros as a thief, and the local government officials confiscate what is left of the family fortune, with the exception of a few coins, which Stavros is able to swallow. Abdul, however, is not done with his exploitation of Stavros. When Stavros is released from custody by the local government, Abdul is waiting for him, informing Stavros that he will murder him after the young man passes the coins he ingested. A stoic Stavros waits until Abdul kneels for his daily prayers, and then he employs his grandmother's knife to kill the man who has threatened his dreams. Although he has lost most of the family treasure, Stavros has just enough money to continue his journey toward Constantinople.

After reaching the city, he finds his cousin Odysseus, who is disappointed that the boy no longer has any money. However, he puts Stavros to work sweeping the floors of the merchant's store, and Odysseus begins to hatch a scheme for marrying Stavros to the daughter of a wealthy businessman. Stavros balks at the plans, which would imprison him in a marriage and prevent him from achieving his ultimate plan of reaching America. He runs away from his cousin's shop and becomes a street urchin struggling to survive. When he sees one of the *hamals*, the human beasts of burden who worked on the docks of Constantinople, collapse, Stavros springs into action to replace the fallen man. Stavros now labors by day as a *hamal*, and at night he washes dishes for a restaurant while living in a hovel and often eating discarded food. But for all his hard work and thrift, in the tradition of Benjamin Franklin's self-made man, it is simply impossible for him to earn enough money to book his passage for America. He is befriended by an older man, Garabet (John Marley), an anarchist who explains to Stavros that he will never be able to succeed within an exploitive capitalist system. The only way to survive in such a society is to steal or overthrow the system. To drive his point home, Garabet takes the innocent Stavros to a prostitute who proceeds to steal his money. He confronts the young woman and realizes that she is as desperate as he. Stavros begins to attend political meetings organized by Garabet in which there is discussion of revolution and the creation of a better world. However, the Turkish authorities attack the anarchists, killing Garabet and wounding Stavros, who is placed in a wagon of corpses to be dumped into the sea. Stavros is able to escape from the wagon, and, swallowing his pride, he returns to the house of his cousin.

Considering Kazan's own history with radical politics in the Communist Party, the depiction of Garabet and anarchism is relatively positive. Responding to the suggestion of Michel Ciment that Vartan the Armenian represented nationalism and Garabet socialist struggle, Kazan asserted:

> There was no outlet for the feeling of anger and rebellion and dislocation in a young man through the means of nationalism; this revolt was crushed immediately, the nationalists being completely outnumbered, terrorized, slaughtered on suspicion. Education was kept from them. The authorities saw to it that they only got to the eighth grade. Nor was there any outlet through anarchism—Garabet represents anarchism,

not socialism—propaganda through deeds, protests, bombing. There were bombings in the streets of Istanbul, but very little programme. It was also squashed without mercy, it had no chance; it had no organization. The young man in the film sees that.[27]

Kazan makes no allusions to his political experience, but it is interesting to speculate whether Kazan somewhat identified with Stavros. He grew disillusioned with the Communist Party and feared the government crackdown that came with McCarthyism, but he still maintained support for many of the progressive principles endorsed by the party. Fear was always a motivating factor for Kazan, and did he, similar to Stavros, decide that to survive it would be necessary to compromise and betray many of those who believed in him?

After rejecting radical politics, we next see Stavros as a well-dressed young merchant for whom his cousin is arranging a marriage to the wealthy family of Aleko Sinnikoglou (Paul Mann). His daughter Thomna is a rather plain young woman, and Stavros is able to negotiate a rather lucrative dowry. The father also surprises the couple with a handsome apartment for them after the marriage. Stavros has now achieved economic security, and Mr. Sinnikoglou tells him that he will eventually be able to retire on a Greek island, where he would be surrounded by grandchildren and grow fat on his wife's cooking. The dream of America, however, still burns brightly for Stavros, and he warns his fiancée not to trust him. Thomna loves Stavros and hopes that her devotion will be able to quash the yearning for America. Despite all her efforts, Stavros will betray her with an adulterous affair that offers the promise of a new life in America.

While working in the carpet store, Stavros is introduced to a wealthy American couple who come annually to Constantinople for the purchase of carpets. Mrs. Sophia Kebabian (Katharine Balfour) is considerably younger than her husband, Aratoon Kebabian (Robert H. Harris), and she is obviously quite bored with business conversations. Stavros offers to escort her back to her hotel while his cousin and Mr. Kebabian complete their negotiations. He spends the afternoon enthralled with magazines about America and stays for dinner. That evening, Stavros accompanies the couple for a sampling of Constantinople's night life, but when Mr. Kebabian falls asleep, Stavros and Mrs. Kebabian seize the opportunity to commence an affair. Mrs. Kebabian agrees to pay for his passage to America if he will accompany the Kebabians on their voyage home and secretly serve as her lover during the journey. As he rushes to buy his ticket, Stavros meets the Armenian to whom he once gave his shoes. Hohanness is obviously suffering from consumption with his constant cough, but he is thrilled to be traveling to America with seven other young men who have been recruited to shine shoes in the promised land.

Before he embarks, however, Stavros tells Thomna of his treachery. He acknowledges that he has done many terrible things to pursue his dream, but Stavros informs Thomna, "In America, I will be washed clean." Thomna loves Stavros and sadly accepts his betrayal. When Ciment mentioned that adultery was a key theme in *America America*, Kazan seemed somewhat uncomfortable, certainly recalling his own relationship with Molly. Kazan mentioned that he was brought up to believe that adultery was a sin, but his experience in life left him with more ambivalent views on the subject. The filmmaker confessed: "I'm both very moral and very unrestrained. I don't think anything is a sin, abstractly. It depends on whom you hurt and how much. Sometimes it's necessary. I think hurting other people is bad, but I don't think you can go through life without hurting other people. All you can do is hurt them as little as you can, or not hurt them if you can possibly help it."[28] These sentiments are similar to those Kazan often expressed to Molly, who seemed often to find herself in the role of Thomna Sinnikoglou.

Although Stavros did not have first-class accommodations aboard the ship, he visited Mrs. Kebabian in her stateroom while her husband slept in the adjoining apartment. Shortly before the ship docks in America, Mr. Kebabian discovers the affair. Feeling betrayed, Mr. Kebabian announces that he is withdrawing a job offer to Stavros, who will now be sent back to Turkey. He asks Stavros if the young man has no sense of honor, to which Stavros replies, "My honor is safe inside me." Wanting to maintain her economic security, Mrs. Kebabian does not intervene on behalf of Stavros, although she does slip him some money and a straw hat.

Meanwhile, Stavros attempts to help his ailing friend Hohanness with passing his medical inspection before disembarking. Hohanness initially passes the test, but following a coughing episode, permission to leave the ship is denied. Stavros, even though he cannot swim, plans to dive into the ocean and make an effort to reach the shore. To thwart this deadly strategy, Hohanness decides to repay Stavros for the kindness he once displayed in giving a stranger the shoes off his feet. The young Armenian leaps overboard to his death, allowing the healthy Stavros to assume his place among the other shoeshine boys. Stavros makes it through the immigration process at Ellis Island, but officials change his name to the more Americanized Joe Arness. Stepping onto the shore, Stavros solemnly falls to his knees and kisses the sacred American soil. Many critics found the scene overly emotional and romanticized. Kazan, however, always defended the shot, telling Jeff Young: "I wouldn't take it out for the world. It actually happened. Believe me, if a Turk could get out of Turkey and come here, even now, he would kiss the ground. To oppressed people, America is still a dream."[29] And besides, it was one of the few parts in *America America* that Molly really liked.[30]

The film concludes with Joe Arness at a shoeshine stand where he is earning money. We see a shot of his family reading a letter from their son and brother, which also contains $50 for them to begin their journey to America. Joe is shown flipping a quarter in the air, urging everyone to come on up. Certainly he is promoting his business, but the call is also for immigrants to line up for the promised land. Kazan then provides a brief narration, explaining that the other members of his family would eventually make it to America, with the exception of his grandfather, who died in the land where he was born. Kazan was quite proud of this most personal of films, but it failed to find an audience despite earning Academy Award nominations for Best Picture, Director, and Screenplay.

Critical response was divided, with those reviewers who disliked the film discovering little heroism in the actions of Stavros. Although Kazan promoted the film with patriotic proclamations about the American dream, some critics found *America America* to be a more derogatory depiction of how the materialism of America failed immigrants. *America America* was also a victim of larger forces beyond the control of a filmmaker. Shortly after the film's premiere, President John F. Kennedy was assassinated in Dallas, Texas, on November 22, 1963. Americans were not in the mood for a serious film that raised challenging questions about the nature of the American dream. In looking back at the immigrant experience of the early twentieth century, the film seemed retrogressive for film viewers. The Oscars that year were swept by the bawdy British comedy *Tom Jones*, and Kazan's film was forgotten.[31]

The mixed reception given *America America* by critics is perhaps best exemplified in the statement of Joan Didion: "*America America* is massively repetitive, insistently obvious, almost interminable, and, perhaps in spite of itself, immensely, miraculously moving."[32] Bosley Crowther of the *New York Times* believed the film was too long, but overall the critic described *America America* as "not only a tribute but also a singing ode to the whole great surging, immigrant wave."[33]

Other reviews were even more enthusiastic. Hollis Alpert of *Saturday Review* credited Kazan with reminding Americans that there was much more to the nation than the conformity of middle-class suburbia. Praising Kazan for his emphasis on the immigrant roots of America, Alpert wrote, "In a more general sense, Kazan has taken the theme of immigration, and developed through this one instance the yearnings, the drives, the will of millions from other places who managed to reach the United States, and whose descendants are still forging its character."[34] *Newsweek* lauded *America America* as one of the best films of the year and agreed with Alpert that it was about time that American filmmakers discovered the nation's immigrant experience. Celebrating Kazan for employing his "extravagant emotional power" to tell the story of his family, *Newsweek* concluded: "And a certain amount of nerve is required; any honest recollection of the dreams of our forefathers is a disturbing experience, for few of us have deserved the sacrifices they made, and fewer still have lived up to the idealistic ardor of their dreams."[35] *Life* was a little lighter in its praise for the film, crediting Kazan for discovering Stathis and providing "a poignant, harrowing and even exhaustive narrative." The popular magazine noted: "But admirers of Kazan can be grateful that the real-life Avraam made the trip and later brought over most of his family one by one. Had he not, Elia Kazan might today be selling rugs in a Turkish bazaar."[36]

Other critics, however, were quite harsh in their reviews of the film. *Time* described *America America* as one of the "more disappointing films" of 1963. The film was panned for its amateur cast, poor dubbing, and a screenplay that was overly theatrical. But *Time* asserted that the most serious problem with the film was the character of Stavros, observing: "The fault is that the slow hardening and corruption of character never becomes organic drama. Whatever he does, Stavros remains Horatio Alger in Constantinople, and the narrative lacks conviction."[37] Pauline Kael of the *New Yorker* also had little positive to say about Kazan's personal cinema. The caustic critic proclaimed that *America America* was "a flabby, overambitious epic, and an epic size failure."[38] Henry Hart of *Films in Review* continued to question Kazan's politics, perceiving *America America* as another of the director's progressive attacks on the United

States and its institutions. Hart complained: "It is about time Elia Kazan stopped biting the hand that has fed him (very well), and devoted his directorial talents to films and plays which exalt, rather than denigrate, American life. *America America* is a beginning. May he put into his next film the things he has been saying in the publicity for *America America*, but which he did not put explicitly into this film itself."[39]

A less polemic and more nuanced critique was incorporated into a review of the film for the *Harvard Crimson* by Eugene E. Leach. Noting that Kazan did a good job of depicting the oppression that drove Stavros from Turkey, Leach argues that the director failed to adequately explain why America offered such hope for the young man. Leach complains that Stavros seemed almost entirely motivated by the dollar sign and has committed so many atrocities to attain financial security: "He has alienated all sympathy when, upon landing in New York harbor, he kisses the dock; one almost wishes that he would get a sliver in his lip."[40] While he originally promoted *America America* as a patriotic cinematic poem to the promise of America, in later interviews Kazan conceded that capitalism had taken its toll on Stavros and Kazan's own family. Joe Kazan, the director's uncle upon whom Stavros was based, did become quite successful in the United States, but he was virtually destroyed by the Depression and became a cynic. Speaking with Ciment, Kazan observed that Stavros's experience also fostered cynicism. There was a great price to be paid for pursuing the American dream. Kazan observed:

> The last thing I show Stavros doing in *America America* is, he gets a quarter tip, throws it up in the air and catches it. You feel he understands what America is. In order to get to America, you have to be tough, you have to go for the money, you have to protect yourself. If your back is to the wall you have to use any means to protect your life. And it's either him or me in capitalism, right? Capitalism is a jungle, right? And it's either he dies or I die, in the jungle, right? That's actually what he felt. That was the lesson of life to him.[41]

This was a heavy dose of cynicism for film audiences in the dark aftermath of the Kennedy assassination, and *America America* failed to resonate with filmgoers. In addition to this artistic and commercial disappointment, Kazan suffered a major personal tragedy in late 1963. Distraught over the death of President Kennedy, Molly Kazan wrote a poem, published in the *Herald Tribune*, eulogizing the fallen leader. Less than a

week later, Molly died, on December 14, 1963, from a cerebral hemorrhage. The usually loquacious Kazan was terse in his comments at Molly's memorial, stating: "This immaculate girl was struck down without
warning, cause or reason, lived without hope of survival for twenty hours,
after which her heart stopped. She was not a member of any church. If she
had any religion, it was the truth, telling it at any cost. She mothered four
fine children, helped playwrights, who are here to acknowledge her support, helped me in everything I did for thirty-one years. She leaves her
own monument."[42]

Following the death of Molly, Kazan went into a period of depression,
while professionally his plans for *America America* to be the first of three
films on the history of his family was thwarted by the commercial failure
of the film. He essentially abandoned his stage and screen endeavors to
pursue a career as a novelist. Kazan, however, never quite seemed to
abandon his dream of making sequels to *America America*. In May 1982,
Kazan was telling Budd Schulberg that he viewed his soon-to-be published novel *The Anatolian* as a sequel to *America America*, and he hoped
to make a film of the novel. Two years later, Kazan told his daughter
Katharine that he was considering going to Turkey to complete his book
Beyond the Aegean, which he also hoped to film as part of the Kazan
family saga. These novels enjoyed modest sales, and they were never
transformed into films.[43]

In 1967, however, Kazan published the semiautobiographical novel
The Arrangement, which was a best seller with over three million copies
in print. In this novel, Kazan's protagonist, Eddie Anderson, rebels
against the conformity of the American dream with a lucrative career in
advertising, which he finds boring, and a loving wife and beautiful home,
which he finds stifling. He seeks to escape the straitjacket of American
capitalism with the aid of a young lover and pursue his passion for writing. Kazan also attempted to resurrect his film career by directing the
adaptation of his novel. While the book was a financial success, the film,
released in 1969, did not fare as well. Kazan believed that his film, which
was autobiographical in its values but not in its details, was a challenge to
the conformity and hypocrisy of middle-class America, which audiences
and critics did not want to confront and recognize in their daily lives. *The
Arrangement* continues the ambivalent personal filmmaking of *America
America*. Kazan told Ciment that during the course of the film, he increasingly identified with Stavros and gradually turned the film "into a

story about myself. I play out the same struggles I've always had: the struggle to find my own dignity, my own self, the struggle to impress other people, the struggle to be rich, and the struggle to remain honest. I always oppose money and purity; I always think, if a person is rich he must be a bastard. Maybe that's from my communist days, maybe it's religious."[44] The ethnicity of Stavros made it possible for many viewers to place some distance between themselves and the protagonist; however, Eddie Anderson was a product of suburbia and a conformist, consumer, capitalist society. Certainly his struggle hit closer to home with many Americans—perhaps exposing their own questions about the validity of the American dream. If Eddie Anderson was Kazan and represented the political, personal, and professional struggles of the filmmaker, it was evident that many viewers were uncomfortable in acknowledging identification with the ambivalence of Kazan and his alter ego displayed on the silver screen.

10

REBELLING AGAINST THE ARRANGED LIFE

The Arrangement (1969)

Following the death of Molly Day Thacher Kazan and the failure of *America America* to find an audience, Elia Kazan went into a period of depression. Although his production of Arthur Miller's *After the Fall* was lauded and earned a Tony Award for Barbara Loden in the Marilyn Monroe role, Kazan was dissatisfied with his position as codirector with Robert Whitehead of the Repertory Theatre of Lincoln Center. Following the poor reception of *The Changeling* in 1965, Kazan resigned as artistic director and announced his retirement from the theater. He entered psychoanalysis and traveled widely, finally settling in Paris, where he wrote *The Arrangement*, an autobiographical novel that became a surprise best seller in 1967. In his personal life, Kazan continued to see other women in addition to Barbara Loden, whom he married in 1967. The plans for a sequel to *America America* were placed on hold following the film's poor showing at the box office, but the commercial success of his novel led Hollywood to express renewed interest in the filmmaker, and Warner Bros. offered Kazan the opportunity to direct the cinematic adaptation of *The Arrangement*.

With its many autobiographical elements, *The Arrangement* was in many ways a sequel to *America America*. Kazan's protagonist, Eddie Anderson, seems to have achieved the American dream. The son of Greek immigrants, he is a successful advertising executive in Los Angeles with a respected side career as an investigative journalist. Eddie has a beautiful home and a wife who dotes on him, but he also pursues numerous affairs. As he becomes increasingly drawn into a relationship with Gwen Hunt, he realizes how disenchanted he is with a life in pursuit of the almighty dollar. Recognizing that he has no sense of who he really is and what he really wants, Eddie attempts to commit suicide and rejects his comfortable upper-middle-class existence. Although the film seems to fit well with the antiestablishment themes of American cinema in the late 1960s, *The Arrangement* was another commercial failure for Kazan as a director. Kazan believed that if he had been able to secure Marlon Brando to play Eddie, rather than Kirk Douglas, film audiences might have been better able to identify with the suffering of the protagonist. The director was also convinced that middle-class audiences were uncomfortable with a film that challenged the hypocrisy of their lives. As for younger audiences, they were drawn to the search for America symbolized by two young hippies on their way to Mardi Gras in the box office smash *Easy Rider* (1969). *The Arrangement* to them seemed more like a middle-age crisis rather than a questioning of the American dream—all booze and no hallucinogenics. Nevertheless, Kazan continued to believe in the picture, asserting: "The film was better than the critics believed it to be but again not conforming to my original vision. Although the book continued to sell—and still does—this film was another financial disaster. I recommend it to you."[1]

Although Kazan initially dismissed descriptions of the film as autobiographical, it clearly referenced the most important personal relationships in the filmmaker's life, even if some details from Eddie Anderson's life were different from those of the director's. Kazan told Michel Ciment: "I wrote about my mother, my father, my youth, elements in my own life. What helped me most was my psychoanalysis, because I'd been psychoanalyzed into articulation, into wishing to speak. It was the most helpful thing that ever happened; the whole thing of just talking. Slowly after about three months, it began to be a story. Then I wrote the book."[2] It is interesting to note that in this interview, Kazan failed to mention Molly Thacher, upon whom the character of Florence Anderson was based, as well as Gwen Hunt, the girlfriend whose inspiration was Barbara Loden. In fact, after completing the novel, Kazan sent copies to his publisher Sol Stein, his psychoanalyst, and Loden, who resented the violation of her privacy.[3] The filmmaker asserted that his greatest failure in life was that he had sacrificed what he wanted to please others—whether it was his father, mother, friends, Molly, studio heads in Hollywood, and perhaps even HUAC, although he does not directly mention informing. Kazan concluded that he should have been more selfish and honest in his life and work.

Nevertheless, Kazan found the writing process to be therapeutic and liberating—but he remained unapologetic. The director turned writer was not about to apologize for his many sexual infidelities, writing in his autobiography:

> Infidelity had saved my life, or that part of my life I most valued. This was drawn not only from my own experience but from that of other men and women I'd known. It accounts, I believe, for the extraordinary popularity the book was to have—most surprisingly—among women. The fact that so many women identified with my male hero, felt as he did, and even walked out of their marriages, which they'd found to be restrictive as he had found his, can't be explained any other way. My hero spoke for them.[4]

Kazan found his voice while writing in Paris, concluding: "Since that day the question has never been whether or not I am a brilliant writer. I know I'm not. But that has been the point of what I am doing. I carry my own memory rod with me, and by that I am a success. In a world where everyone is trying—as I had for so many years—to please someone else—a boss, an ideology, a mate, a leader, a critic, a backer—I had finally found a way of living by pleasing only myself."[5] Describing the writing process, Kazan told Haskel Frankel of the *Saturday Review* that he had more pleasure in writing *The Arrangement* "than anything else I've ever done." Kazan wrapped up his interview with Frankel by remarking: "I feel as if I am starting all over again—with exhilaration, new power. That wonderful feeling of gee, I have a voice and I can make it heard."[6]

These celebrations of the independence he found in writing did not mean that Kazan was totally unconcerned with the novel's reception. In a letter to daughter Judy Kazan, the budding novelist spoke of the contract negotiations his attorney was pursuing with various publishers, observing that he could get more money from Random House and Dell, but he felt a certain loyalty to Stein for publishing *America America*, "and I wouldn't have a guilty feeling of having by-passed a man who had once done me some good." He concluded by telling Judy that he was rather enjoying the entire negotiating process.[7] As usual, editing was a painful process, and publisher Sol Stein helped Kazan cut his lengthy manuscript in half, but the novel was still a hefty five-hundred-page volume.[8] Kazan was both surprised and delighted when *The Arrangement* became the number one book on the *New York Times* Best Seller list in March 1967 and remained in the top ten for thirty-seven weeks. Kazan was also delighted with a reception in New York City's Brentano's Bookstore, where the filmmaker was reunited with his authors—Tennessee Williams, Budd Schulberg, and Arthur Miller. Kazan related: "The most generous of them, as ever, was Tennessee. I doubt that Miller ever read the book, if he has, he's never mentioned it to me. But he was affable and cordial, if a bit bewildered. He'd never thought of me as an author."[9]

The reviews of the novel were rather mixed, with some critics dismissing the book as another sexually exploitive novel in the tradition of Harold Robbins, author of *The Carpetbaggers* (1961). For example, Eliot Fremont-Smith of the *New York Times* quipped: "The best thing about the novel is its rollicking zest, Mr. Kazan never tires. The worst thing is that he doesn't." Fremont-Smith found *The Arrangement* excessive, with Kazan simply attempting to do too much with both literary devices and action. The reviewer concluded: "It is chock-full of action, sex, punchy set-piecing, yards of conversation, all in a sort of amalgam of the styles of Norman Mailer, Hemingway, and Harold Robbins—and it, too, should have few commercial worries."[10] *Time* magazine was even more critical of the novel, calling *The Arrangement* "a muddled, massive mistake."[11]

Other reviews were a bit more evenhanded. Writing in the *Saturday Review*, Granville Hicks argued that if Kazan "has proved to be less than a master of the form he has adopted, he has at least shown an awareness of the novel's possibilities of this age." The esteemed critic even found some parts of the book to be "excellent," but he concluded that the major fault of the book was its lack of originality. Feelings of discontent that one abandoned personal desires in favor of pursuing the American dollar were not uncommon, and Hicks lamented that Kazan failed to pose his questions "in some fresh way that might give us a new insight."[12] A review in the *Times Literary Supplement* agreed with the arguments set forth by Hicks, asserting that *The Arrangement* was typical fiction for the sons of immigrants with themes of assimilation and betrayal. Kazan had

little new to offer in addressing these issues, which were "mere parenthe-
ses within this strenuous, energetic, but trite fiction."[13]

The most effusive review of *The Arrangement* was penned by Eleanor
Perry in *Life* magazine. Perry provided a positive depiction of the novelist's protagonist, writing: "One may disapprove of Eddie Anderson. His
whole life is a series of phony arrangements: his marriage, his work, his
sexual escapades, his friendships. But nobody can deny his humanity. . . .
By the end of the book he has achieved what is most needed on this shaky
planet—a new working model of a human being. This is a novel to
change your life by."[14] Perry's high words of praise were employed to
publicize the novel, but the review that meant the most to Kazan was by
his friend James Baldwin in the *New York Review of Books*.

The African American novelist and political activist was a correspon-
dent with Kazan, who was advising Baldwin on a screenplay he was
developing on the life of Malcolm X. In a letter to Baldwin, Kazan
complained that he was prostituting himself to promote *The Arrangement*, while major newspapers assigned reviews of the book to writers
who were critics of Kazan's work and politics.[15] The *New York Review of
Books*, however, gave the book to Baldwin, who provided a generally
favorable commentary on *The Arrangement*. Baldwin found Kazan's
novel difficult to describe, asserting that the book was "terribly naked"
and "uncomfortably direct" with "a certain raw gracelessness," as Kazan
tried to address "the chasm we experience in life between what one
wished to become and what one has become." Rather than writing a
novel, Baldwin perceived Kazan as talking to his readers; however, the
critic concluded that the filmmaker turned novelist had an important message to convey. Baldwin wrote:

> He is trying to tell us something, and not only for his sake—for, then,
> *The Arrangement* would be nothing more than an unexpected and as-
> serting tour de force from an emotional man of the theater—but also
> for ours. The tone of the book is extremely striking, for it really does
> not seem to depend on anything that we think of as a literary tradition,
> but on something older than that: the tale being told by a member of
> the tribe to the tribe. It has the urgency of a confession and the stam-
> mering authority of a plea.[16]

The message that Kazan was attempting to deliver to the tribe is that
we have allowed our dreams and desires to be sacrificed on the altar of

commerce. Kazan and his protagonist Eddie Anderson saw this in the tragedy of their immigrant fathers, who sacrificed everything in the pursuit of the American dream. Eddie denounces his successful advertising career and comfortable marriage to embark upon a voyage of self-discovery. Of course, he is considered to be crazy for doing this and ends up institutionalized. In a passage that conveys Kazan's message, Eddie tells one of his doctors: "All this talk about our Christian civilization. We have a business civilization. The idea is not to love your brother but to get the better of him, and do it so there won't be any blood to wash off your hands in public. Everybody knows that's the way it is. But we live in pretense. The pretense and the facts, and the gulf in between is getting bigger every year. Well, I've stopped pretending, and you'd be amazed how much that eliminates of what a person usually does all day."[17]

Despite the denunciation of a capitalist civilization where everyone must become a salesman to survive, Kazan was unable to practice what he preached, and he was drawn back into the Hollywood system and seduced by the almighty dollar. In an interview with Jeff Young, Kazan conceded that like Eddie following a career in advertising, he sold out when he agreed to make *The Arrangement* for Warner Bros.[18] In a lecture titled "The Cinema in America," delivered at Wesleyan University on May 7, 1971, Kazan outlined the story of how *The Arrangement* was sabotaged by the pursuit of wealth. Kazan related that the reception of *The Arrangement* convinced him that he now had the freedom to pursue a second career as a writer, in which he could exercise greater independence. However, when the carrot of a generous financial deal spread over ten years was offered by Warner Bros., Kazan agreed to direct his novel for the screen. Seeking to explain his actions, Kazan asserted:

> A living in the performance arts is precarious, tenure (you've heard that word before), tenure is uncertain, cost of living, children, a second wife, a second family, love of travel, books, country living, all, all come very, very high. And there was the oldest dread I had: that I might sometime be forced to do work I abominated just to pay the bills. I've done my share of poor work, but not for those reasons. Besides I still loved films, wanted to make more and now—one of my own! Why not?[19]

The seduction of Kazan was underway as the high purchase price paid for the novel ensured that the film would be a big-budget production.

Kazan would be unable to rely on the unknowns he liked to cast. He tried to obtain Brando, whom the studio now found untenable, and Barbara Loden, but Kazan ended up with Kirk Douglas and Faye Dunaway, coming off her acclaim for *Bonnie and Clyde* (1968). Production costs were high as the studio sought to protect its large investment. Time was of the essence, and there was simply little opportunity for rehearsals or experimentation. According to Kazan, what was lost in the film was a sense of modesty, as the director explained: "The scale of human affairs, the small area of the single human psyche. That was being swamped, the privacy of private problems. In short, the scale of humanity." He had written a book to disturb people and cause them to question the compromises made in their lives, but Hollywood wanted a film that offended no one and entertained a mass audience. Although Kazan still found much to admire in the cinematic adaptation of *The Arrangement*, he believed that he had compromised too much. He told his university audience: "I was far out on the wrong road. I had to face that I had someway betrayed myself. I made a discovery—that money is the root of all evil. Not original with me? Right! We keep learning the same lesson over and over."[20]

Despite being unable to fully implement the ideas outlined in his novel, making the filming of *The Arrangement* somewhat of an American tragedy in its own right, Kazan believed that Marlon Brando might have saved the film, and he made a considerable effort to recruit the actor for his cinematic adaptation of the novel. Kazan met with Brando and gave him a copy of the book. After reading the novel, the actor was not sure that he was right for the part, but he might be willing to take "a stab at it." To dissuade the director from pursuing Brando, Warner Bros. had Kazan screen the actor's performances in Charlie Chaplin's *A Countess from Hong Kong* (1967) and John Huston's *Reflections in a Golden Eye* (1967). Kazan found Brando's acting in *A Countess from Hong Kong* to reflect the thespian's growing disenchantment with his profession. Nevertheless, Kazan wrote Brando a lengthy letter urging the actor to commit to the film. Flattering Brando, Kazan wrote: "I think when you have been in good form, you have been the best actor we have." He also revealed to Brando that Warner Bros. had tried to discourage his interest in the actor for the part of Eddie Anderson, but the filmmaker "concluded as before— at the top of your form, the absolute top, you'd be the best guy I knew for it, if, that is, you'd be willing and eager to break down some old habits and go some directions that were new for you, in effect enlarge yourself."[21] Among the reservations that Kazan communicated directly to Bando was a concern about the actor's weight. The director asserted:

> Now I don't really know whether you want to go back to the way you were—as far as weight goes. It's very tough after forty as I know from my own experience. And except for a kind of vanity, there isn't much point to it. It means cutting out a lot of the more enjoyable things in life. Christ, I won't urge it on you. But I don't want Eddie plump. And since so much of his pain is brought out through sex, there is something about the hefty or plump image that goes against this. I can't afford to deceive myself about this.[22]

While Brando remained noncommittal toward *The Arrangement*, as well as toward dropping weight, Kazan remained optimistic that he could sway the reluctant actor. However, his casting plans were shattered when Brando met with the director following the assassination of Martin Luther King Jr. in April 1968. Brando was an activist who campaigned for Native American rights and marched alongside King in the civil rights movement. He despaired for the future of America and explained to Kazan that he was simply not interested in doing *The Arrangement*. He walked Kazan back to his car and gave his old director a kiss on the cheek. Kazan relates that he drove away "planning to call him in a few days. I saw the man in the rearview mirror, walking to his home and going in: he looked desolate. I never saw Marlon Brando again, haven't seen him to this day."[23]

With Brando unavailable, Kazan turned to Kirk Douglas for the role of Eddie Anderson. He initially hit it off with Douglas, who as the son of immigrants shared with Kazan a similar troubled relationship regarding his father. He told Jeff Young that he enjoyed a good professional association with Douglas, who worked really hard on the picture. But in the final analysis, Douglas did not "suggest the vulnerability that the character had in the book, and as a result the damn picture didn't jell."[24] In his autobiography, Kazan was still lamenting the loss of Brando. He explained that it was essential for the film to depict the despair of Eddie Anderson. The problem with Douglas was that he radiated "indomitability," while Brando, even with all of his success and fame, was still unsure of himself. Kazan concluded: "Kirk without knowing it gave the lie to the part throughout—even in the way his clothes sat on him, even in the way he tied his ties, certainly in the way he walked. I wished I had Marlon, fat as he was."[25] Also without Brando, Kazan determined that Barbara Loden was no longer right for the role of Gwen, and he replaced her with Faye Dunaway, Loden's understudy in *After the Fall*—a decision that had significant repercussions for the relationship between Loden and Kazan.

While struggling with casting for the film, Kazan also battled with Warner Bros. over the screenplay for *The Arrangement*. He agreed to collaborate with playwright Arthur Laurents, which was a strange match. Laurents was critical of Kazan for his HUAC testimony and found the director to be condescending in his approach to the writer. The playwright told Richard Schickel that he accepted the assignment because he needed the money, and he thought that Kazan's novel was "a potboiler that could make a good hot fudge sundae of a movie."[26] Instead, Kazan viewed the material as a serious commentary on the American dream. The director eventually rejected Laurent's screenplay and inserted his own script, which drew heavily on flashbacks. While the novel is a sustained first-person narrative provided by Eddie Anderson, the film is told through a series of flashbacks, beginning with Eddie's automobile accident/suicide. Kazan told Michel Ciment that starting with the accident "created the basis for a psychological mystery story." Why was Eddie doing this? The director also believed that the flashbacks were necessary in order to establish Eddie's relationship with his parents—"the mother encouraged him to become an artist and to have faith in himself. The father taught him the other orientation: he always acted tough."[27] Nevertheless, this structure tends to delete much of Eddie's voice, depriving the film of the novel's political impact with its critique of the American dream.

The Arrangement begins with the shot of a wealthy middle-aged couple, Eddie Anderson (Kirk Douglas) and Florence Anderson (Deborah Kerr), in suburban Los Angeles arising from their twin beds and greeting one another with a perfunctory morning kiss.[28] After showering separately in their own bathrooms, they have breakfast outside, where they are served by a maid and embrace their eighteen-year-old daughter, Ellen (Diane Hull). Eddie then kisses his family good-bye and jumps into his sports car to commence his daily commute to work. These opening shots depict a sense of affluence, but there is little warmth to the Anderson family—establishing the theme that wealth does not necessarily provide happiness. As Eddie drives, he is constantly changing channels on the car radio. A sense of historical context is fostered as we hear reports regarding the launch of an American spacecraft, the American bombing campaign in Vietnam, and advertisements for Zephyr Cigarettes, the "clean cigarette." Eddie drives into a tunnel, where his small sports car is between two large trucks, and he suddenly swerves underneath one of the eighteen-wheelers.

Eddie survives the crash, but it is clear that the accident was an attempted suicide as Eddie mutters to himself that he was a coward for ducking when his car went under the truck. The doctors confirm that Eddie has not suffered brain damage, and he is released from the hospital to continue his recuperation at home, where he spends most of his time sitting beside the family swimming pool. He is unresponsive and makes no effort to explain his actions. His wife, Florence, remains patient and seemingly supportive of her husband. He is also visited by his boss, Mr. Finnigan (Charles Drake), and other executives from the advertising agency where Eddie is employed. Eddie is quite hostile to these men as he watches a nature television show depicting predators on the plains of Africa devouring their prey. This motif is employed several other times during the film and symbolically gets at the picture's theme of Eddie being devoured as he is unable to escape the clutches of a materialistic culture that seeks to crush his individuality. Some critics found the metaphor for the advertising world to be unnecessary and a distraction. Kazan, however, believed: "Underneath our patina of culture and politeness I've seen a lot of people being torn up or even worse. The fact that blood doesn't flow and that the wound isn't visible doesn't mean that it's not deep. It's a desperate world. I saw my father's back broken in the Depression much worse than if he'd had a knife stuck in his side. I saw him killed. I don't know any other metaphor for it."[29] Eddie's response to the hyenas in business suits is that he is not going back to work. Florence, recognizing the threat that such a decision would pose to her lifestyle, quickly interjects that Eddie did not really mean to utter this rejection of American materialism.

The reasons for Eddie's discontent are explained in a series of flashbacks. We are introduced to Eddie as an advertising executive who responds to research linking his tobacco client with cancer by designing a successful campaign for Zephyr Cigarettes as the "clean cigarette." At the office, he is attracted to a beautiful young woman, Gwen (Faye Dunaway), who challenges Eddie's advertising campaigns and urges him to reach his full potential rather than prostitute himself to companies such as Zephyr. They commence an affair in which the couple is shown frolicking nude on the beach, taking photographs that Florence will later discover. Eddie promises Gwen that he will leave his wife, but he fails to initiate any actions that would terminate his marriage. The affair comes to an end when Eddie has Gwen accompany him to New York as a research assistant to interview right-wing politician Chet Collier (Barry Sullivan) for a magazine profile that Eddie is preparing—his career as a writer is a topic that is better developed in the novel. When Eddie concludes his interview with the wealthy politician, Gwen decides that she will stay with Collier, who is a much better developed character in the novel. Gwen's action ends the relationship, and Eddie returns to his marriage, but he has lost sexual interest in Florence, leading to his attempt to end his meaningless life in the automobile accident.

Back in the present, Eddie explains to Florence that a large part of his attraction to Gwen was that she encouraged him to reach his full potential by figuring out what he really wanted to do with his life. Florence tells him that she can help him change as well, but this is something that she, comfortable in her materialistic consumer lifestyle, will be unable to do. She attempts to seduce Eddie, who, thinking of Gwen, is aroused, but when he opens his eyes and sees Florence's face, Eddie is unable to consummate the sexual act. Eddie, however, does try to please his wife by returning to the office, where he is enthusiastically greeted. Despite his best efforts, Eddie is unable to renew his interest in advertising, telling the people from Zephyr Cigarettes that their campaign to deny the link between smoking and lung cancer is "bullshit." He is taken off the account, and his behavior becomes more erratic. Eddie purchases a small plane and buzzes the high-rise offices of the advertising company—a scene that holds even greater impact after the events of 9/11. Following his arrest, he is released into the care of Florence and her psychiatrist, Dr. Liebman (Harold Gold), and attorney, Arthur (Hugh Cronyn)—both of whom are clearly interested in Florence. To protect Florence, Arthur has Eddie sign a legal paper turning over the couple's assets to his wife.

Meanwhile, Eddie is called to New York City, where his father, Sam (Richard Boone), is hospitalized, dying from arteriosclerosis. The second half of the film concentrates on the relationship between Sam and Eddie, and the influence of Kazan's own family history is quite evident. Sam is a Greek rug merchant who lost most of his wealth during the Depression. He spends his days in the hospital haranguing his wife for taking an Irish lover whom Sam imagines while also scheming his return to the business world. It is a sad ending for an immigrant who has put all of his faith in the materialism of the American dream. Sam was critical of Eddie for going to college, with the support of his mother Thomna (Anne Hegira), but now that Eddie has made a great deal of money in the advertising world, Sam is proud and calls him "big shot" while constantly asking Eddie how much money he has. Torn between pity and his old resentment and fear of his father, Eddie promises to help Sam get out of the hospital.

First, however, he attempts to locate Gwen, whom he discovers has a baby and is living with Charles (John Randolph Jones). Gwen refuses to reveal the identity of the baby's father, but she explains to Eddie that she is considering marrying Charles because he loves the baby and understands that she needs to see other men. Although Gwen informs Eddie that she "will never risk everything again on someone like you," they make love. In the novel, Gwen confesses that Chet Collier is the father of her child and Charles is the younger brother of Chet. This lack of explanation tends to make Charles a rather confusing figure in the film.

After seeing Gwen, Eddie learns that his family is considering committing Sam to a rest home, which would destroy what is left of his spirit. Eddie kidnaps his father from the hospital and takes Sam to the rather dilapidated family home overlooking Long Island Sound. Gwen and her baby join Eddie and Sam at the family home, where Eddie and Gwen resume their sexual liaison. While the couple is engaging in rather violent sex, they are discovered by Florence and Eddie's sister-in-law, Gloria (Carol Rossen), who are searching for the missing Sam. A nude Eddie chases Florence and Gloria out of the house, followed by hysterical laughter from both Eddie and Gwen. Any sense of domestic bliss, however, is destroyed when Sam demands that his son provide him with a loan so that he may return to his career as a rug merchant. Eddie tries to explain that he has lost his job and Florence controls the couple's finances. Sam does not believe his son, and their confrontation leads Eddie to remember how his father had terrorized him and his mother in pursuit of the dollar—even striking his mother when she supported her son's college dreams. Eddie shouts that he is ashamed of his father, and he retreats to the sound in a rowboat, accompanied by Gwen. While they are on the water, Florence and Gloria return with hospital attendants to take Sam from the home.

After Gwen also departs, Eddie is left alone in the family home, where he is plagued by dreams from his troubled childhood and images of his former self as Eddie the advertising executive. Hoping to reconcile her parents, Ellen arrives and takes her father to Florence's New York City apartment, where Eddie finds his wife in the company of her admiring psychiatrist and lawyer. An interesting subplot dealing with Florence's disapproval of Ellen's relationship with a young black man is dropped from the film and might have made *The Arrangement* more appealing to younger audiences. Eddie is finally able to get Florence alone and suggests that they give up all their possessions and live in a small New York City apartment. She asks him what he plans on doing with his life, and Florence cannot understand his reply of "nothing." Florence cannot imagine a future without the comforts of a bourgeois lifestyle. Eddie flees, recognizing that Florence is one of the hyenas who wants to devour him.

Seeking to purge himself of his past, Eddie returns to the family home and burns the house down, destroying Sam's most prized possession—his business records. By focusing on Sam's dying desire to return to his home in Turkey, the novel offers a more sympathetic treatment of the old man destroyed by American capitalism. Eddie then goes to see Gwen and asks her to marry him, but their conversation is interrupted by Charles, who shoots Eddie. While he is recovering from his wounds, Eddie is taken to court by Florence and her attorney, Arthur, who succeed in getting Eddie committed to a mental institution. Seeking only to do nothing, Eddie does not fight the proceedings, and he seems reasonably happy isolated in the sanatorium. Gwen, however, recognizes that Eddie is not insane for rejecting American materialism and searching for his own muse. She has found him a job and place to live—the conditions that will allow for his release.

The film concludes with a funeral for Sam. Gwen is there alongside Eddie, while Florence is now with Arthur. Sam died just looking for another chance in life, but it is not too late for Eddie. The burial site is alongside a busy freeway, and the sounds of American commerce drown out the words of a priest as the camera pans back to reveal the hustle and bustle of American capitalism. Kazan was proud of the film's conclusion, noting: "What is better in the film is the ending; the funeral with the thruways all around and going by. The man who came over here, went through all this misery and raised a family, died right in the middle of a traffic jam! And the way the family's gathered there, all the opposing elements, who don't look at each other, and then separate."[30] Kazan found the novel's ending to be a little melodramatic as Gwen and Eddie marry, have a child of their own, operate her uncle's liquor store in rural North Carolina, and Eddie begins to pursue a writing career. They find happiness in their rejection of the pursuit of wealth that destroyed Sam and almost devoured Eddie.

But seemingly neither ending would have saved *The Arrangement* from the critics who rejected Kazan's personal film questioning the American dream. One of the film's few positive reviews came from Roland Gelatt in *Saturday Review*. Gelatt termed the film old-fashioned, but he confessed "to having relished every cornball minute of it."[31] Writing in *Film Quarterly*, Joseph McBride found some positive qualities in *The Arrangement*, especially the relationship between Sam and Eddie. Overall, it was difficult to understand Eddie's motivation without the sustained personal narrative of the novel. McBride, however, suggested: "If we remember *America America*, though, we may be able to keep in focus. What may seem like a slam against contemporary America—the nightmare highways, gadget houses, and so on—is nothing more to Kazan than the logical extension of the immigrant's impossible dream." Nonetheless, McBride concluded that this motivation was often unclear in the film, although the critic agreed with Kazan that Marlon Brando in the title role might have provided the pathos for a more sympathetic audience identification with the troubled Eddie Anderson.[32]

Far more typical of media reaction was Vincent Canby's piece in the *New York Times*. Canby attributed the film's failure to its source material, describing Kazan's novel as reading "like a short story that has been inflated by pointless plot digressions and by fat paragraphs of banal dialogue, recorded with the sort of fidelity that might better be given radio signals from Venus." Acknowledging that some filmmakers such as Francois Truffaut were able to transform material from their personal stories into fascinating cinema, Canby concluded: "Kazan seems to have turned his search for identity into a callous soap opera, unworthy of Kazan's true talent."[33] Roger Ebert of the *Chicago Sun-Times* dismissed *The Arrangement* as "one of those long, ponderous, star-filled 'serious' films that were popular in the 1950s, before we began to value style more than the director's good intentions." Unlike most critics, however, Ebert praised the work of Douglas and Dunaway in an incredibly weak script.[34]

Louise Bartlett of *Films in Review* was even more vicious in her attack on the film, accusing Kazan of pandering to the growing countercultural critique of American values and institutions. She argued: "Kazan's film, like his novel, uses and espouses the hippie shibboleths of social irresponsibility, sexual license and degeneracy, and mindless negativism. Since no one but himself had anything to do with major decision-making, this film is an unusual instance of self-revelation, and an unpleasant sight."[35] Pauline Kael of the *New Yorker* did not perceive Kazan's work as a part of the nation's cultural wars in the 1960s. Instead, she insisted that the problem with *The Arrangement* was Kazan's ego. She compared *The Arrangement* with Ayn Rand's *The Fountainhead*, but Kael argued that Rand's hero, Howard Roark, was stronger and more admirable than the whining Eddie Anderson. The critic concluded that Kazan's film even more than the book was "a noisy glorification of anguish over selling out, with such an exaggerated valuation of the loss to the world of the hero's wasted creativity that one does not know which way to look." The difficulty with *The Arrangement*, according to Kael, was that Kazan wanted to make an artistic statement about not abandoning one's values and ideas, but in order to make his picture within the studio system, it was necessary for Kazan to compromise and create a film that would appeal to a mass audience. Kael asserted: "The movie represents what successful people dissatisfied with themselves and their work are very likely to turn out when they want to show 'truth' and their integrity." She urged Kazan to scale down his massive ego and do a small film well, as he was capable of doing, even if the source material was not his own.[36]

When *The Arrangement* failed at the box office, Kazan concluded that Kael was right and that he was guilty of "selling out" his vision in order to get the film made. Nevertheless, Kazan maintained that the film offered more than critics and film audiences were willing to acknowledge. Noting that he had never received such vitriolic attacks on his work, Kazan proclaimed that he made *The Arrangement* to disturb rather than entertain people. He maintained that the major characters depicted in the film were prototypes rather than individuals, for they were intended to represent "the social masks of our day and of our country in our day." For example, Florence is the typical upper-middle-class wife whose good intentions destroy her marriage. On the other hand, Eddie represents the divided self as he is torn between conformity and rebellion. Again focusing on Eddie's immigrant background, Kazan observes, "He aspires to be a typical American and yet he is inevitably an outsider."[37]

Kazan insisted that *The Arrangement* was the most "social" or contemporary film he had ever made. Commenting on the political unrest in the streets of America in 1969, Kazan expressed sympathy with the countercultural youth rebellion, observing: "They are the well-educated children of middle-class America. And devout idealists. To show them simply as rioters or even revolutionaries is to enforce a false impression." On the other hand, cinematic stereotypes of the establishment contributed little to the national dialogue. The issue, according to Kazan, was that most filmmakers tended to evade these social problems by addressing them through the metaphor of a Western or war picture. Thus, the audience could ignore the difficulties confronting contemporary life by assuming that the message of these films was about another time or place. Instead, Kazan wanted to confront his audiences and make them think about the masks they assumed every day. Kazan proclaimed: "I tried to make a film where the people on the screen are the same, the epitomization of the people watching the screen. I tried to make everything as familiar and as typical as possible. I accepted the danger of banality. But above all I wanted the audience to jump a little, yes to embarrassment, to see themselves and ask: is that what makes me tick too? Are these my own standards? My values? Is that my situation? Is that the truth about me?" Kazan concluded that he did not want the audience for *The Arrangement* to exit the film without being forced to confront the uncomfortable arrangements in their own lives. The director insisted: "The climax of my film simply says that our society condemns a man who breaks the mold and is erratic and finally dangerous, and therefore in one way or another restrains him."[38]

In its critique of American materialism and depiction of a society that sought to thwart the nonconformist individual, *The Arrangement* would appear to well reflect the antiestablishment values challenging traditional American politics, values, and institutions such as Hollywood. Ken Kesey's *One Flew Over the Cuckoo's Nest* (1962) and Joseph Heller's *Catch-22* (1961) became cultural icons during the 1960s, with heroes who were deemed insane because they questioned conformity and war. In this vein, Kazan informed Jeff Young that he was opposed to psychoanalysts who emphasized that the individual must adjust to society. The filmmaker complained: "They cripple the rebel. A man is insane if he says this way of living, this society is not worth adjusting to. He should be in rebellion, it's healthy."[39] This antiestablishment sense of rebellion in the 1960s worked well for Kesey, Heller, Bob Dylan, Dennis Hopper, and Peter Fonda in *Easy Rider* (1969), as well as countless other artists, writers, and filmmakers, but not Elia Kazan.

Kazan's biographer Richard Schickel, who termed *The Arrangement* as an even worse film of a bad novel, notes that the writer and director's work seemed to reflect the changing times, arguing that "the book spoke to the contempt many people felt for their society, their government, their own materialism." Schickel argues that Kazan was tapping into the zeitgeist of the era and identified with many criticisms of American life found in the New Left and protest politics. The biographer, however, argues that much of the novel's cultural relevance was lost in Kazan's film adaptation of his book. Schickel concludes: "In Kazan's adaptation one loses sight of what made the book a best-seller, its legitimate criticisms of mid-century America—its materialism, the way people used one another while pretending to love one another. Yes, the picture offered a couple of nice satirical versions of TV commercials and billboards hawking cigarettes, but they did not have the passionate contempt that colored the pages of the book."[40]

Film scholar Brian Neve also observes Kazan's identification with cultural and political protests of the 1960s. Neve points out that Kazan attended the 1968 Democratic National Convention wearing a political button for insurgent South Dakota senator George McGovern, and his observation of the police attacking protesters in the streets of Chicago encouraged the director to pen an article "sympathetic to what he saw as the revolution by the children of the middle class against their parents' materialism, dollar orientation, and personal hypocrisies."[41] There were some political references in the film, such as the autographed picture of Richard Nixon in the office of Eddie's boss at the advertising agency, and Gwen decorated her New York City apartment with photographs of Bob Dylan and Allen Ginsberg, along with various countercultural mottos such as "Escape while there is still time." Neve concludes that if the film employed the novel's ending, with Eddie and Gwen dropping out of traditional society and finding a place in the countryside, it might have resonated with the youth culture, but in the final analysis *"The Arrangement*, perhaps because the crisis that inspired it dates from the late fifties and because the conflicts are inside Eddie's head, fails to engage with, translate to, the wider social mayhem of America at the time."[42] It was difficult for a young person with a hippie, countercultural, or revolutionary perspective to identify with the middle-aged and wealthy Eddie Anderson. Kazan seemed to be blending his critique of American business civilization with a midlife male crisis. The trappings of the counterculture in regard to drugs and music were also missing from the film, with Eddie consuming a steady dose of hard liquor while the soundtrack includes music from Greece and the Middle East, but there are no strains of rock and roll. In addition, the marketing of the film seemed to focus on an arrangement between a business executive and his mistress. The idea that Kazan and Eddie were rebelling against the arranged life society imposes upon us was certainly not apparent in film posters concentrating on steamy sex scenes between Douglas and Dunaway.[43]

Despite some sympathies with youthful protest, Kazan was really a man of the 1930s whose worldview was shaped by the Great Depression and World War II. Rather than looking forward to the Age of Aquarius, Kazan was still coming to grips with how American capitalism had destroyed the dreams of Stavros and his father. In an interview with Michel Ciment, Kazan argued: "In this society, there are thousands and thousands of people who earn their living doing something, which they not only detest, but know is killing them. They sell their lives to make a living. A lot of these men have a secret hope that someday they'll write something or do something they respect. There are all kinds of secret, forlorn, incapable artists in this society." However, Kazan believed that the story of Eddie Anderson provided hope for these forlorn people, as at the end of the film Eddie is able to reclaim his soul. Kazan concluded: "It's a happy ending, even though it's painful. You have to pay for happiness. He sacrifices a lot: a home, a decent wife, money, security; and he doesn't know where he is at the end. But he's more stable within himself."[44] An advertising campaign for *The Arrangement* emphasizing these themes might have better resonated with audiences in the turbulent late 1960s.

But Kazan was an older man who was looking backward and concentrated on the destructive impact of the Great Depression on immigrant parents and how their children were forced to become salesmen of some type to fit within the materialistic culture of a capitalist America. This is similar to the critique of the American experience that Kazan embraced when he joined the Communist Party in the 1930s, and these ideas were still an important element in his films. In his novel, Kazan has Eddie Anderson join the Communist Party in the 1930s before he goes off to fight in World War II—Kazan did not serve in the military—but there is no mention of informing or the impact of McCarthyism. Yet this issue still seemed to weigh upon Kazan, as at the conclusion of his interview with Ciment, he introduces the topic of the blacklist. Complaining that too many films are based on metaphors rather than directly confronting the truth as *The Arrangement* did, Kazan commented: "I have often wondered why no one of the Hollywood Ten has ever written a film or novel about their experiences. I think a work telling the outrages of the McCarthy period, as seen by people who suffered terribly by it, would have been welcomed." The problem was that filmmakers and writers in the 1930s and 1940s, including himself, were so focused on getting a bit of social criticism into their films, they forgot about the larger truths. Kazan argued: "And that became a habit of mind, in all these people—a way of thinking; and a way of working. Of all of us, myself included. It was one thing I had to confront and change."[45]

This hardly constituted an apology for Kazan's HUAC testimony, but these comments certainly indicate that his actions continued to concern him. On the other hand, if *The Arrangement* was his effort to finally tell the whole truth and indict the conformity and materialism of American culture and capitalism, it was a huge failure. The disastrous reviews and box office returns for *The Arrangement* essentially terminated Kazan's Hollywood career. Returning to his writing as a novelist, Kazan nevertheless remained interested in filmmaking. In 1971, he would make a small independent film, *The Visitors*, with his son Chris, examining questions of informing within the context of the Vietnam War, which was tearing the nation apart. Five years later, he was lured back to Hollywood by producer Sam Spiegel to direct the film version of F. Scott Fitzgerald's *The Last Tycoon*. Although today this film is favorably viewed by many critics and film historians, the box office failure assured that *The Last Tycoon* was Kazan's last film.

11

THE FINAL FILMS

The Visitors (1971) and *The Last Tycoon* (1976)

After the poor reception given to *The Arrangement* by film audiences as well as critics, Kazan was disenchanted with Hollywood, while the studios were coming to view the director as box office poison. While Kazan continued to pursue his new career as a writer, he remained interested in film. His feelings toward the film industry following *The Arrangement* were well captured in his autobiography as Kazan insisted: "After the experience, I decided not to even make another film in Hollywood. But I didn't want to give up filmmaking. I would show myself and the men who controlled the industry that films could be made inexpensively, that the process was essentially simple and didn't need the pumped-up costs, the services of coddled stars, and the pressure by the men who bring the money."[1] Kazan's experiment with independent, low-budget cinema, which culminated in making *The Visitors* (1971) with his son Chris, was also fostered by the experience of his increasingly independent wife Barbara Loden producing the film *Wanda* (1971) outside of the studio system.

Working with cameraman Nick Proferes, whom Kazan later assumed to be having an affair with his wife, Loden was able to make *Wanda* on a budget of under $200,000. The film about a young woman without money struggling to survive in capitalist America was shot on 16 mm film with a small crew, an unknown cast outside of Loden, and a largely improvised script and employed natural locations similar to Italian neorealism. The film garnered some decent reviews acknowledging Loden's potential as a filmmaker, but *Wanda*'s distribution beyond New York City was limited. The film was better received in Europe, winning a prize at the Venice Film Festival and encouraging Loden to pursue other independent film projects, which were not as well accepted.[2] Kazan offered to help his wife with the film, but he confessed to students at Wesleyan University that Loden required little assistance. Kazan concluded: "She showed herself to be an excellent director and has since received all the praise she deserved for that. I helped some around the edges, but, as the days passed, less and less, until finally, not at all. I stayed home and worked on my book mornings, and swam with the kids in the afternoons. I babysat, while she made *Wanda*. Women's Lib please note." Kazan observed, however, that *Wanda*, despite earning praise, did very little business and could not be made within the Hollywood system. The filmmaker argued: "So now I had to face the elemental facts. I was not going to be able to make the films I wanted to make, not in the old way, not in this time of an industry that was dying and desperately trying to find a way to revive itself."[3] The lessons of *The Arrangement* and *Wanda* were that Kazan would only be able to make the films he wanted outside of the Hollywood system.

These conclusions led Kazan to the making of *The Visitors*. In describing the origins of the film to Jeff Young, Kazan noted that he was discussing with his son Chris a piece in the *New Yorker* by Daniel Lang about a young soldier in Vietnam who reported two of his fellow soldiers for raping and killing a young Vietnamese woman.[4] They were court martialed and found guilty, although their sentences were later reduced on appeal. Kazan remarked to his son that he wondered what would happen if the imprisoned soldiers were released and they went to visit their comrade who had informed on them.[5] Chris found the idea fascinating, and after approximately three weeks he returned with a completed film script, which he asked his father to direct. Kazan asserted: "I was really flattered and pleased when he asked me. I think most kids want to get their old man out of their lives as quickly as possible and forget him, or recover from the wounds the old man has inflected, psychic and physical. And here was Chris including me in this project. I thought it over and said I'd direct it."[6]

Chris's screenplay, however, was a rather bleak story in which the two soldiers released from the stockade beat the informant and rape his common-law wife, and Kazan was unable to raise funds with which to make the picture. So he decided that he would follow the example of *Wanda* and produce a low-budget personal film. Accordingly, Kazan took out a loan for $170,000 to complete the film—supposedly a sum less than what Faye Dunaway earned for *The Arrangement*.[7] To reduce costs, the cast and crew could not be paid union-scale salaries. Nick Proferes, who worked with Loden on *Wanda*, served as the cameraman, and he was assisted by a soundman, camera assistant, lighting assistant, and a jack-of-all-trades to do everything else. The only experienced actor was Patrick McVey, who was getting little work, while the rest of the cast consisted of Patricia Joyce from the Yale drama program, Steve Railsback and James Woods from the Actors Studio, and a Puerto Rican cab driver named Chico Martinez, who wanted to become an actor. To further save money, *The Visitors* would be filmed at the Connecticut homes of Elia and Chris Kazan, where the cast and crew could be housed as well. The film was completed in a few weeks, and Kazan was delighted with the experience, proclaiming that he had rediscovered the joy of filmmaking. Seeking to establish a positive family relationship that had eluded Kazan with his father, the director told Jeff Young: "One of the reasons I feel so loyal to this picture is that it was the product of a good relationship between me and my son. The irony was that we had more artistic freedom with a nothing budget than I had with all the studio resources on *The Arrangement*."[8] Describing the filming experience of *The Visitors* in his autobiography, Kazan concluded: "When *The Visitors* was done and edited—by the cameraman—I was proud of it. It had been an exhilarating experience, I came out of it refreshed, not exhausted. We'd made the first film to deal with the effect of the Vietnam War on the people at home."[9]

Yet this was one of the major problems with the film, as it was unclear as to exactly what statement *The Visitors* wanted to communicate about the conflict in Southeast Asia that was dividing American society and culture. The film begins with Bill Schmidt (James Woods) and Martha Wayne (Patricia Joyce) lying in bed on a snowy Saturday morning when their sleep is interrupted by the crying of their baby. Reflecting the changing mores of the 1960s, the young couple is not married, and they reside in the Connecticut countryside home of Martha's father, Harry Wayne (Patrick McVey), who also lives on the property and spends most of his evenings writing Western novels that no longer sell as well as his earlier books.[10] There is a certain coldness in the relationship between Bill and

Martha. While Bill is gone to purchase a newspaper, two visitors arrive. The two young men, Tony Rodriguez (Chico Martinez) and Mike Nickerson (Steve Railsback), introduce themselves to Martha as old friends of Bill who served with him in Vietnam, and she invites them to wait for her husband and stay for dinner. Bill is visibly uncomfortable when he discovers the visitors, and he later explains to Martha that Tony and Mike are the soldiers he reported to military authorities for raping and murdering a young Vietnamese woman. They were convicted but released early from the stockade due to legal issues with their prosecution. The visitors are initially cordial, complimenting Bill on his attractive wife and nice home—elements of reintegration into civilian life, which Tony and Mike were unable to attain while in prison. Bill explains that the home belongs to Martha's father, while he has been forced to accept a job with a helicopter manufacturing plant—maintaining a connection with the Vietnam War, which he wanted to put behind him. While Mike takes a nap, Bill and Tony walk around the grounds, and Tony assures Bill that the visitors are not a threat to him or his family.

The three Vietnam veterans decide to pay Harry a visit, and the film offers an interesting critique of American masculinity. A World War II veteran, Harry is immediately drawn to the simmering threat of masculinity presented by Mike and Tony. Pointing out that Bill never likes to talk about his war experience, Harry bonds with Mike and Tony. Their bonding, however, is interrupted by the whimpering of Harry's dog, which has been mauled by a neighbor's Great Dane. While Bill tends to the injured dog, the warriors decide to take action. Mike goes to his car and retrieves a rifle. He kills the Great Dane with a single shot, and the men then carry the dead animal and deposit it on the neighbor's porch. The detachment with which this killing was undertaken is foreboding regarding the intentions of the visitors, but they have removed a threatening animal that once attacked Martha, whose safety was not protected by Bill.

Tony, Mike, and Harry then pursue further male bonding while drinking heavily and enjoying the violence of a televised football game. Bill seems less interested in the game, and while Martha prepares dinner, he goes upstairs to take care of the baby. It is fascinating to note that the powerful anti–Vietnam War documentary *Hearts and Minds* (1974) would later indict American football culture as encouraging the violence that characterized the American approach to Vietnam. As Harry becomes more intoxicated, he begins to lament the changes in America that are softening the nation. He asserts that the United States must stand up to Communist aggression in Southeast Asia, but the visitors are not really interested in these political arguments. Then Harry asks them what happened in Vietnam. Mike explains that the girl they killed was a Viet Cong sympathizer and a threat to the American soldiers, but Bill informed on them anyway. Harry retorts that he always suspected that Bill was "half queer." Bill's manhood is further challenged at dinner when he prefers his meat well done, while Mike and Tony, of course, want their steak as raw as possible.

After a day of male comradery, Harry is drunk, cuts his hand while carving the meat, and stumbles back to his cottage, leaving the visitors alone with Bill and Martha. While Bill is clearing the dinner dishes, Tony engages him in a serious conversation regarding his job prospects as a mechanic. Meanwhile, Martha puts the baby to bed, and she is left alone with Mike. Clad in a miniskirt and proudly championing her opposition to the Vietnam War, Martha appears to be the stereotypical hippie female from the 1960s. She criticizes Mike for his actions in Vietnam, but the veteran counters that she does not understand what he and other Americans went through in the jungles of Southeast Asia. Martha begins to soften toward Mike, and she reclines on a couch in a sexually provocative pose. Mike then finds some music on the radio and asks her to dance. The two are moving in slow, sexual rhythm to the music with Martha's head on Mike's shoulder. When Bill discovers them, he hits Mike, and the two men go outside to continue their fight. Their violent encounter takes place behind a car and is not shown on the screen, but Mike emerges bloodied after knocking Bill unconscious. He then chases Martha upstairs, where he proceeds to rape her. Tony drags Bill's unconscious body out of the snow and into the house, and he prepares to leave. Mike, however, motions for Tony to have his turn with Martha. Meanwhile, Mike wanders outside, urinates in the snow, and flashes back to the rape of the Vietnamese girl. The rape scene with Martha was disturbing and misogynist, suggesting that Martha, by being sexually provocative, in some way invited the attack, and *The Visitors* would be compared to the rape scene in Sam Peckinpah's *Straw Dogs* (1971). After the visitors have beaten Bill and raped Martha, they leave. Bill regains consciousness and asks Martha, "You all right?" The distance between the two has only grown.

Kazan recognized that the subject matter of *The Visitors* would be difficult for many film viewers. In terms of marketing the film, Kazan urged Chris to proceed carefully. The director asserted: "This is a very powerful picture. It is not 'entertainment,' it is an experience." He believed that the support of the critics would be crucial for a film as challenging as *The Visitors*. Therefore, his father suggested that Chris only show the film to the important critics, such as Vincent Canby of the *New York Times*, one at a time in a quiet projection room. The filmmaker concluded: "The public should not even see the film until the reviews are out. If there ever was a film to which the public has to be brought by the critics this is it. The critics have to tell (instruct!) the public that this is an exceptional film, an experience they must not miss, the film of the day. I think they will. If it is shown without this kind of intellectual sponsorship, the public will merely see it as entertainment. They have to be prepared in order to take the film on its proper level."[11]

Kazan, however, was most disappointed by both film critics and audiences in their reactions to *The Visitors*. The film opened at the Little Carnegie Theatre in New York City, and Kazan was shocked when part of the crowd booed *The Visitors*. Kazan was at a loss as how to explain the reasons for this reaction. He speculated that the audience was primarily composed of leftists who continued to punish his informing—which is certainly a theme of the film—or perhaps they "resented our rather scoffing attitude toward the girl 'peacenik.'" The director concluded: "But that wouldn't account for the intensity of the hostile reaction. As the audience moved out, I stood in the back of the theatre, waiting for someone to come up and explain why the film had been received so hatefully. No one did."[12] The crowds dwindled after the premiere, and United Artists, in charge of distributing the film, withdrew it from New York City after only eight days and made little effort to find other venues for exhibiting *The Visitors* in the United States.

The critics, upon whom Kazan had been depending, had little good to say about the picture. Hollis Alpert of the *Saturday Review* described *The Visitors* as "neither needed nor welcome." The critic credited Kazan with contributing realism to the production with his direction, but his craftsmanship was wasted on a banal script. The father was especially disappointed that many reviews singled out Chris's writing as the weakest element in the film. Finding it bothersome that Martha seemed to encourage her sexual assault, Alpert argued, "Although *The Visitors* purports to show the brutalizing effects of the war on American soldiers and civilians alike, there is little in it that can be regarded as enlightening; and its effect, message-wise, is akin to receiving a telegram from Western Union that has been delivered several months late."[13] Writing in *New York Magazine*, Judith Crist agreed with Alpert's sentiments. She found *The Visitors* to be a "cheapjack *Straw Dogs*" that simply regurgitated violent revenge themes from earlier Hollywood movies. Crist described *The Visitors* as "pretentiously trying to make a portentous comment about Vietnam veterans, while dragging in a bit of women's lib here, a dash of machismo there, a 'nowness' that is strictly vintage forties." Again, Chris Kazan came in for some heavy-handed criticism as Crist argued *The Visitors* was "from the first, a hopeless task: brick needs straw and a director needs a script. Perhaps such family ventures should be confined to 8 mm. films—and the family vault."[14]

One of the few reviews with anything positive to say about the film was by Vincent Canby in the *New York Times*. While taking Chris Kazan to task for spelling out simplistic points that the audience should have already grasped, Canby praised Kazan's young actors, especially Railsback as Mike, "who looks like the sort of nice, clean-cut, small-town American boy who could eat a piece of apple pie with one hand and cut a friend's throat with the other."[15] The *New York Times* critic concluded: "*The Visitors* is a far from great film. It insists on saying too much about large issues when it should keep quiet and it's ambiguous when one has the right to expect explicit answers. Yet, it is an extremely moving film, partly, I think, because everything—from the physical production to the melodrama—is kept in small scale, as if not to get in the way of, or to confuse, its very legitimate expression of a major American sorrow."[16]

A positive review from Canby in the *Times*, however, could not rescue *The Visitors*, which United Artists quickly pulled from theaters. Kazan was perplexed by the poor reception given the film, but perhaps the problem with the picture was the ambiguity the filmmaker and his son brought to the complex issues of the Vietnam War, violence, and women's liberation, which were polarizing American society in the early 1970s. In terms of the historical context in which *The Visitors* was made and released, it is worth noting that in March 1971, First Lieutenant William L. Calley Jr. was found guilty of murdering hundreds of South Vietnamese civilians during what became known as the My Lai Massacre, which occurred in March 1968. Defenders of Calley insisted that the politicians who placed young American soldiers in Vietnam were the ones who should be held accountable rather than common soldiers whose lives were threatened and who were only following orders and implementing the strategy of increasing the enemy body count. Debate over the war was exacerbated by President Richard Nixon's invasion of Cambodia in May 1970, along with the ensuing shooting of protesting students at Kent State and Jackson State Universities. Although the Cold War liberals who supported the anti-Communist crusade, and provided an environment in which HUAC could thrive, were architects of the war in Vietnam, Kazan was a critic of the conflict in Southeast Asia—providing further evidence regarding the persistence of his progressive principles.

Explaining to Jeff Young the purpose of *The Visitors*, Kazan maintained:

> The picture is about the price of the Vietnam War on the soul of the American people. It's an antiwar picture. If you teach a generation of young people to think life is cheap and that the answer to problems is violent confrontation, that's the way they are going to turn out at home as well as on the battlefield. The film makes this point in almost primal terms. The important thing to me was to try to make the villains, the two visitors, not heavies, not psychos, not criminals, not bastards, not monsters, but absolutely typical and characteristic young American boys. What so shocked the American public about My Lai was for the first time we saw that butchery and monstrosity committed in war can be done by someone as ordinary and familiar as Lieutenant William Calley. [17]

In suggesting that the Vietnam War brutalized and dehumanized young American soldiers, Kazan was attempting, in the rhetoric of the Weather Underground, to bring the war home. The ideas of the domino theory and containment of Communism endorsed by Cold War liberals were missing from Kazan's analysis of Vietnam and its impact on American society.

The Visitors, however, is ambiguous in assigning the responsibility for the growing acceptance of violence in American society. The film text seems to imply that the embracing of militarism from World War II, the mayhem of football, and the culture of guns and hunting contributed to an American masculinity that rationalized rape and the subjugation of women. Thus, Kazan told Michel Ciment that Martha's father was a naive old man who wanted the Vietnam generation to celebrate the masculinity and violence that tamed the American West and brought victory in World War II. Kazan argued: "That psychology—we intervened, we're going to save Europe, we're going to make the world safe for democracy—really has something so arrogant about it, combined with stupidity. What the hell, let's make our own country safe for democracy, since we still haven't got democracy in many respects here."[18] Yet, whether Mike and Tony were desensitized by both the Vietnam War and American cultural attitudes, the fact remains that in seeking to explain, and some might say excuse, the actions of Mike and Tony, Bill and Martha seem to come off as weak figures who got what was coming to them rather than sensitive individuals who opposed the brutality of the Vietnam War.

In a 1973 article for *Film Quarterly*, Julian Smith credits *The Visitors* with providing a more realistic depiction of the Vietnam veteran in contrast with early exploitation films, which often had those returning from the war joining outlaw motorcycle gangs and engaging in a wide range of violent antisocial behavior. The idea of the Vietnam veteran as a noble warrior who was denied victory by spineless politicians was developed after the war in the Rambo series, featuring Sylvester Stallone, and the Chuck Norris *Missing in Action* films, which were also used to reinvigorate support for war and militarism in American culture. Smith, however, was somewhat dismissive of the violence in *The Visitors*, writing: "In today's perspective it is all very casual, every day, and realistic, unlike the majority of the returned veteran stories that build to violent and generally fatal climaxes. No one gets seriously hurt in *The Visitors*, for it is not a film that takes refuge in the kind of extreme catharsis or violent resolution audiences have been trained to expect."[19]

However, it seems a bit flippant to suggest that no one is seriously hurt in a violent gang rape. In her seminal work *From Reverence to Rape*, film critic Molly Haskell argues that in response to the growing women's liberation movement, many males were threatened, and cinematic rape fantasies were a way to bring these independent women under control. Perhaps the most notorious film in this regard is Sam Peckinpah's *Straw Dogs* in which the meek Dustin Hoffman asserts his manhood by killing the men who entered his home and raped his wife—even though the film proposes that the sexually provocative female elicited the rape.[20] Foster Hirsch, writing in *Film Quarterly*, argued, however, that *The Visitors* was not as simplistic as Peckinpah's conclusion that violence equated with masculinity. Hirsch argues that *The Visitors* indicated that violence might in some cases be justified, but the film spent "most of its time satirizing a John Wayne conception of American masculinity." The critic maintains that the visitors and Martha's father, who spend their time drinking, watching sports, fondling guns, and reveling in male camaraderie, are "decidedly inferior to the quiet hero who doesn't need to declare his manliness so defensively."[21] As for Kazan, he attempted to explain Martha's attraction to Mike by observing that something was missing in her relationship with Bill. Kazan concluded: "She marches in the antiwar parades, but misses in her lover the violence and strength that would have made him shoot the dog when it threatened her. She bullies the man, and at the same time she wishes he were stronger."[22]

This perspective seems to almost justify rape and equates violence and masculinity. Nevertheless, Kazan insisted that what he and Chris wanted to convey with the conclusion of the film was more metaphorical. Referring to the last line of the film, "Are you all right?," Kazan explained: "Like a lot of Chris's work, the line has a double meaning. It's like saying to America the Vietnam War never happened: we lost 55,000 men, wiped out a civilian population and spent billions of dollars—but it never happened. We cancel our experiences. But it did happen, and there was a price. She slowly turns and looks at him as if to say, are you kidding? It's a very bitter tough ending. I admire it a lot."[23] This antiwar message nevertheless tends to become obscured with the film's diversion into the topic of American masculinity. As Brian Neve observes, this sense of confusion was partly due to Kazan's continuing struggles with his decision to inform on his comrades. Neve argues: "Whether influenced by his own traumatic testimony or not, Kazan as a director seems in this film to distrust his own liberalism. In his film it is Bill, the informer, who most would see as doing the right thing, yet the script and director clouded this essential issue."[24]

Kazan's HUAC testimony and the Hollywood blacklist continued to haunt the director after he convinced United Artists to place *The Visitors* in competition at the Cannes Film Festival following a positive reaction from European critics. Placed in competition for the festival's prestigious grand prize, the Palme d'Or, *The Visitors* enjoyed a favorable audience response, and this time there was no booing and hissing. However, the chair of the jury committee to award the festival prize was director Joseph Losey, who left the United States when subpoenaed by HUAC and continued his filmmaking career in the United Kingdom. Losey was no admirer of Kazan, who said that he learned from other committee members that Losey sabotaged awarding the prize to *The Visitors*. Kazan responded: "I didn't expect a left intellectual to forget in 1972 what had happened in 1952, because I hadn't forgotten either. I shed no tears, ate the most tender part of the greatest fish in the Mediterranean, the *loup de mer*, breached bottles of my favorite wine, Chateau de Sancerre, and never saw Joe Losey."[25]

Kazan also faced censure from the Directors Guild for employing nonunion performers and crew in the production of *The Visitors*. According to the bylaws of the Directors Guild, Kazan was assessed a fine, which he paid without protest, but he urged the organization to amend their rules in order to better support independent filmmaking. However, after the failures of the big-budget *The Arrangement* and the independently made *The Visitors*, Kazan was not exactly in great demand as a filmmaker and he returned to writing, publishing *The Assassins* (1972), *The Understudy* (1974), *Acts of Love* (1978), *The Anatolian* (1982), and finally *Beyond the Aegean* (1994). These books enjoyed modest success but did not achieve the best-seller status of *The Arrangement*. Meanwhile, his personal life was again deteriorating as Barbara Loden sought a more independent life apart from her husband. According to Kazan, the couple remained married but stopped sleeping together. Ignored by Hollywood, Kazan's major cinematic connection was with Wesleyan University, to which he donated his papers. He was provided with a small campus office and often gave lectures to students who did not appear to care about his past politics. Film scholar Jeanine Basinger helped organize the Kazan papers and got to know the director reasonably well. She informed Kazan biographer Richard Schickel that the filmmaker missed Molly and was growing increasingly resentful toward the film industry during the 1970s, observing: "I felt he was young and energetic, but he couldn't act on it, he didn't feel he was any longer a part of the movie world." He reportedly told Basinger, "Tell your students they'll throw you away eventually."[26]

Kazan, nevertheless, was drawn back to Hollywood for what proved to be the last hurrah when he was contacted by producer Sam Spiegel, with whom he collaborated in the making of *On the Waterfront*. Spiegel wanted Kazan to direct *The Last Tycoon*, based on F. Scott Fitzgerald's unfinished novel, which was published a year after the author's death in 1940 by his friend and literary critic Edmund Wilson. The novel was loosely based on the short life and career of MGM legendary producer

Irving Thalberg, who was referred to as "the boy wonder" for his ability to assess what film audiences in the 1920s and 1930s wanted to see on the silver screen. Born with a congenital heart condition, Thalberg understood that he had a short life expectancy, but the film tycoon still insisted on laboring long hours, which contributed to several heart attacks and his death at age thirty-seven in 1936. In his portrait of film producer Monroe Stahr, Fitzgerald made several significant departures from Thalberg's biography. Thalberg married actress Norma Shearer in 1927, and the union produced two children. Instead, Fitzgerald has Stahr concentrating exclusively on his work following the death of his wife, actress Minna Davis. His humanity, however, is reawakened by the mysterious Kathleen Moore, but his pursuit of love renders him vulnerable to the pecuniary interests of studio executives and their financial backers. Fitzgerald also planned for Stahr to perish in an airplane crash, but Kazan helped design a conclusion that seems more fitting for the film as well as Kazan's career in cinema. [27]

When Spiegel approached Kazan about directing the film, Harold Pinter and Mike Nichols had already prepared a script, but Nichols decided to withdraw from the project, and the producer wanted to recruit his old friend Kazan in hopes of re-creating the box office magic of *On the Waterfront*. Kazan accepted the assignment without even reading the Pinter screenplay, which was a faithful—perhaps too faithful—adaptation of the Fitzgerald novel. After the terrible Hollywood experience with *The Arrangement*, it is somewhat surprising that the director agreed on a return to the film capital for a project in which he essentially would be directing someone else's work. The decision was made for personal rather than artistic reasons. His relationship with Barbara was deteriorating, and another woman he was seeing lived in California. The most important factor, however, was the declining health of his mother. For her final days, the son wanted to relocate her from the frigid North to the mild Southern California climate. He would have a nurse to watch her during the day, and every evening Kazan could go home and visit with his mother. Kazan relates that he met Spiegel in the producer's office and was offered an expensive cigar. Describing the meeting, Kazan remarked: "What a whore you are! For a two-buck cigar; and I laughed. An hour later I'd agreed to take my mother to California—and make a film of *The Last Tycoon* which should have remained on the bookshelves like my own novel, *The Arrangement*." [28]

Although Kazan had little control over the screenplay, he did make significant contributions to the casting of *The Last Tycoon*. In addition, while the film is about Fitzgerald's creation Monroe Stahr rather than Kazan, it is difficult not to read some autobiographical elements into the film. Similar to Kazan, Fitzgerald's novels, such as *The Great Gatsby* and *The Last Tycoon*, focus on the price one pays for pursuing the elusive American dream. And when one sees the studio executives, attorneys, union leaders, and bankers lined up against Stahr's prestige picture, which may not bring any profits to the studio, it is easy to recall the challenges Kazan confronted in making many of his films. Film scholar Brian Neve notes that similar to Stahr, Kazan was frustrated by the "sense of his diminishing opportunity to make the films he wanted to make."[29]

Kazan tried to convince Spiegel that it was necessary to make changes in the script regarding the love story between Stahr and Kathleen Moore, but the director concluded that Spiegel was too impressed with Pinter's literary reputation to insist on revisions. Kazan complained to Pinter that the love story was too vague and skimpy, as if it were taking place "under water." To which, the writer replied, "Isn't that where it always happens."[30] Finding it impossible to deal with Pinter, Kazan concentrated on the casting of the major roles. Model Ingrid Boulting was cast as Kathleen Moore, while Theresa Russell was selected for the role of Cecilia Brady, who has a crush on Stahr and is the daughter of studio chief Pat Brady. It seems that Spiegel had sexual designs on both women, which were not realized, and the producer was disappointed with them in the film. On the other hand, Kazan was pleased with their work on the picture. He believed that the criticisms of Boulting were more due to the weakness of the script rather than her acting abilities. Kazan also clashed openly with Spiegel over the selection of Robert De Niro to play Stahr. While he had never met De Niro before the film, Kazan had a hunch that the actor was the right man for the part. The two men worked well together, and Kazan was pleased with De Niro's performance, which he had to constantly defend against the concerns expressed by Spiegel.[31]

In his notes on the character of Monroe Stahr and correspondence with De Niro, Kazan demonstrates numerous parallels that one might draw with the filmmaker's career. In his production notes, Kazan perceived Stahr as a young man with a mission dedicated to making films a higher art form. But he is combating a mercenary and reactionary crowd only concerned with earning a profit on the pictures. In the process of pursuing his mission, Stahr becomes a ruthless businessman who loses sight of his humanity, which is reawakened by an image of beauty with Kathleen. Nevertheless, in the final analysis it is suggested that Stahr finds it difficult to commit to Kathleen over his obligations to the studio and his career. In responding to Kathleen, however, Stahr realizes "how dried up and toughened and serene he has become, he reaches back to regain his humanity. When he does this he exposes, what he has never exposed before, his vulnerability. His naked neck. When he exposes this, he is killed."[32]

Seeking to convey these themes to De Niro, Kazan wrote: "Stahr is determined to single-handedly and against the tide of all those money-fuckers around him, to carry out his mission." Kazan went on to argue that Stahr, similar to Thalberg, wanted motion pictures to be recognized as an art form. Speaking of Thalberg, Kazan commented: "He wanted to give the world he was engaged in respect and thereby give his own life dignity. In that end he was a controlled, quietly determined, unshakeable visionary. Even a revolutionary." Perhaps perceiving elements of his own life and career in the work of Thalberg and Stahr, Kazan concluded his letter to De Niro by proclaiming: "Stahr is a terrific part, something you have never attempted. I know you can do it. But nothing of that much size and meaning is easy. It will take a lot of work, good happy work. And thought and care and experiment—and work."[33] Kazan was delighted by De Niro's work ethic and performance, although he constantly had to address the reservations expressed by Spiegel. For example, Spiegel complained that he had over $5 million of his own money riding on De Niro, who was exceedingly "willful and arrogant." He reminded the director that De Niro was not his choice, but in a backhanded compliment, the producer told Kazan, "There's no director in the world except you who could have influenced me to take a chance on Bobby."[34]

In addition to fighting off Spiegel's efforts to replace De Niro, Kazan was dealing with the deteriorating health of his mother, who died in mid-November 1975. He wrote a formal note to her family in Greece, asserting: "She was eighty-seven years old and had had a good life, eventful and I think satisfying. All anyone could ask for, I believe. I mourn her but I also rejoice that her life was as worthy as it was. She never did anything of which she might have been ashamed. She was a fine example of how to live and how to die to everyone who knew her."[35] This communication, however, failed to acknowledge that Athena Kazan had suffered greatly at the hands of her domineering husband. Kazan also recognized that in moving her from New York to California for her final days, he had resigned her to die in bitterness, "alone and far from home." As for *The Last Tycoon*, Kazan vowed that he would return to the set and "just finish the film."[36]

While completing *The Last Tycoon*, Kazan was hardly a happy individual, and on January 7, 1976, he complained to Spiegel about his treatment on the set. He described filming an evening scene outside the studio. While De Niro was provided with a trailer and there was a truck for the technicians, Kazan was left sitting on a curb with a cup of coffee and a doughnut. Kazan complained: "About ten o'clock, Sam, I must confess that despite my fondness for the producer and my respect for the film he was making, I began to lose interest. In fact, I began to want to go home. I didn't because that would have been a breach of discipline and a bad example to all. But I began to wish for the night's work to be over. That is the first time on this picture that I felt that way."[37] Despite these misgivings, Kazan did complete the picture with Spiegel. In fact, in an interview with *Film Comment*, Kazan had nothing but good things to say about *The Last Tycoon* with its nearly $8 million budget. He praised the writing of Pinter and the work ethics of both De Niro and Spiegel. Kazan was also impressed by Ingrid Boulting's performance, which was panned by many critics, observing: "She accomplished what I wanted to do. I always thought of Kathleen as an apparitional figure, not a real person—someone to whom he could attach his romanticism. She's not a human figure. I never meant her to be like an ordinary girl. She's been whipped, and she's full of mysterious pain." Kazan concluded his interview with *Film Comment* by complaining about the increasing violence of American films. The director argued: "I think a picture like *The Last Tycoon* is a test of a critic. I don't think I'm being tested in it, or Harold's being tested in it, and certainly Fitzgerald's not being tested. But it's a test of a critic's sensitivity; for they basically, I think, have become debased, as the audience has become debased. They think that there's got to be a piece of violence every so often"—which Kazan estimated to be about every five minutes.[38]

Film critics and audiences, however, failed to pass Kazan's test. Spiegel was worried about the distributors' negative reaction to the film, and Kazan urged the producer not to tinker with the film in response to these criticisms. Some distributors were evidently upset that *The Last Tycoon* was so different from *On the Waterfront*. Observing that such comparisons were meaningless, Kazan told Spiegel: "Our love story is narrative more than drama and is in all ways ambivalent, dealing with wisps of meaning and half-truths. The basic issue is never dealt with up front, never altogether confronted. That is Harold's way." Thus, it was appropriate that the pace of *The Last Tycoon* was slow in contrast with the violent melodramas dominating Hollywood productions. The director insisted: "I like *The Last Tycoon* the way I do a couple of my close friends, appreciating that they are quite different from most people I know. Our film is like no other. It is packed with deeper meanings, one piled on another. And it has its own beauty. I'm proud I made it."[39]

Nevertheless, *The Last Tycoon* is often a difficult film to follow, with its many characters whose motivations are often left underdeveloped or unexplained. The film begins with Monroe Stahr (Robert De Niro), the young production head of International World Films, tirelessly supervising numerous projects at the studio.[40] Stahr advises Latin-lover leading man Rodriguez (Tony Curtis) on a delicate problem of impotency for the star. Meanwhile, Stahr reassures French actress Didi (Jean Moreau) that she is still a beautiful starlet with much to offer, removing director Red Ridingwood (Dana Andrews) from her film for failing to elicit the type of performance of which Didi was still capable. He also deals with a prima donna British scriptwriter Boxley (Donald Pleasance), who complains about the hack writers with whom he is surrounded in Hollywood—perhaps representing some of Fitzgerald's negative experiences as a scriptwriter in the film capital. Stahr will eventually fire the hard-drinking and disruptive Boxley. He also has to fight off the advances of Cecilia Brady (Theresa Russell), daughter of studio head Pat Brady (Robert Mitchum). Although Irish rather than Jewish, Brady seems to represent Louis B. Mayer, who was often jealous of Thalberg's success and warned his daughters to stay away from the young producer. The confident Stahr also dismisses the objections of Brady and studio attorney Fleishacker (Ray Milland) to his prestige picture set in Latin America, which will undoubtedly lose money. Brady and Fleishacker insist that the New York City bankers backing the studio are adamantly opposed to the picture, but the confident producer dismisses their concerns.

Devoted entirely to his work following the death of his wife, film star Minna Davis, Stahr's humanity is reawakened when he goes to inventory damage suffered by the studio during an earthquake. He observes two young female visitors to the studio who were stranded on the golden head of the goddess Sira floating through the damaged studio. One of the women reminds Stahr of his wife, and he has his staff locate her the next day. He calls her and arranges a meeting, but he has the wrong woman. However, she introduces him to her blond friend with an English accent, who refuses to give Stahr her name or invite him into her home. A few days later at the writers' ball, Stahr again sees the young woman and pursues her, learning that her name is Kathleen Moore (Ingrid Boulting). She agrees to meet Stahr the next day, and he takes Kathleen to his uncompleted beach house, whose construction was halted following the death of his wife. The couple makes love, but Kathleen remains quite mysterious regarding her background. She speaks of a relationship with a wealthy man—"a real king"—who betrayed her by insisting that she sleep with his friends. After they depart the next day, Kathleen leaves Stahr a letter explaining that she is about to marry another man and cannot see Stahr again.

Stahr is distraught and begins to ignore his work at the studio, but he is revived by a phone call from Kathleen, who agrees to meet him again at the beach house. They make love, but Kathleen makes it clear that she still plans to marry the other man, who promises to provide her "the quiet life" she now desires. Stahr cannot bring himself to ask Kathleen not to leave him, which leads Kazan to suggest that work will always take precedence despite the humanity Kathleen reawakens in the producer. Meanwhile, Stahr presides over the successful premiere of Didi's film, but he remains attached to the memory of Kathleen, who phones and agrees to a weekend rendezvous. However, when screening a new film, Stahr receives a telegram from Kathleen, which reads: "I was married at noon today. Goodbye." With the disappearance of Kathleen, the apparition of love and beauty that was missing from his life, Stahr encounters difficulty fulfilling his duties at the studio.

Cecilia serves as the hostess for an important meeting between Stahr and Brimmer (Jack Nicholson), an East Coast Communist organizer who is attempting to unionize the studio's writers. Stahr opposes the unionization of the writers, referring to them as children, while it is producers like himself who really make the films. Brimmer retorts: "They're still the farmers in this business. They grow the grain, but they're not invited to the feast." Drinking heavily, Stahr grows increasingly frustrated with Brimmer, who beats the producer in Ping-Pong and flirts with Cecilia.

Stahr attempts to start a fight, but Brimmer lays him out with one punch, and Cecilia puts the inebriated producer to bed. Considering Kazan's tumultuous relationship with the Communist Party, the encounter with Brimmer makes for an interesting scene. The principles espoused by Brimmer in the exchange with Stahr would seem to better represent the progressive ideas of Kazan, who respected writers. However, Brimmer appears somewhat disingenuous, and this becomes more evident the following day when he joins forces with the more reactionary businessmen opposed to Stahr's art and prestige picture.

Brady invites Stahr to an emergency meeting of the studio's board of directors, where the producer is told that his prestige picture will not be made and he will not represent the studio in negotiations with Brimmer and the writers. He is ordered to take a long rest, and after a brief visit to his office, where he imagines Kathleen married, Stahr walks across a quiet and vacant studio on Sunday morning and disappears into a dark soundstage—suggesting that old directors and producers just fade away. Kazan insisted that he was quite proud of this final shot, which said more about him than the film's protagonist. Kazan asserted that he recognized that the final shot of *The Last Tycoon* was the end of his career in cinema. In his autobiography, the director remarked: "It was the end, the fade-out of the film I was making and the end for me and my time as a director. I walked away from the shot and the crew and entered my office. As I began to pack my books, my records, and my diaries to send back east, it hit me that this was indeed my last film and that it was a kind of death for me, the end of a life in the art where I'd worked for so long. It was all over, and I knew it."[41] While this was, indeed, Kazan's final scene, it did not stop the director from trying to resurrect his film career with a sequel to *America America* over the next fifteen years.

While *The Last Tycoon* earned mixed reviews from the critics, it proved to be a box office flop and marked the last film for producer Sam Spiegel. Perceiving *The Last Tycoon* as a prestige picture, some reviewers believed that they should like the film but most could not bring themselves to praise the movie. Writing in *Film Comment*, Brendan Gill acknowledged the good intentions of Kazan and his collaborators to make a significant film of an important writer's last literary work. In the final analysis, Gill nevertheless determined that *The Last Tycoon* was a failure "on so grand a scale that we are unable to find a discreet path around it, pretending it doesn't exist."[42] As usual, Pauline Kael was more direct in her condemnation of the film, describing *The Last Tycoon* as "a series of disastrous mistakes by intelligent, gifted, well-meaning people." As for the director, Kael argued: "Kazan's work seems to be a reaction against the shrill energy he has sometimes used to keep a picture going. He's trying for something quiet and revelatory, but he seems to have disowned too much of his own temperament. Though the picture certainly has promising characters, they remain potential, tentative."[43] Reviewing the film for *Saturday Review*, Judith Crist was every bit as critical as Kael, maintaining that Kazan, Pinter, Spiegel, and De Niro "made a faithful, lavish, and bloodless transcription to film of Fitzgerald's literary fragment and reduced what has endured as an insightful study of a man and an industry into an insipid little love story."[44]

Vincent Canby of the *New York Times*, however, found *The Last Tycoon* to have some merit despite its slow pace. Differing with many of his colleagues, Canby praised the film for its allegiance to Fitzgerald's original work, writing: "*The Last Tycoon* preserves original feeling and intelligence. The movie is full of echoes. We watch it as if at a far remove from what's happening, but that too is appropriate: Fitzgerald was writing history as it happened."[45] Dewitt Bodeen of *Films in Review* was even more enthusiastic in his praise, concluding, "A fascinating film, *The Last Tycoon* commands your attention, and is one of the year's best from Hollywood."[46] Robert Hatch of the *Nation* disagreed, arguing that *The Last Tycoon* was a promising picture, but it proved almost impossible for the filmmakers to convey what Fitzgerald was after in his characterization of Monroe Stahr, where "once in a while a personality transcends definition to become an aura. Or, in his inflated terms, that infallibility induces awe and invites destruction." While this personification might have eluded the filmmakers, Hatch concluded that *The Last Tycoon* was "a cool, somewhat fragmented view of Hollywood" that was still worth seeing.[47] Jay Cocks of *Time* was also ambivalent about *The Last Tycoon*. Claiming that the film displayed some of Kazan's "most assured work in a decade," Cocks was disappointed that Kazan and Pinter went "swarmy on the romantic episodes, where Fitzgerald struggled for—and found—a saving, tough-minded detachment."[48]

Perhaps the most insightful review of *The Last Tycoon* was provided by Barbara and Leonard Quart in *Cineaste*. Their general evaluation of the film was little different from that of other critics, observing that *The Last Tycoon* was "a literate, intelligent, but uneven film, one which frequently strikes a chord of deep romantic yearning, while at other times it seems almost embalmed, without any movement or resonance." However, what Barbara and Leonard Quart contribute to the discussion of *The Last Tycoon* is the notion that both Fitzgerald and Kazan were obsessed with the pursuit of the American dream and the toll placed upon the individual, who often found the dream to be a nightmare. This perspective restores some authorship to Kazan, whose work on *The Last Tycoon* is often viewed as simply implementing the ideas of Pinter and Spiegel. The Quarts argue: "Fitzgerald—like director Elia Kazan—always had a powerful response to the dream of America, to the notion of unlimited mobility, to the idea of creating or willing a self, an imagination, a career, out of nothing." And for Kazan, Fitzgerald, Thalberg, and Monroe Stahr, Hollywood provided a fertile ground to manipulate and explore the American dream. However, with the opportunity of the dream comes the potential for destruction. In the conclusion of the film, Stahr, who in the vision of Kazan seeks to fulfill a mission of making films works of art that are accessible to the masses, is destroyed by the coarse forces of conformity and materialism that reduce the dream to the bottom line of profitability. Thus, the Quarts note: "Stahr's final defeat comes at the hands of his partners, the cost-conscious, corporate money-men—callous men, without taste or love for their product, people he has always treated with quiet disdain."[49] In this scenario, it is possible to perceive Kazan's critique of American consumerism and capitalism as it applied to Willy Loman, George Kazan, Stavros Topouzoglou, Eddie Anderson, and the director himself. Thus, *The Last Tycoon*, although not as personal as many of his other films, fits well into the canon of Kazan's post-HUAC testimony films in which the self-avowed anti-Communist director nevertheless provided a progressive critique of capitalism and the myth of the American dream—underscoring the theme of ambivalence in Kazan's life and work.

While *The Last Tycoon* proved to be Kazan's last film, he did not fade away as silently as Monroe Stahr walking into the darkened soundstage. He kept pursuing projects, such as a remake of *A Face in the Crowd* or a sequel to *America America*. Kazan evidently came the closest to resurrecting his cinematic career in 1990 with a film version of his novel *Beyond the Aegean* in which Stavros returns to Anatolia during the 1920s when Greece and Turkey were waging war over the territory. To shoot the film in Greece, Kazan would need the cooperation of the Greek government, and the filmmaker believed that this permission was denied due to his HUAC testimony. Greek actress Melina Mercouri was the minister of culture, youth, and sports, who was also married to the black-listed director Jules Dassin, and Kazan blamed the couple for blocking his film project. Richard Schickel agreed with Kazan's suspicions and observed that the failure to make the film was "a bitter blow to Kazan," whose energy seemed to decline.[50]

Kazan continued to pursue his career as a novelist, but his later works never enjoyed the commercial success of *The Arrangement*. He also suffered major setbacks in his personal life. Kazan dropped divorce proceedings against Barbara when she was diagnosed with cancer, and he traveled with her on many journeys to discover an elusive cure, which are outlined in his autobiography. Barbara Loden died in 1980, and two years later Kazan seemed to find happiness with Frances Rudge in his third marriage. In 1993, however, much of his vitality was sapped with the premature death of his son Chris. Kazan's final years were quiet, but he could never quite escape the shadow of HUAC and the blacklist, as the furor over his 1999 Lifetime Achievement Award well attests.

As America put McCarthyism and the blacklist in the rearview mirror, many expected that Kazan would issue some type of apology for his informing, and the director's autobiography was eagerly anticipated. Although his 1985 autobiography expressed considerable ambiguity regarding his testimony and cooperation with HUAC, a proud and belligerent Kazan refused to make the abject public apology that many expected. Kazan was not a man to express regrets, but his comments on actor Tony Kraber, whom Kazan named in his testimony, reflects the degree of ambivalence we often see in *A Life*. Following an exchange of notes with Kraber after the death of Molly, Kazan reflected: "It had just been a game of power and influence, and I'd been taken in and twisted from my true self. I'd fallen for something I shouldn't have, no matter how hard the pressure and no matter how sound my reasons. The simple fact was that I wasn't political—not then, not now—I only wish that I could have been as generous and decent as Tony had been with me."[51]

Although his comments on Kraber come close to an apology, Kazan clung to his denunciation of the Communist Party as a threat to democratic institutions. In his interview book released in 1999, Jeff Young tried to push Kazan to express some regrets or at least better explain his reasons for cooperating with HUAC. As the two men were wrapping up their interviews, Young posed a question that seemed to catch the director off guard. Noting that Kazan only named names of which the committee was already aware, Young asked him: "If you truly believed that there was a Communist conspiracy and that it presented a real danger to our country, why did you stop there? Why didn't you go further? Why didn't you tell them things that they didn't already have, get rid of all those Red bastards?" According to Young, a defiant Kazan proclaimed that he did not have to explain his actions to anyone, and "then his head dropped forward and he passed out cold." Young argued that Hollywood figures drawn into the blacklist controversy were committed to a self-image that they wanted to preserve at all costs. Thus, in the split second during which Kazan "went from bright, clear awareness to unconsciousness, his psyche spoke very loudly. Our exploration of the blacklist and his testimony had come to an end."[52]

In a 2011 retrospective of Kazan's work, *Cineaste* editor Dan Georgakas viewed Kazan's motivation as less complex, agreeing with Victor Navasky that Kazan named names because he wanted to continue making films in Hollywood. Of course, as Erik S. Lunde suggested in the *Journal of American History*, neither Kazan nor anyone else in Hollywood should have been compelled by a government entity to divulge their political views or denounce friends and associates in order to be employed.[53] It was a violation of American principles to which Kazan surrendered. Nevertheless, Georgakas argued, regardless of how one perceives Kazan's political behavior: "The indispensable reality is that for nearly sixty years Kazan positioned himself at the center stage in American cultural life. . . . His Hollywood films, which involve complex readings of various aspects of American society and characters that are often fragile but always complex and engaging, won popular and critical acclaim at home and abroad."[54]

Whether Kazan's decision to legitimize HUAC's inquisition into the political beliefs of citizens in a democracy was offset by the art he was able to produce as he continued to make films is a topic of considerable debate. A close examination of Kazan's post-HUAC testimony films nevertheless reveals that the director, even after publicly denouncing the Communist Party in 1952, maintained a progressive and somewhat Marxist perspective in his cinema, questioning the American dream and capitalism. Thus, Kazan's biographer Richard Schickel, despite his more conservative political inclination, lauds the director's post-HUAC films, noting that Kazan's later works concentrated on "the question of what constituted loyalty both to friends, obviously, but also the obsessive concentration on father-son relationships, the differences between America as an ideal and America as a reality."[55] As Kazan often suggested, perhaps ambivalence is the key concept for understanding his life and work. He feared his father, yet Kazan refused to follow his wishes and pursue a career as a merchant. He loved Molly Thacher, yet pursued extramarital affairs, which he ambiguously argued saved his first marriage. He was terrified by authority, yet his cinematic heroes were rebels who challenged the patriarchy and establishment. He made a film supposedly celebrating his family and the immigrant experience, but in the final analysis *America America* raised serious questions as to whether the efforts of Stavros and Kazan's own father to achieve the American dream were worth the sacrifice. He cooperated with HUAC and named names, but in his post-testimony films Kazan often presented a more radical critique of American capitalism and democracy.

His legacy of ambivalence, however, was somewhat negated in his 2003 *New York Times* obituary, which did not lead with any reference to his HUAC testimony. Instead, the obituary begins: "Elia Kazan, the immigrant child of a Greek rug merchant who became one of the most honored and influential directors in Broadway and Hollywood history, died at his home in Manhattan. He was 94."[56] Despite his interrogation of the American dream, the *New York Times* chose to emphasize the immigrant mobility of Kazan's family as the son of a rug merchant becomes one of the nation's most influential artists. The American dream is a difficult myth to dispel, but Elia Kazan's post-HUAC testimony films offer no regrets or apologies for questioning the fundamental tenets of an American democracy in which there is a considerable gap between the national myth and the reality of daily life in the United States.

NOTES

INTRODUCTION

1. Wolfe, "Reviving a False History."
2. Schlesinger, "Hollywood and Hypocrisy."
3. Navasky, *Naming Names*, 200.
4. Goldstein, "Many Refuse to Clap as Kazan Receives Oscar."
5. *Letter to Elia*, and Weinraub, "Time Frees the Hollywood One."
6. Kazan, "A Statement" [paid advertisement].
7. Haskell "Pete" Wexler, quoted in Schickel, *Elia Kazan*, 453.
8. Kazan, *A Life*, 218.
9. Ibid., 449.
10. Ibid., 460.
11. Ibid., 462.
12. For Clifford Odets, see Brenman-Gibson, *Clifford Odets*, and Kazan, *A Life*, 662–65.
13. Kazan, *A Life*, 685.
14. For overviews of Kazan's life and work, see Baer, *Elia Kazan Interviews*; Ciment, *Elia Kazan*; Ciment, *Kazan on Kazan*; Dobrowski, *Kazan Revisited*; Girgus, *Hollywood Renaissance*; Kazan, *A Life*; Neve, *Elia Kazan*; Pauly, *An American Odyssey*; Schickel, *Elia Kazan*; and Young, *Kazan*.
15. Clurman, *Fervent Years*, 294.
16. Young, *Kazan*, 51.
17. Kazan, *A Life*, 374–76.
18. Ciment, *Elia Kazan*, 72.
19. Pauly, *An American Odyssey*, 124.
20. Ciment, *Elia Kazan*, 171.

21. Elia Kazan to Martin J. Quigley, August 16, 1951, in Devlin and Devlin, *Selected Letters*, 169–71.

22. Kazan, *A Life*, 420–21.

23. Neve, *Elia Kazan*, 40–58.

24. Barson and Heller, *Red Scared*, 90–110.

25. Michaels, *Elia Kazan*, 27–28.

26. Hey, "Ambivalence as a Theme in *On the Waterfront* (1954)," 159–89.

27. Young, *Kazan*, 217.

28. Murphy, *Tennessee Williams and Elia Kazan*.

29. Kazan, *Kazan on Directing*, 193–94.

30. McGinniss, *The Selling of the President, 1968*; and Goodlad, Kaganovsky, and Rushing, *Madmen, Madworld*.

31. Ciment, *Kazan*, 50.

32. Baer, *Elia Kazan Interviews*, 147–49.

33. Neve, *Elia Kazan*, 126–27.

34. Kazan, *Kazan on Directing*, 209.

35. Molly Thacher Day Kazan helped her husband produce a novel of the film script, which enjoyed solid sales. Kazan, *America America*.

36. Ciment, *Elia Kazan*, 231.

37. Kazan, *A Life*, 731–33.

38. Ciment, *Elia Kazan*, 126–31.

39. For *The Visitors*, see Neve, *Elia Kazan*, 172–80.

40. For *The Last Tycoon*, see Kazan, *A Life*, 765–81.

1. *VIVA ZAPATA!* (1952) AND COLD WAR LIBERALISM

1. Elia Kazan to HUAC, April 9, 1952, in Devlin and Devlin, *Selected Letters*, 181–82.

2. For Steinbeck, see Jackson J. Benson, *The True Adventures of John Steinbeck*; Steinbeck, *In Dubious Battle*; Tedlock and Wicker, *Steinbeck and His Critics*; and Wartzman, *Obscene in the Extreme*.

3. Morsberger, *John Steinbeck*, 6 and 206.

4. Kazan, *Kazan on Directing*, 170.

5. Schickel, *Elia Kazan*, 242–43, and Kazan, *A Life*, 396–97.

6. Kazan to the editor of the *Saturday Review*, April 5, 1952, in Devlin and Devlin, *Selected Letters*, 178–80.

7. Kazan, *A Life*, 398–99.

8. Ibid., 420–21.

9. Kazan to Darryl F. Zanuck, January 24, 1952, in Devlin and Devlin, *Selected Letters*, 175–76.

10. Kazan, *A Life*, 451.

11. For the casting of *Viva Zapata!*, see Morsberger, *John Steinbeck*, 13–15.

12. Kazan, *Kazan on Directing*, 166–67.

13. Brando, *Songs My Mother Taught Me*, 170–71.

14. Manso, *Brando*, 318.

15. Skidmore and Smith, *Modern Latin America*, 230–33.

16. Young, *Kazan*, 92–93.

17. Pauly, *American Odyssey*, 147.

18. Ciment, *Kazan on Kazan*, 89.

19. For an overview of the Mexican Revolution, see Meyer and Sherman, *The Course of Mexican History*, 483–566.

20. For an analysis of the *Viva Zapata!* script, see Michaels, *Elia Kazan*, 55–58.

21. Crowther, "Marlon Brando Plays Mexican Rebel Leader."

22. "*Viva Zapata!*," *Holiday*, 105; and "*Viva Zapata!*," *Life*, 594.

23. "*Viva Zapata!*," *New Yorker*, 105; and "*Viva Zapata!*," *New Republic*, 21.

24. Hobson, "Trade Winds," 6.

25. Ciment, *Kazan on Kazan*, 94.

26. Beals, "Letter to the Editor," 28.

27. Kazan to editor of the *Saturday Review*, April 5, 1952, in Devlin and Devlin, *Selected Letters*, 178–80.

28. Schickel, *Elia Kazan*, 240–41.

29. Baer, *Elia Kazan Interviews*, 166–67.

30. Ciment, *Kazan on Kazan*, 93–94.

31. Neve, *Elia Kazan*, 58. In a debate in the film journal *Cineaste*, Dan Georgakas defended the progressive principles of *Viva Zapata!* in opposition to Peter Biskind and agreed with the conclusions reached by Neve. See Biskind, "Ripping Off Zapata," 11–15, and Georgakas, "Still Good after All These Years," 16–17.

32. Womack, *Zapata and the Mexican Revolution*, 420.

33. Brunk, *Emiliano Zapata*, 238–39.

34. Kazan, *Kazan on Directing*, 171.

35. Ciment, *Kazan on Kazan*, 97.

2. KAZAN AND THE ANTI-COMMUNIST FILM GENRE

1. Ross, *Hollywood Left and Right*, 6–7.

2. Hellman, *Scoundrel Time.*

3. Trumbo, *Time of the Toad*, 18; see also Ceplair and Trumbo, *Dalton Trumbo.*

4. Kanfer, *A Journal of the Plague Years*, 173.

5. Ceplair and Englund, *The Inquisition in Hollywood*, 377.

6. Navasky, *Naming Names*, 427.

7. Roffman and Purdy, "The Red Scare in Hollywood," 202.

8. Ceplair and Englund, *The Inquisition in Hollywood*, 422.

9. Kazan, *A Life*, 476.

10. Kazan, *Kazan on Directing*, 233.

11. Kazan, *A Life*, 482.

12. Ibid., 478.

13. For background information on Fredric March and Adolphe Menjou, see Menjou, *It Took Nine Tailors*; Peterson, *Fredric March*; Quirk, *Films of Fredric March*; and Tranberg, *Fredric March.*

14. Kazan, *A Life*, 479.

15. Kazan to Darryl Zanuck, May 18, 1952, in Devlin and Devlin, *Selected Letters*, 185–86.

16. Kazan to Robert Sherwood, April 21, 1952, in Devlin and Devlin, *Selected Letters*, 184.

17. Kazan to Molly Day Thatcher, August 15, 1952, in Devlin and Devlin, *Selected Letters*, 192–94.

18. Ciment, *Kazan on Kazan*, 85.

19. Young, *Kazan*, 112–13.

20. Schickel, *Elia Kazan*, 274–76.

21. Ibid.

22. Kazan to Gerd Oswald, August 1, 1952, in Devlin and Devlin, *Selected Letters*, 193–94.

23. *Man on a Tightrope.*

24. For an analysis of the screenplay for *Man on a Tightrope*, see Michaels, *Elia Kazan*, 58–61.

25. Kazan to Darryl Zanuck, May 18, 1952, in Devlin and Devlin, *Selected Letters*, 186.

26. "Red Terror Stalks the Circus," *New York Times.*

27. Knight, "Political Circus," 30.

28. Kazan, *A Life*, 485.

3. THE AMBIVALENCE OF INFORMING

1. Kazan, *A Life*, 409–10.

2. On Roy Brewer and the Hollywood labor wars, see Ceplair and Englund, *The Inquisition in Hollywood*; Horne, *Class Struggle in Hollywood*; and Nielson and Mailes, *Hollywood's Other Blacklist*.

3. Kazan, *A Life*, 411.

4. On Harry Bridges, see Larrone, *Harry Bridges*; Schwartz, *Solidarity Stories*; and Ward, *Harry Bridges on Trial*.

5. Kazan, *A Life*, 412.

6. Ciment, *Kazan on Kazan*, 102.

7. Schickel, *Elia Kazan*, 223–24.

8. Miller, *Timebends*, 308.

9. For background information on Budd Schulberg, see Schulberg, *Moving Pictures*.

10. Gottfried, *Arthur Miller*, 179, and Schickel, *Elia Kazan*, 225–30.

11. Kazan to Budd Schulberg, November 1952, in Devlin and Devlin, *Selected Letters*, 204–8.

12. Kazan to Darryl Zanuck, December 30, 1952, in Devlin and Devlin, *Selected Letters*, 218–21. For the waterfront priest Father Corridan, see Allen, *Waterfront Priest*, and Ward, *Dark Harbor*.

13. Kazan, *A Life*, 508–9.

14. Kazan, *Kazan on Directing*, 177–80.

15. Kazan, *A Life*, 516. For Sam Spiegel, see Cavassoni, *Sam Spiegel*.

16. Brando, *Songs My Mother Taught Me*, 194–96.

17. Kazan, *Kazan on Directing*, 179–80.

18. Kazan, *A Life*, 527.

19. *On the Waterfront*; Braudy, *On the Waterfront*; Michaels, *Kazan*, 61–64; and Rapf, *On the Waterfront*.

20. Hey, "Ambivalence as a Theme in *On the Waterfront*," 184.

21. Anderson, "The Last Sequence of *On the Waterfront*," 127–30.

22. Biskind, *Seeing Is Believing*, 175–82.

23. Young, *Kazan*, 120.

24. For the post–World War II union movement, see Dray, *There Is Power in a Union*; Dubofsky, *Labor in America*; Freeman, *Working-Class New York*; and Zieger, *The CIO, 1935–1955*.

25. For the role of religion in the Cold War, see Herzog, *The Spiritual-Industrial Complex*; Inboden, *Religion and American Foreign Policy*; Kirby, *Religion and the Cold War*; and Muehlenbeck, *Religion and the Cold War*.

26. Schulberg, "Collision with the Party Line," 6–8 and 31–37.

27. Ceplair and Englund, *The Inquisition in Hollywood*, 324.

28. Ross, *Hollywood Left and Right*, 4. For the Communist Party in America, see Klehr, *Heyday of American Communism*, and Ottonelli, *The Communist Party of the United States*.

29. Kael, *For Keeps*, 434–39; see also Kael, "The Story of Delinquency."

30. Weiler, *"On the Waterfront."*

31. Rogow, *"On the Waterfront,"* 25.

32. *"On the Waterfront," Commonweal*, 485–86; and *"On the Waterfront," Time*, 824.

33. "Union Leader Sues *Waterfront," New York Times*.

34. Baer, *Elia Kazan Interviews*, 138–39.

35. Kazan, *A Life*, 529.

36. Girgus, *Hollywood Renaissance*, 168–69.

4. FATHERS AND SONS AND THE COST OF PURSUING THE AMERICAN DREAM

1. Steinbeck to Pat Covici, May 28, 1952, quoted in Benson, *True Adventures of John Steinbeck*, 722.

2. Kazan to John Steinbeck, May 18, 1953, in Devlin and Devlin, *Selected Letters*, 226–28.

3. Steinbeck to Ritchie Lovejoy, March 2, 1955, quoted in Benson, *True Adventures of John Steinbeck*, 773.

4. Schickel, *Elia Kazan*, 319.

5. Young, *Kazan*, 199.

6. Ciment, *Kazan on Kazan*, 121–22.

7. Kazan, *A Life*, 534.

8. Ibid., 538.

9. Ciment, *Kazan on Kazan*, 126.

10. Kazan, *Kazan on Directing*, 186.

11. Young, *Kazan*, 198.

12. Dalton, *James Dean*, 162. For additional background on Dean, see Alexander, *Boulevard of Broken Dreams*; Howlett, *James Dean*; and Spoto, *Rebel*.

13. Chafe, *Unfinished Journey*, 136–37.

14. Michaels, *Elia Kazan*, 65–68; *East of Eden*.

15. Ciment, *Kazan on Kazan*, 121.

16. Kazan to Stephen B. Tully, January 4, 1954, in Devlin and Devlin, *Selected Letters*, 257.

17. Ciment, *Kazan on Kazan*, 128.

18. Ibid., 127–28.

19. Kazan, *A Life*, 20–23.

20. Ibid., 99.

21. Schickel, *Elia Kazan*, 253.

22. Kazan, *A Life*, 356–58.

23. Ibid., 9.

24. *"East of Eden," Newsweek*, 90.

25. *"East of Eden," Time*, 98.

26. Rogow, *"East of Eden,"* 25.

27. Hatch, *"East of Eden,"* 294.

28. Hartung, *"East of Eden,"* 604.

29. Crowther, *East of Eden*, and McCarten, *East of Eden*, 140–41.

30. *"East of Eden," Newsweek*, 90.

31. Kazan to Helen Bower, March 22, 1955, in Devlin and Devlin, *Selected Letters*, 298.

32. Dalton, *James Dean*, 340.

33. Schickel, *Elia Kazan*, 374.

34. Ibid., 318.

35. Kazan, *Kazan on Directing*, 186.

36. Young, *Kazan*, 219.

37. Kazan to Darryl Zanuck, December 14, 1954, in Devlin and Devlin, *Selected Letters*, 285–87.

5. SEXUALITY AND THE NEW SOUTH

1. Chadwick, "Sex, Sex, and More Sex."

2. Ciment, *Kazan on Kazan*, 121.

3. Schickel, *Elia Kazan*, 314.

4. Neve, *Elia Kazan*, 113.

5. Kazan, *A Life*, 495. On the relationship between Kazan and Tennessee Williams, see Murphy, *Tennessee Williams and Elia Kazan*.

6. Lahr, *Tennessee Williams*, 243.

7. Ibid., 245.

8. Kazan to Steven B. Trilling, May 31, 1952, in Devlin and Devlin, *Selected Letters*, 191–92.

9. Kazan to Audrey Wood, April 9, 1954, in Devlin and Devlin, *Selected Letters*, 261.

10. Kazan to Tennessee Williams, August 30, 1955, in Devlin and Devlin, *Selected Letters*, 310–12.

11. Kazan to Molly Day Thacher, November 29, 1955, in Devlin and Devlin, *Selected Letters*, 324–27.

12. Kazan to Tennessee Williams, July 29, 1955, in Devlin and Devlin, *Selected Letters*, 308–9.

13. Bubbeo, "Baby Doll Carroll Baker in Huntington."

14. Kazan, *A Life*, 562.

15. Quoted in Lahr, *Tennessee Williams*, 319.

16. *Baby Doll*, and Michaels, *Elia Kazan*, 68–71.

17. Lahr, *Tennessee Williams*, 320.

18. Kazan to Jack Warner, November 15, 1955, in Devlin and Devlin, *Selected Letters*, 317–19.

19. "Cardinal Scores *Baby Doll* Film," *New York Times*.

20. Kazan to Jack Warner, July 25, 1956, in Devlin and Devlin, *Selected Letters*, 338–39.

21. McCarten, "*Baby Doll*," 59.

22. Knight, "Williams-Kazan Axis," 22–24.

23. Crowther, "Streetcar on Tobacco Road," *New York Times*.

24. Hatch, "*Baby Doll*," 567.

25. "*Baby Doll*," *Time*, 61.

26. "Bitter Dispute over *Baby Doll*," *Life*, 60–65. See also "Trouble with *Baby Doll*," *Time*, 100.

27. Finley, "The Children's Hour," 62.

28. Ciment, *Kazan on Kazan*, 81.

29. Schickel, *Elia Kazan*, 334–35.

30. Kolin, "Civil Rights and the Black Presence," 3.

31. Neve, *Elia Kazan*, 110–11.

32. Ciment, *Kazan on Kazan*, 75.

33. Agee, *Now Let Us Praise Famous Men*.

6. A RETURN TO PROGRESSIVE PRINCIPLES AND THE SHAPE OF THINGS TO COME

1. Young, *Kazan*, 224.

2. Quoted in Schickel, *Elia Kazan*, 336. For Will Rogers, see Rogers and Day, *The Autobiography of Will Rogers*; White, *Will Rogers*; and Yagada, *Will Rogers*.

3. Ciment, *Kazan on Kazan*, 112.

4. Quoted in Ciment, *Elia Kazan*, 41–53.

5. Kazan to Molly Day Thacher, September 27, 1955, in Devlin and Devlin, *Selected Letters*, 312–14.

6. Kazan to Budd Schulberg, October 6, 1955, in Devlin and Devlin, *Selected Letters*, 314–16.

7. Young, *Kazan*, 236–38.

8. Kazan, *A Life*, 571–72.

9. Ibid.

10. Mills, *White Collar*; Packard, *The Hidden Persuaders*; Riesman, Glazer, and Denney, *The Lonely Crowd*; Whyte, *The Organization Man*; and Wilson, *The Man in the Gray Flannel Suit*.

11. Neve, *Elia Kazan*, 116.

12. Ciment, *Elia Kazan*, 50–51.

13. Ciment, *Kazan on Kazan*, 113.

14. For Lyndon and Lady Bird Johnson, see Cairo, *Master of the Senate*; Caroli, *Lady Bird and Lyndon*; and Russell, *Lady Bird*.

15. Ross, *Hollywood Left and Right*, 154.

16. Kazan to H. William Fitelson, September 10, 1956, in Devlin and Devlin, *Selected Letters*, 340; see also Singer, *Arthur Godfrey*.

17. Kazan to Ben Kalmenson, May 20, 1957, in Devlin and Devlin, *Selected Letters*, 353–55.

18. *A Face in the Crowd*, and Michaels, *Elia Kazan*, 58–71.

19. Young, *Kazan*, 253.

20. Ciment, *Kazan on Kazan*, 118, see also Williams, *Huey P. Long*.

21. Neve, *Elia Kazan*, 121.

22. Young, *Kazan*, 235.

23. For *Meet John Doe*, see Carney, *American Vision*; Capra, *The Name above the Title*; and Wolfe, *Meet John Doe*.

24. Kazan to Budd Schulberg, June 3, 1957, in Devlin and Devlin, *Selected Letters*, 356–57.

25. Kazan, *Kazan on Directing*, 200–201.

26. Hatch, "*A Face in the Crowd*," 533–34.

27. McCarten, "More TV Villainy," 86–88.

28. Crowther, "Rise of a TV Personality."

29. "Guitar-Thumping Demagogue," *Life*, 68–72.

30. "Loud-Lunged Satire," *Newsweek*, 161.

31. "*A Face in the Crowd*," *Time*, 92.

32. Hart, "*A Face in the Crowd*," 350.

33. Quoted in Kazan, *A Life*, 567.

34. Ibid., 568.

35. Ibid., 567.

36. Kazan to Budd Schulberg, May 26, 1982, in Devlin and Devlin, *Selected Letters*, 595–96.

37. Rosenberg, "*Face in the Crowd* Saw the Danger."

38. Hoberman, "*A Face in the Crowd*."

39. Schickel, *Elia Kazan*, 343.

7. LOOKING BACKWARD AND THE COST OF PROGRESS

1. Ciment, *Elia Kazan*, 88.

2. Kazan, *A Life*, 660–61.

3. Kazan to Robert Ardrey, March 9, 1957, in Devlin and Devlin, *Selected Letters*, 342–44.

4. Kazan to Paul Osborn, July 20, 1959, in Devlin and Devlin, *Selected Letters*, 408–10.

5. Ibid.

6. Ciment, *Kazan on Kazan*, 130–31.

7. Kazan, *Kazan on Directing*, 204.

8. Young, *Kazan*, 257–58.

9. Schickel, *Elia Kazan*, 368–69.

10. Kazan, *A Life*, 598.

11. For Montgomery Clift see Bosworth, *Montgomery Clift*; Girelli, *Montgomery Clift*; and Lawrence, *The Passion of Montgomery Clift*.

12. Kazan, *A Life*, 597.

13. Ciment, *Kazan on Kazan*, 134–35.

14. Kazan, *A Life*, 599–600.

15. Kazan to Spyros Skouras and Buddy Adler, December 12, 1959, in Devlin and Devlin, *Selected Letters*, 412–15.

16. Kazan to Tennessee Williams, February 26, 1958, in Devlin and Devlin, *Selected Letters*, 368–69.

17. *Wild River*, and Michaels, *Elia Kazan*, 74–77. For the Tennessee Valley Authority as well as the New Deal documentaries, see Callahan, *TVA*; McDonald and Muldowny, *TVA and the Dispossessed*; Selnick, *TVA and the Grass Roots*; and Snyder, *Pare Lorentz and the Documentary Film*.

18. Sitkoff, *New Deal for Blacks*.

19. Young, *Kazan*, 260.

20. Weiler, "Kazan Film Is Drawn from Two Novels."

21. Knight, "*Wild River*," 26–27.

22. Hart, "*Wild River*," 356–57.

23. McCarten, "River Stay 'Way from My Door," 99.

24. Hatch, "*Wild River*," 520.

25. "*Wild River*," *Time*, 47.

26. Young, *Kazan*, 258.

27. McLachian and Dawson, "The Politics of *Wild River* and Elia Kazan."

28. Schickel, *Elia Kazan*, 371.

29. Kazan, *A Life*, 601.

30. Kazan to Budd Schulberg, October 11, 1960, in Devlin and Devlin, *Selected Letters*, 434–35.

8. ANTICIPATING THE YOUTH REBELLION OF THE 1960s

1. Ciment, *Kazan*, 91. For William Inge, see Bryer, *William Inge*; McClure, *Memories of Splendor*; and Voss, *A Life of William Inge*.

2. Kazan, *A Life*, 461.

3. Ciment, *Kazan on Kazan*, 140.

4. Kazan notebook, February 6, 1960, as cited in Kazan, *Kazan on Directing*, 208–13.

5. Ibid.

6. Ciment, *Kazan on Kazan*, 141.

7. Kazan, *A Life*, 601.

8. Ciment, *Kazan on Kazan*, 139.

9. Ibid., 141–42.

10. Kazan, *Kazan on Directing*, 213.

11. Ciment, *Kazan on Kazan*, 142–44.

12. Young, *Kazan*, 267–68.

13. Schickel, *Elia Kazan*, 377–79.

14. For background information on Natalie Wood, see Finstad, *Natasha*; Lambert, *Natalie Wood*; and Wood, *Natalie*.

15. For Warren Beatty, see Amburn, *Sexiest Man Alive*; Biskind, *Star*; Finstad, *Warren Beatty*; Ross, *Hollywood Left and Right*, 315–16; and Thomson, *Warren Beatty and Desert Eyes*.

16. Kazan to Jack Warner, January 4, 1961, in Kazan, *Kazan on Directing*, 213–16.

17. Kazan to Jack Warner, February 27, 1961, in Devlin and Devlin, *Selected Letters*, 439–41.

18. Kazan to Clifford Odets, June 20, 1961, in Devlin and Devlin, *Selected Letters*, 443.

19. Kazan to Richard Lerderer, October 16, 1961, in Devlin and Devlin, *Selected Letters*, 452–54.

20. *Splendor in the Grass*, and Michaels, *Elia Kazan*, 78–80.

21. Kazan, *A Life*, 604.

22. Wordsworth, *Ode*.

23. Ciment, *Kazan on Kazan*, 144.

24. Kazan to William Inge, June 7, 1963, in Devlin and Devlin, *Selected Letters*, 498–501.

25. Crowther, "*Splendor in the Grass*."

26. "*Splendor in the Grass*," *Newsweek*, 112.

27. Knight, *Splendor in the Grass*, 36.

28. Hatch, "*Splendor in the Grass*," 363.

29. "*Splendor in the Grass*," *Time*, 95. Beatty and Wood supposedly began an affair during filming, which Kazan encouraged by sending Wood's husband Robert Wagner away during location shooting.

30. Gill, "*Splendor in the Grass*," 177–78.

31. Neve, *Elia Kazan*, 142.

32. Young, *Kazan*, 265.

33. Kazan to Clifford Odets, February 7, 1967, in Devlin and Devlin, *Selected Letters*, 465.

34. Ciment, *Kazan on Kazan*, 139.

9. THE ANATOLIAN SMILE AND THE IMMIGRANT EXPERIENCE

1. Ciment, *Elia Kazan*, 92.

2. Kazan to Tennessee Williams, June 8, 1955, in Devlin and Devlin, *Selected Letters*, 300–302.

3. Kazan to John Steinbeck, August 27, 1960, in Devlin and Devlin, *Selected Letters*, 226–27.

4. Behrman, "Effrontery of a Director," in Kazan, *America America*, 2–15.

5. Kazan, *Kazan on Directing*, 219.

6. Kazan, *A Life*, 618–19.

7. Ibid., 650.

8. Kazan to Molly Day Thacher, August 2, 1961, in Devlin and Devlin, *Selected Letters*, 445–47.

9. Elia Kazan, "Man for a Part," *New York Herald Tribune*, December 8, 1963, as cited in Ciment, *Elia Kazan*, 118.

10. Kazan to Warren Beatty, February 7, 1962, in Devlin and Devlin, *Selected Letters*, 466–67.

11. Kazan, "Man for a Part," in Ciment, *Elia Kazan*, 118–23. This more detailed account differs from Kazan's claim in his memoir that he simply discovered Stathis while the young Greek was sweeping a floor in Athens.

12. Kazan, *A Life*, 629.

13. Kazan to William Fitelson, September 5, 1961, in Devlin and Devlin, *Selected Letters*, 448–49.

14. Ciment, *Kazan on Kazan*, 146.

15. For the Armenian genocide, see Balakian, *The Burning Tigris*; Sony, *"They Can Live in the Desert but Nowhere Else"*; and Kevorkian, *The Armenian Genocide*.

16. Kazan to Meserref Hekimoglou, May 8, 1960, in Devlin and Devlin, *Selected Letters*, 473–75.

17. Kazan to Molly Day Thacher, August 6, 1962, in Devlin and Devlin, *Selected Letters*, 480–82.

18. Kazan, *A Life*, 645.

19. Schickel, *Elia Kazan*, 397.

20. Kazan to Molly Day Thacher, October 22, 1962, in Devlin and Devlin, *Selected Letters*, 483–44.

21. Kazan to Molly Day Thacher, November 15, 1962, in Devlin and Devlin, *Selected Letters*, 485–87

22. Kazan to Haskell "Pete" Wexler, November 27, 1962, in Devlin and Devlin, *Selected Letters*, 487–88.

23. Schickel, *Elia Kazan*, 395–96.

24. Kazan, *A Life*, 661.

25. A 1963 note by Kazan, quoted in Ciment, *Elia Kazan*, 124–25.

26. *America America*; see also Michaels, *Elia Kazan*, 81–84.

27. Ciment, *Kazan on Kazan*, 151.

28. Ibid., 150–51.

29. Young, *Kazan*, 273.

30. Kazan, *A Life*, 647.

31. For a discussion of the reasons for the failure of *America America*, see Kazan, *Kazan on Directing*, 222.

32. Didion, "*America America*," 64.

33. Crowther, *"America America."*

34. Alpert, "Come on You!," 29 and 62.

35. "Kazan Kazan," *Newsweek*, 74.

36. "Ode to an Uncle's Homeric Journey," *Life*, 113–14.

37. "An Odyssey Retraced," *Time*, 78.

38. Kael, "Kazan's Latest Arrangement," 211–17.

39. Hart, "*America America*," 44–45.

40. Leach, "*America America* at the Paris Cinema."

41. Ciment, *Kazan on Kazan*, 148–49.

42. Kazan, *A Life*, 677. For Molly Kazan's poem, "Thanksgiving, 1963," see Devlin and Devlin, *Selected Letters*, 512–13.

43. Kazan to Budd Schulberg, May 26, 1982, in Devlin and Devlin, *Selected Letters*, 595–96; and Kazan to Katharine Kazan, April 1984, in Devlin and Devlin, *Selected Letters*, 601–2.

44. Ciment, *Kazan on Kazan*, 145–46.

10. REBELLING AGAINST THE ARRANGED LIFE

1. Ciment, *Elia Kazan*, 94.

2. Ciment, *Kazan on Kazan*, 155.

3. Schickel, *Elia Kazan*, 420.

4. Kazan, *A Life*, 732.

5. Ibid., 735.

6. Frankel, "Son of the Oven Maker," 25.

7. Kazan to Judy Kazan, January 1967, in Devlin and Devlin, *Selected Letters*, 537–38.

8. Kazan, *The Arrangement*.

9. Kazan, *A Life*, 746.

10. Fremont-Smith, "All about Eddie."

11. "One Man's Family," *Time*, 92.

12. Hicks, "*The Arrangement*," 25.

13. "The State of the Union," *Times Literary Supplement*.

14. Eleanor Perry, "A Phony's Fight to Get Human," 25.

15. Kazan to James Baldwin, February 17, 1967, and November 29, 1967, in Devlin and Devlin, *Selected Letters*, 542–44 and 547–50.

16. Baldwin, "God's Country."

17. Kazan, *The Arrangement*, 511.

18. Young, *Kazan*, 294–95.

19. Kazan, "The Cinema in America."

20. Ibid.

21. Kazan to Marlon Brando, July 12, 1967, in Devlin and Devlin, *Selected Letters*, 544–47.

22. Ibid.

23. Kazan, *A Life*, 752.

24. Young, *Kazan*, 293. For Kirk Douglas, see Douglas, *I Am Spartacus!*; Douglas, *The Ragman's Son*; and Thomas, *Films of Kirk Douglas*.

25. Kazan, *A Life*, 753.

26. Schickel, *Elia Kazan*, 423–24.

27. Ciment, *Kazan on Kazan*, 157.

28. *The Arrangement*, and Michaels, *Elia Kazan*, 84–87.

29. Young, *Kazan*, 297.

30. Ciment, *Kazan on Kazan*, 157.

31. Gelatt, "Kazan's Rearrangement," 68.

32. McBride, "*The Arrangement*."

33. Canby, "Kazan's *The Arrangement*."

34. Ebert, "*The Arrangement*."

35. Bartlett, *"The Arrangement,"* 639.

36. Kael, "Kazan's Latest Arrangement."

37. Kazan to Michel Ciment, 1969, in Kazan, *Kazan on Directing*, 223–27.

38. Ibid.

39. Young, *Kazan*, 298.

40. Schickel, "A Worse Movie of a Bad Book," *Life*, December 12, 1969, as cited in Schickel, *Elia Kazan*, 424–28.

41. Kazan, "Political Passion Play, Act II," 26–27.

42. Neve, *Elia Kazan*, 169–71.

43. It is interesting to note the similarities between the AMC television series *Mad Men* and Kazan's *The Arrangement*. Although fans of the television series have commented on these connections via the Internet, the show's creator, Matthew Weiner, has not acknowledged the influence. The lead character of *Mad Men* is Don Draper (Jon Hamm), an advertising executive who in the 1960s becomes increasingly discontented with the mask of his upper-middle-class lifestyle and seeks escape through alcohol, sexual promiscuity, and experiments with the counterculture. For an analysis of *Mad Men*, see Goodlad, Kaganovsky, and Rushing, *Madmen, Madworld*.

44. Ciment, *Kazan on Kazan*, 157–58.

45. Ibid.

11. THE FINAL FILMS

1. Kazan, *A Life*, 754.

2. Schickel, *Elia Kazan*, 432–33.

3. Kazan, "The Cinema in America," May 7, 1971, lecture at Wesleyan University, in Ciment, *Elia Kazan*, 140.

4. Lang, "Casualties of War," 61–146. In 1989, Brian De Palma made *Casualties of War* into a well-received film featuring Sean Penn and Michael J. Fox.

5. As it turns out, Private Erickson, a fictitious name employed by Lang, did fear that his former comrades-in-arms might, indeed, attempt to do him and his family harm after being released from the stockade. Tom Fitzpatrick, "There Is Yet More to *Casualties of War*."

6. Young, *Kazan*, 304.

7. Kazan, *A Life*, 755.

8. Young, *Kazan*, 305.

9. Kazan, *A Life*, 756.

10. Michaels, *Elia Kazan*, 87–89, and *The Visitors*.

11. Kazan to Chris Kazan and Nick Proferes, June 2, 1971, in Devlin and Devlin, *Selected Letters*, 361–63.

12. Kazan, *A Life*, 786.

13. Alpert, "*The Visitors*," 23.

14. Crist, "Blues in the Nightmare," 54–55.

15. Canby, "*The Visitors* Portrays Ordeal."

16. Ibid.

17. Young, *Kazan*, 306. For the My Lai Massacre, see Belknap, *The Vietnam War on Trial*; Hersh, *My Lai 4*; and Oliver, *The My Lai Massacre in American History*.

18. Ciment, *Kazan on Kazan*, 165–67.

19. Smith, "Between Vermont and Violence," 15.

20. Haskell, *From Reverence to Rape*, and Prince, *Savage Cinema*.

21. Hirsch, "*The Visitors*," 63–64.

22. Ciment, *Kazan on Kazan*, 167.

23. Young, *Kazan*, 311.

24. Neve, *Elia Kazan*, 177.

25. Kazan, *A Life*, 758. For Joseph Losey, see Caute, *Joseph Losey*, and Prime, *Hollywood Exiles in Europe*.

26. Schickel, *Elia Kazan*, 436–37.

27. For F. Scott Fitzgerald, see Bruccolie and Smith, *Some Sort of Epic Grandeur*; Fitzgerald and Wilson, *The Last Tycoon*; and Moyers, *Scott Fitzgerald*. For Irving Thalberg, see Flamini, *Thalberg*; Vieira, *Hollywood Dreams Made Real*; and Vieira, *Irving Thalberg*.

28. Kazan, *A Life*, 762.

29. Neve, *Elia Kazan*, 189.

30. Kazan, *A Life*, 766.

31. For a discussion of casting for *The Last Tycoon*, see Schickel, *Elia Kazan*, 438–40.

32. Notes on Monroe Stahr in *The Last Tycoon* in Ciment, *Elia Kazan*, 143–47.

33. Kazan to Robert De Niro, April 15, 1975, in Devlin and Devlin, *Selected Letters*, 571–72.

34. Kazan, *A Life*, 770.

35. Kazan to Maria Kalkanis and Stellio Yeremia, November 24, 1975, in Devlin and Devlin, *Selected Letters*, 573–74.

36. Kazan, *A Life*, 777–78.

37. Kazan to Sam Spiegel, January 7, 1976, in Devlin and Devlin, *Selected Letters*, 574–79.

38. Silver and Corliss, "Hollywood under Water," 40–44.

39. Kazan to Sam Spiegel, August 3, 1976, in Devlin and Devlin, *Selected Letters*, 577–79.

40. Michaels, *Elia Kazan*, 89–92, and *The Last Tycoon*.

41. Kazan, *A Life*, 781.

42. Gill, *"The Last Tycoon,"* 44–45.

43. Kael, *"The Last Tycoon,"* 211–16.

44. Crist, "Murder in the Reverential Degree," 77–78.

45. Canby, *"Tycoon* Echoes 30s Hollywood."

46. Bodeen, *"The Last Tycoon,"* 633–34.

47. Hatch, *"The Last Tycoon,"* 637.

48. Cocks, *"The Last Tycoon,"* 106.

49. Quart and Quart, *"The Last Tycoon,"* 45–46.

50. Schickel, *Elia Kazan*, 446.

51. Kazan, *A Life*, 685.

52. Young, *Kazan*, 331–32.

53. Lunde, *"A Life,"* 288.

54. Georgakas, "Kazan, Kazan," 4–9.

55. Schickel, *Elia Kazan*, 455.

56. Rothstein, "Elia Kazan, Influential Director, Is Dead at 94."

BIBLIOGRAPHY

Agee, James. *Now Let Us Praise Famous Men*. 1941. New York: Mariner Books, 2001.

Alexander, Paul. *Boulevard of Broken Dreams: The Life, Times, and Legend of James Dean*. New York: Viking, 1994.

Allen, Raymond. *Waterfront Priest*. New York: Holt, 1955.

Alpert, Hollis. "Come on You!" *Saturday Review* 46 (December 28, 1963): 29 and 62.

———. "*The Visitors*." *Saturday Review* 55 (February 19, 1972): 23.

Amburn, Ellis. *The Sexiest Man Alive: A Biography of Warren Beatty*. New York: HarperEntertainment, 2002.

America America. Directed by Elia Kazan. Los Angeles: 20th Century Fox Home Video, 2010. DVD.

Anderson, Lindsay. "The Last Sequence of *On the Waterfront*." *Sight and Sound* 24 (1955): 127–30.

The Arrangement. Directed by Elia Kazan. Burbank, CA: Warner Home Video, 1997. DVD.

Baby Doll. Directed by Elia Kazan. Los Angeles: 20th Century Fox Home Video, 2010. DVD.

"*Baby Doll*." *Time* 68 (December 24, 1956): 61.

Baer, William, ed. *Elia Kazan Interviews*. Jackson: University Press of Mississippi, 2000.

Balakian, Peter. *The Burning Tigris: The Armenian Genocide and America's Response*. New York: HarperCollins, 2003.

Baldwin, James. "God's Country." *New York Review of Books*, March 23, 1967.

Barson, Michael, and Steven Heller. *Red Scared: The Communist Menace in Propaganda and Popular Culture*. San Francisco, CA: Chronicle Books, 2001.

Bartlett, Louise. "*The Arrangement*." *Films in Review* 20 (December 1969): 639.

Beals, Carlton. "Letter to the Editor." *Saturday Review* 35 (May 24, 1952): 28.

Belknap, Michael R. *The Vietnam War on Trial: The My Lai Massacre and the Court Martial of Lieutenant Calley*. Lawrence: University Press of Kansas, 2012.

Benson, Jackson J. *The True Adventures of John Steinbeck, Writer*. New York: Penguin, 1984.

Biskind, Peter. "Ripping Off Zapata: Revolution Hollywood Style." *Cineaste* 7 (Spring 1976): 11–15.

———. *Seeing Is Believing: How Hollywood Taught Us to Stop Worrying and Love the Fifties*. New York: Pantheon Books, 1983.

———. *Star: The Life and Wild Times of Warren Beatty*. New York: Simon and Schuster, 2010.

"The Bitter Dispute over *Baby Doll*." *Life* 42 (January 7, 1957): 60–65.

Bodeen, Dewitt. "*The Last Tycoon*." *Films in Review* 27 (December 1976): 633–34.

Bosworth, Patricia. *Montgomery Clift: A Biography*. New York: Harcourt Brace Jovanovich, 1978.

Brando, Marlon, with Robert Lindsey. *Songs My Mother Taught Me*. New York: Random House, 1994.

Braudy, Leo. *On the Waterfront*. London: British Film Institute, 2005.

Brenman-Gibson, Margaret. *Clifford Odets, American Playwright: The Years from 1906 to 1940*. New York: Athenaeum, 1981.

Bruccolie, Matthew J., and Scottie Fitzgerald Smith. *Some Sort of Epic Grandeur*. Columbia: University of South Carolina Press, 2002.

Brunk, Samuel. *Emiliano Zapata: Revolution and Betrayal in Mexico*. Albuquerque: University of New Mexico Press, 1995.

Bryer, Jackson R. *William Inge: Reminiscences on the Plays and the Man*. Jefferson, NC: McFarland, 2014.

Bubbeo, Daniel. "Baby Doll Carroll Baker in Huntington." *Newsday*, June 21, 2011. Accessed October 25, 2015. http://www.newsday.com/entertainment/movies/baby-doll-carroll-baker-in-huntington-1.2971728.

Cairo, Robert. *Master of the Senate: The Years of Lyndon Johnson*. New York: Knopf, 2003.

Callahan, North. *TVA: Bridge over Troubled Water, a History of the Tennessee Valley Authority*. South Brunswick, NJ: A. S. Barnes, 1980.

Canby, Vincent. "Kazan's *The Arrangement*." *New York Times*, November 19, 1969.

———. "*Tycoon* Echoes 30s Hollywood." *New York Times*, November 18, 1976.

———. "*The Visitors* Portrays Ordeal of a Threatened G. I." *New York Times*, February 3, 1972.

Capra, Frank. *The Name above the Title: An Autobiography*. New York: Vintage, 1985.

"Cardinal Scores *Baby Doll* Film." *New York Times*, December 17, 1956.

Carney, Raymond. *American Vision: The Films of Frank Capra*. Cambridge: Cambridge University Press, 1986.

Caroli, Betty Boyd. *Lady Bird and Lyndon: The Hidden Story of a Marriage That Made a President*. New York: Simon and Schuster, 2015.

Caute, David. *Joseph Losey: A Revenge on Life*. London: Faber and Faber, 1994.

Cavassoni, Natasha. *Sam Spiegel: The Incredible Life and Times of Hollywood's Most Iconoclastic Producer, the Miracle Worker Who Went from Penniless Refugee to Showbiz Legend, and Made Possible "The African Queen," "On the Waterfront," "The Bridge over the River Kwai," and "Lawrence of Arabia."* New York: Simon and Schuster, 2003.

Ceplair, Larry, and Steven Englund. *The Inquisition in Hollywood: Politics in the Film Community, 1930–1960*. Berkeley: University of California Press, 1979.

Ceplair, Larry, and Christopher Trumbo. *Dalton Trumbo: Blacklisted Hollywood Radical*. Lexington: University Press of Kentucky, 2015.

Chadwick, Bruce. "Sex, Sex, and More Sex: A 1950s Bedsheet Scorcher." History News Network, September 21, 2015. Accessed September 22, 2015. http://historynewsnetwork.org/article/160680.

Chafe, William. *The Unfinished Journey: America since World War II*. New York: Oxford University Press, 2003.

Ciment, Michel, ed. *Elia Kazan: An American Odyssey*. London: Bloomsbury, 1988.

———. *Kazan on Kazan*. New York: Viking Press, 1974.

Clurman, Harold. *Fervent Years: The Group Theatre and the 30s*. 1945. New York: Da Capo, 1995.

Cocks, Jay. "*The Last Tycoon*." *Time* 18 (December 6, 1976): 106.

Crist, Judith. "Blues in the Nightmare." *New York Magazine* 5 (February 7, 1972): 54–55.

———. "Murder in the Reverential Degree." *Saturday Review* 64 (December 11, 1976): 77–78.

Crowther, Bosley. "*America America*." *New York Times*, December 26, 1963.

———. "*East of Eden*." *New York Times*, March 10, 1955.

———. "Marlon Brando Plays Mexican Rebel Leader in *Viva Zapata!*" *New York Times*, February 8, 1952.

———. "The Rise of a TV Personality." *New York Times*, May 29, 1957.

———. "*Splendor in the Grass*." *New York Times*, October 11, 1961.

———. "Streetcar on Tobacco Road; Williams-Kazan *Baby Doll*." *New York Times*, December 19, 1956.

Dalton, David. *James Dean: The Mutant King*. New York: St. Martin's Press, 1974.

Devlin, Albert J., and Marlene J. Devlin, eds. *The Selected Letters of Elia Kazan*. New York: Knopf, 2014.

Didion, Joan. "*America America*." *Vogue* 143 (February 1, 1964): 64.

Dobrowski, Lisa. *Kazan Revisited*. Middletown, CT: Wesleyan University Press, 2011.

Douglas, Kirk. *I Am Spartacus! Making a Film, Breaking the Blacklist*. New York: Open Media, 2012.

———. *The Ragman's Son*. New York: Simon and Schuster, 1988.

Dray, Philip. *There Is Power in a Union: The Epic Story of Labor in America*. New York: Anchor, 2011.

Dubofsky, Melvyn. *Labor in America: A History*. New York: Wiley-Blackwell, 2010.

East of Eden. Directed by Elia Kazan. Los Angeles: 20th Century Fox Home Video, 2010. DVD.

"*East of Eden*." *Newsweek* 45 (March 7, 1955): 90.

"*East of Eden*." *Time* 65 (March 21, 1955): 98.

Ebert, Roger. "*The Arrangement*." *Chicago Sun-Times*, December 24, 1969.

A Face in the Crowd. Directed by Elia Kazan. Los Angeles: 20th Century Fox Home Video, 2010. DVD.

"*A Face in the Crowd*." *Time* 69 (June 3, 1957): 92.

Finley, James Fenton. "The Children's Hour." *Catholic World* 185 (April 1957): 62.

Finstad, Suzanne. *Natasha: The Biography of Natalie Wood*. New York: Three Rivers Press, 2002.

———. *Warren Beatty: A Private Man*. New York: Three Rivers Press, 2006.

Fitzgerald, F. Scott, and Edmund Wilson. *The Last Tycoon: An Unfinished Novel*. 1941. New York: Charles Scribner's Sons, 1960.

Fitzpatrick, Tom. "There Is Yet More to *Casualties of War*." *Phoenix New Times*, August 30, 1989.

Flamini, Roland. *Thalberg: The Last Tycoon and the World of M-G-M*. New York: Crown, 1994.

Frankel, Haskel. "Son of the Oven Maker." *Saturday Review* 50 (March 4, 1967): 25.

Freeman, Joshua B. *Working-Class New York: Life and Labor since World War II*. New York: New Press, 2001.

Fremont-Smith, Eliot. "All about Eddie." *New York Times*, February 21, 1967.

Georgakas, Dan. "Kazan, Kazan." *Cineaste* 36 (Fall 2011): 4–9.

———. "Still Good after All These Years." *Cineaste* 7 (Spring 1976): 16–17.

Gelatt, Roland. "Kazan's Rearrangement." *Saturday Review* 52 (November 22, 1969): 68.

Gill, Brendan. "*The Last Tycoon*." *Film Comment* 13 (January–February 1977): 44–45.

———. "*Splendor in the Grass*." *New Yorker* 37 (October 14, 1961): 177–78.

Girelli, Elisabetta. *Montgomery Clift: Queer Star*. Detroit, MI: Wayne State University Press, 2013.

Girgus, Sam. *Hollywood Renaissance: The Cinema of Democracy in the Era of Ford, Capra, and Kazan*. Cambridge: Cambridge University Press, 1998.

Goldstein, Patrick. "Many Refuse to Clap as Kazan Receives Oscar." *Los Angeles Times*, March 22, 1999.

Goodlad, Lauren M. E., Lilya Kaganovsky, and Robert A. Rushing, eds. *Madmen, Madworld: Sex, Politics, Style & the 1960s*. Durham, NC: Duke University Press, 2013.

Gottfried, Martin. *Arthur Miller: His Life and Work*. New York: Da Capo, 2003.

"Guitar-Thumping Demagogue." *Life* 42 (May 27, 1957): 68–72.

Hart, Henry. "*America America*." *Films in Review* 15 (January 1964): 44–45.

———. "*A Face in the Crowd*." *Films in Review* 8 (August–September 1957): 350.

———. "*Wild River*." *Films in Review* 11 (June–July 1960): 356–57.

Hartung, Philip. "*East of Eden*." *Commonweal* 61 (March 11, 1955): 604.

Haskell, Molly. *From Reverence to Rape: The Treatment of Women in the Movies*. New York: Penguin, 1974.

Hatch, Robert. *"Baby Doll." Nation* 183 (December 29, 1956): 567.

———. *"East of Eden." Nation* 180 (April 2, 1955): 294.

———. *"A Face in the Crowd." Nation* 184 (June 15, 1957): 533–34.

———. *"The Last Tycoon." Nation* 223 (December 11, 1976): 637.

———. *"Splendor in the Grass." Nation* 193 (November 4, 1961): 363.

———. *"Wild River." Nation* 190 (June 11, 1960): 520.

Hellman, Lillian. *Scoundrel Time.* Boston: Little, Brown, 1976.

Hersh, Seymour. *My Lai 4: A Report on the Massacre and Its Aftermath.* New York: Random House, 1970.

Herzog, Jonathan P. *The Spiritual-Industrial Complex: America's Religious Battle against Communism in the Early Cold War.* New York: Oxford University Press, 2011.

Hey, Kenneth R. "Ambivalence as a Theme in *On the Waterfront* (1954): An Interdisciplinary Approach to Film Study." In *Hollywood as Historian: American Film in a Cultural Context,* edited by Peter Rollins. Lexington: University Press of Kentucky, 1977.

Hicks, Granville. *"The Arrangement." Saturday Review* 50 (March 4, 1967): 25.

Hirsch, Foster. *"The Visitors." Film Quarterly* 26 (Summer 1973): 63–64.

Hoberman, J. *"A Face in the Crowd:* A Harbinger of Things to Come." *Village Voice,* February 26, 2008.

Hobson, Laura. "Trade Winds." *Saturday Review* 35 (March 1, 1952): 6.

Horne, Gerald. *Class Struggle in Hollywood, 1930–1950: Moguls, Mobsters, Reds, and Trade Unionists.* Austin: University of Texas Press, 2001.

Howlett, John. *James Dean: A Rebel Life.* Medford, NJ: Plexus Publishing, 2015.

Inboden, William, III. *Religion and American Foreign Policy, 1945–1960: The Soul of Containment.* Cambridge: Cambridge University Press, 2010.

Kael, Pauline. *For Keeps: 30 Years at the Movies.* New York: Penguin, 1966.

———. "Kazan's Latest Arrangement." *New Yorker* 45 (November 22, 1969): 211–17.

———. *"The Last Tycoon." New Yorker* 52 (November 29, 1976): 211–16.

———. "The Story of Delinquency: *On the Waterfront, East of Eden, Blackboard Jungle.*" In *I Lost It at the Movies,* 44–61. Boston: Atlantic-Little Brown, 1990.

Kanfer, Stefan. *A Journal of the Plague Years.* New York: Athenaeum, 1971.

Kazan, Elia. *America America.* New York: Stein and Day, 1962.

———. *The Arrangement.* New York: Stein and Day, 1967.

———. "The Cinema in America." In *Kazan: An American Odyssey,* edited by Michel Ciment, 132–42. London: Bloomsbury, 1988.

———. *Kazan on Directing.* New York: Vintage, 2010.

———. *A Life.* New York: Knopf, 1988.

———. "Political Passion Play, Act II." *New Yorker* 1 (September 23, 1968): 26–27.

———. "A Statement" [paid advertisement]. *New York Times,* April 12, 1952.

"Kazan Kazan." *Newsweek* 62 (December 23, 1963): 74.

Kevorkian, Raymond. *The Armenian Genocide: A Complete History.* London: I. B. Tauris, 2011.

Kirby, Dianne. *Religion and the Cold War.* New York: Palgrave Macmillan, 2013.

Klehr, Harvey. *Heyday of American Communism: The Depression Decade.* New York: Basic Books, 1985.

Knight, Arthur. "Political Circus." *Saturday Review* 36 (May 30, 1953): 30.

———. *"Splendor in the Grass." Saturday Review* 44 (September 6, 1961): 36.

———. *"Wild River." Saturday Review* 43 (June 1960): 26–27.

———. "The Williams-Kazan Axis." *Saturday Review* 39 (December 29, 1956): 22–24.

Kolin, Philip C. "Civil Rights and the Black Presence in *Baby Doll.*" *Literature Film Quarterly* 24 (1996): 3–15.

Lahr, John. *Tennessee Williams: Mad Pilgrimage of the Flesh.* New York: Norton, 2014.

Lambert, Gavin. *Natalie Wood.* New York: Faber and Faber, 2004.

Lang, Daniel. "Casualties of War." *New Yorker* 48 (October 18, 1969): 61–146.

Larrone, Charles P. *Harry Bridges: The Rise and Fall of Radical Labor in the U.S.* Lancaster, UK: Gazelle Books, 1973.

The Last Tycoon. Directed by Elia Kazan. Hollywood: Paramount Home Entertainment, 2003. DVD.

Lawrence, Amy. *The Passion of Montgomery Clift*. Berkeley: University of California Press, 2010.

Leach, Eugene L. "*America America* at the Paris Cinema." *Harvard Crimson*, March 12, 1964. Accessed March 1, 2015. www.thecrimson.com/article/1864/3/12/america-ameerica-pelia-Kazan-put-a/.

Letter to Elia. Directed by Martin Scorsese. Los Angeles: 20th Century Fox Home Video, 2010. DVD.

"Loud-Lunged Satire." *Newsweek* 49 (June 3, 1957): 161.

Lunde, Erik S. "*A Life*." *Journal of American History* 76 (June 1989): 288.

Man on a Tightrope. Directed by Elia Kazan. Los Angeles: 20th Century Fox Home Video, 2010. DVD.

Manso, Peter. *Brando*. New York: Hyperion, 1994.

McBride, Joseph. "*The Arrangement*." *Film Quarterly* 23 (Summer 1970): 52–54.

McCarten, John. "*Baby Doll*." *New Yorker* 32 (December 29, 1956): 57.

———. "*East of Eden*." *New Yorker* 31 (March 19, 1955): 140–41.

———. "More TV Villainy." *New Yorker* 33 (June 8, 1957): 86–88.

———. "River Stay 'Way from My Door." *New Yorker* 36 (June 4, 1960): 99.

McClure, Arthur F. *Memories of Splendor: The Midwestern World of William Inge*. Topeka: Kansas State Historical Society, 1989.

McDonald, Michael J., and John Muldowny. *TVA and the Dispossessed: The Resettlement of Population in the Norris Dam Area*. Knoxville: University of Tennessee Press, 1981.

McGinniss, Joe. *The Selling of the President, 1968*. New York: Trident Press, 1969.

McLachian, Wilson, and M. Dawson. "The Politics of *Wild River* and Elia Kazan." Left Field Cinema, 2008–2009. Accessed February 17, 2014. www.leftfieldcinema.com/analysis-the-politics-of-wild-river-and-elia-kazan.

Menjou, Adolphe. *It Took Nine Tailors: An Autobiography*. New York: McGraw Hill, 1948.

Meyer, Michael C., and William L. Sherman. *The Course of Mexican History*. New York: Oxford University Press, 1995.

Michaels, Lloyd. *Elia Kazan: A Guide to References and Resources*. Boston: G. K. Hall, 1985.

Miller, Arthur. *Timebends: A Life*. New York: Grove Press, 1987.

Mills, C. Wright. *White Collar: The American Middle Classes*. New York: Oxford University Press, 1951.

Morsberger, John, ed. *John Steinbeck: Zapata*. New York: Penguin, 1993.

Moyers, Jeffrey. *Scott Fitzgerald: A Biography*. New York: Harper Perennial, 2014.

Muehlenbeck, Philip, ed. *Religion and the Cold War: A Global Perspective*. Nashville, TN: Vanderbilt University Press, 2012.

Murphy, Brenda. *Tennessee Williams and Elia Kazan: A Collaboration in the Theatre*. Cambridge: Cambridge University Press, 1992.

Navasky, Victor S. *Naming Names*. New York: Viking Press, 1980.

Neve, Brian. *Elia Kazan: The Cinema of an American Outsider*. New York: I. B. Tauris, 2008.

Nielson, Mike, and Gene Mailes. *Hollywood's Other Blacklist: Union Struggles in the Studio System*. London: British Film Institute, 1995.

"Ode to an Uncle's Homeric Journey." *Life* 56 (March 6, 1954): 113–14.

"An Odyssey Retraced." *Time* 83 (January 3, 1964): 78.

Oliver, Kendrick. *The My Lai Massacre in American History and Memory*. Manchester, UK: Manchester University Press, 2006.

"One Man's Family." *Time* 89 (March 4, 1967): 92.

On the Waterfront. Directed by Elia Kazan. Los Angeles: 20th Century Fox Home Video, 2010. DVD.

"*On the Waterfront*." *Commonweal* 60 (August 20, 1954): 485–86.

"*On the Waterfront*." *Time* 61 (August 9, 1954): 824.

Ottonelli, Fraser. *The Communist Party of the United States from the Depression to World War II*. New Brunswick, NJ: Rutgers University Press, 1991.

Packard, Vance. *The Hidden Persuaders*. New York: David McKay, 1957.

Pauly, Thomas H. *An American Odyssey: Elia Kazan and American Culture*. Philadelphia: Temple University Press, 1983.

Perry, Eleanor. "A Phony's Fight to Get Human." *Life* 62 (February 17, 1967): 25.

Peterson, Deborah. *Frederic March: Craftsman First, Star Second*. New York: Praeger, 1986.

Prime, Rebecca. *Hollywood Exiles in Europe: The Blacklist and Cold War Film Culture*. New Brunswick, NJ: Rutgers University Press, 2014.

Prince, Stephen. *Savage Cinema: Sam Peckinpah and the Rise of Ultraviolent Movies*. Austin: University of Texas Press, 1998.

Quart, Leonard, and Barbara Quart. "*The Last Tycoon*." *Cineaste* 7 (Winter 1977): 45–46.

Quirk, Lawrence J. *Films of Frederic March*. Secaucus, NJ: Citadel Press, 1971.

Rapf, Joanna. *On the Waterfront*. Cambridge: Cambridge University Press, 2003.

"Red Terror Stalks the Circus in *Man on a Tightrope*." *New York Times*, June 5, 1953.

Riesman, David, Nathan Glazer, and Reuel Denney. *The Lonely Crowd: A Study of the Changing American Character*. New Haven, CT: Yale University Press, 1950.

Roffman, Peter, and Jim Purdy. "The Red Scare in Hollywood." In *Hollywood's America: United States History through Its Films*, edited by Steven Mentz and Randy Roberts. New York: Brandywine Press, 1993.

Rogers, Will, and Donald Day. *The Autobiography of Will Rogers*. New York: Avon, 1975.

Rogow, Lee. "*East of Eden*." *Saturday Review* 38 (March 19, 1955): 25.

———. "*On the Waterfront*." *Saturday Review* 37 (July 24, 1954): 25.

Rosenberg, Howard. "*Face in the Crowd* Saw the Danger." *Los Angeles Times*, August 14, 2000.

Ross, Steven J. *Hollywood Left and Right: How Movie Stars Shaped American Politics*. New York: Oxford University Press, 2011.

Rothstein, Mervyn. "Elia Kazan, Influential Director, Is Dead at 94." *New York Times*, September 29, 2003.

Russell, Jane Jarboe. *Lady Bird: A Biography of Mrs. Johnson*. New York: Scribner, 2014.

Schlesinger, Arthur A., Jr. "Hollywood and Hypocrisy." *New York Times*, February 29, 1999.

Schickel, Richard. *Elia Kazan: A Biography*. New York: HarperCollins, 2005.

Schulberg, Budd. "Collision with the Party Line." *Saturday Review* 30 (August 1952): 6–8.

———. *Moving Pictures: Memories of a Hollywood Prince*. New York: Ivan R. Dee, 2003.

Schwartz, Harvey, ed. *Solidarity Stories: An Oral History of the ILWU*. Seattle: University of Washington Press, 2009.

Selnick, Philip. *TVA and the Grass Roots, a Study in the Sociology of Formal Organization*. Charleston, SC: Forgotten Books, 2012.

Silver, Charles, and Mary Corliss. "Hollywood under Water: Elia Kazan and *The Last Tycoon*." *Film Comment* 13 (January–February 1977): 40–44.

Singer, Arthur J. *Arthur Godfrey: The Adventures of an American Broadcaster*. Jefferson, NC: McFarland, 2006.

Sitkoff, Harvard. *A New Deal for Blacks: The Emergence of Civil Rights as a National Issue: The Depression Decade*. New York: Oxford University Press, 2008.

Skidmore, Thomas E., and Peter H. Smith. *Modern Latin America*. New York: Oxford University Press, 1984.

Smith, Julian. "Between Vermont and Violence: Film Portraits of Vietnam Veterans." *Film Quarterly* 26 (Summer 1973): 15–20.

Snyder, Robert. *Pare Lorentz and the Documentary Film*. Norman: University of Oklahoma Press, 1968.

Sony, Grigor. "*They Can Live in the Desert but Nowhere Else*": *A History of the Armenian Genocide*. Princeton, NJ: Princeton University Press, 2015.

Splendor in the Grass. Directed by Elia Kazan. Los Angeles: 20th Century Fox Home Video, 2010. DVD.

"*Splendor in the Grass*." *Newsweek* 58 (October 16, 1961): 112.

"*Splendor in the Grass*." *Time* 78 (October 13, 1961): 95.

Spoto, Donald. *Rebel: The Life and Times of James Dean*. New York: HarperCollins, 1996.

"The State of the Union." *Times Literary Supplement*, May 18, 1967.

Steinbeck, John. *In Dubious Battle*. New York: Viking, 1938.

Tedlock, F. W., Jr., and C. V. Wicker, eds. *Steinbeck and His Critics*. Albuquerque: University of New Mexico Press, 1957.

Thomas, Tony. *The Films of Kirk Douglas*. New York: Citadel Press, 1998.

Thomson, David. *Warren Beatty and Desert Eyes*. New York: Vintage, 1988.

Tranberg, Charles. *Frederic March: A Consummate Actor*. Albany, GA: BearManor Media, 2015.

"The Trouble with *Baby Doll*." *Time* 69 (January 14, 1957): 100.

Trumbo, Dalton. *The Time of the Toad: A Study of Inquisition in America and Two Related Pamphlets*. New York: Perennial Library, 1972.

"Union Leader Sues *Waterfront*." *New York Times*, March 18, 1955.

Vieira, Mark A. *Hollywood Dreams Made Real: Irving Thalberg and the Rise of M-G-M*. New York: Abrams, 2008.

———. *Irving Thalberg: Boy Wonder to Producer Prince*. Berkeley: University of California Press, 2009.

The Visitors. Directed by Elia Kazan. Eugene, OR: Timeless Media Group, 2014. DVD.

Viva Zapata! Directed by Elia Kazan. Los Angeles: 20th Century Fox Home Video, 2010. DVD.

"*Viva Zapata!*" *Holiday* 22 (May 1952): 105.

"*Viva Zapata!*" *Life* 32 (February 25, 1952): 594.

"*Viva Zapata!*" *New Republic* 126 (February 25, 1952): 21.

"*Viva Zapata!*" *New Yorker* 27 (February 16, 1952): 105.

Voss, Ralph E. *A Life of William Inge: The Strains of Triumph*. Lawrence: University Press of Kansas, 1989.

Ward, Estolv Ethan. *Harry Bridges on Trial*. Charleston, SC: Forgotten Books, 2009.

Ward, Nathan. *Dark Harbor: The War for the Waterfront*. New York: Farrar, Straus and Giroux, 2010.

Wartzman, Rick. *Obscene in the Extreme: The Burning and Banning of John Steinbeck's* The Grapes of Wrath. New York: Public Affairs, 2008.

Weiler, A. H. "Kazan Film Is Drawn from Two Novels." *New York Times*, May 27, 1960.

———. "*On the Waterfront*." *New York Times*, July 29, 1954; Weinraub, Bernard. "Time Frees the Hollywood One." *New York Times*, January 12, 1999.

White, Richard D., Jr. *Will Rogers: A Political Life*. Lubbock: Texas Tech University Press, 2011.

Whyte, William H., Jr. *The Organization Man*. New York: Simon and Schuster, 1956.

Wild River. Directed by Elia Kazan. Los Angeles: 20th Century Fox Home Video, 2010. DVD.

"*Wild River*." *Time* 75 (June 6, 1960): 47.

Williams, T. Harry. *Huey P. Long*. New York: Knopf, 1969.

Wilson, Sloan. *The Man in the Gray Flannel Suit*. New York: Da Capo Press, 1956.

Wolfe, Alan. "Reviving a False History." *Los Angeles Times*, March 21, 1999.

Wolfe, Charles, ed. *Meet John Doe*. New Brunswick, NJ: Rutgers University Press, 1989.

Womack, John, Jr. *Zapata and the Mexican Revolution*. New York: Knopf, 1969.

Wood, Lana. *Natalie: A Memoir by Her Sister*. New York: Putnam, 1984.

Wordsworth, William. *Ode: Intimations of Immortality from Recollections of Early Childhood*. Boston: D. Lanthrop, 1884.

Yagada, Ben. *Will Rogers: A Biography*. Norman: University of Oklahoma Press, 2000.

Young, Jeff, ed. *Kazan: The Master Director Discusses His Films*. New York: Newmarket Press, 1999.

Zieger, Robert. *The CIO, 1935–1955*. Chapel Hill: University of North Carolina Press, 2000.

INDEX

ABOUT THE AUTHOR

Ron Briley taught history and film studies for thirty-eight years at Sandia Preparatory School in Albuquerque, New Mexico, where he also served as assistant head of school. In addition, Briley was an adjunct professor of history at the University of New Mexico, Valencia campus, for twenty years. He is the recipient of the New Mexico Golden Apple Award for Excellence in Teaching as well as national teaching awards from the Organization of American Historians, American Historical Association, National Council for History Education, and Society for History Education. The recipient of Fulbright awards to the Netherlands, Yugoslavia, and Japan, Briley has also served on numerous committees for the Organization of American Historians and the American Historical Association. A distinguished lecturer for the Organization of American Historians, he is the author of five books and numerous scholarly articles and encyclopedia entries on the history of sport, music, and film. Briley is also a frequent contributor to the History News Network. During his spare time, Briley enjoys being with his family, reading and writing history, watching films, and following his beloved Houston Astros.